SERVICE SUCCESS!

Lessons from a Leader on How to Turn Around a Service Business

Daniel I. Kaplan

with

Carl Rieser

John Wiley & Sons, Inc.

New York • Chichester • Brisbane • Toronto • Singapore

Copyright © 1994 by Daniel I. Kaplan and Carl Rieser.
Published by John Wiley & Sons, Inc.

Library of Congress Cataloging in Publication Data:

Kaplan, Daniel I., 1943–
    Service success! lessons from a leader on how to turn around a service
    business / Daniel I. Kaplan with Carl Rieser.
        p.   cm.
    Includes bibliographical references and index.
    ISBN 0-471-59129-7
    1. Service industries—Management.   2. Service industries—Quality
    control.   I. Rieser, Carl.   II. Title.   III. Hitting one
    thousand singles.
    HD9980.5.K37   1994
    658.5—dc20   93-27197

To Frank A. Olson,
whose leadership qualities
guided me through the years

Foreword

For some time, there has been ample evidence across all sectors that we have an urgent need to find new approaches to managing our institutions. This realization, coupled with what we have learned from Japanese management practices, has fathered the concept known as total quality management, or "TQM." A new way to think about the process of management, TQM is built on five basic precepts:

1. Focus on the customer.
2. Develop a style of management by facts.
3. Push continuous improvement.
4. Seek total involvement of the whole organization.
5. Provide systemic support for the work force.

Most of the initial attempts at implementing the concepts of total quality management were in the manufacturing arena. In the early 1980s, American industry discovered Dr. W. Edwards Deming, the brilliant statistician and management expert. After World War II, the Japanese had Deming come to Japan and help companies implement statistically based methods for measuring and assuring both quality and continuous process improvement. Manufacturing activities usually entail repetitive processes that lend themselves to statistical measurement, and much of the early emphasis was in this area. Manufacturing companies also began experimenting with "quality circles" or "employee involvement teams." For the first time since the introduction of mass production, line workers were being encouraged to bring their minds and hearts to the job, not simply their muscles.

In the past five years, there have been efforts to expand the TQM concept to include more sophisticated statistical tools in engineering, design, and marketing; greater use of multidisciplinary work teams; and partnering with a reduced number of suppliers. Although the results of this broad movement have been mixed, there seems to be a growing appreciation of what can be achieved by approaching management in new ways. This has been less true, however, in the service sector. Service businesses often do not have the systematic, repetitive processes found in manufacturing operations. There are estimates, for example, that as much as 90 percent of "service work" in this country involves some kind of rework. Managers in the service sector therefore have found it easy to dismiss the process-improvement disciplines of continuous improvement. As a result, TQM innovation has lagged over most of the past decade in the services.

This has serious implications for our productivity. More than three-quarters of all working Americans today are employed in the service sector, which is the fastest growing segment of the economy and likely to continue so. In view of what has happened in the banking industry, no service business can ignore the need to improve the competence and effectiveness of its management practices. Yet with few exceptions, service organizations are just beginning to awaken to new customer-focused management approaches that involve the disciplines of continuous improvement.

One of those exceptions is the Hertz Equipment Rental Corporation (HERC), run by a senior executive in the service business who has been living the principles of total quality management over the past decade, with remarkable results. Although Daniel I. Kaplan, the president of HERC, never employs the term "total quality management," he lives it. To borrow from the vernacular of modern business, he "walks the talk," both literally and figuratively, as readers come to appreciate when they witness the transformation of HERC described in this book.

TQM goes by different names in different quarters. In some organizations, it is known as "QM," for "quality management," in others as "TQ," for "total quality." It also goes by such names as "customer-driven quality," "continuous quality improvement," or "continuous process improvement." Names come and go, and given the Western world's impatience and its passion for new packaging, almost inevitably the expression TQM, too, will pass. Dan Kaplan has a simple and graphic phrase for it: "hitting 1,000 singles," which he defines as an ethic of "making tomorrow better than today." But no matter what label the concept is given, everyone is still talking about the same thing: management excellence. In that light, *managing for total quality*, which is what this book is all about, will never go out of fashion.

Nor was there ever greater need for the concept than at this moment in history. Until we can manage our businesses and all our institutions to be fully competitive with the best in the world—meaning fastest to market, lowest real cost per unit, highest long-term quality, and stable or growing world-wide market shares—we will be a nation at risk. And the most clear-thinking and farsighted of our German and Japanese trading partners would agree that a weak United States means a weakened world. We do no one a favor in the long term by failing to establish a fully competitive management system.

In this book, Dan Kaplan provides a straight-talking, eminently practical case study of managing for excellence. His customer focus is unequivocal, and it is based on hard facts. "Customer focus" is not simply a question of good intentions. Virtually all the people in any organization want to please their customers and believe they do. But Dr. Deming wisely asks, "How do they know?" In other words, what data do you have to show who your customer is, what he or she wants or needs, how well you are meeting these needs? Dan Kaplan relates in instructive detail how he drives these and other questions in his company.

The key management issue of *continuous improvement* is embedded in the opening strategies and details of the book. At HERC, key determinables are measured and tracked. Throughout the organization, there is a well-defined understanding of what is expected and how it will be monitored. And all this is directed at meeting the customers' needs better than any competitor—and also better than HERC met them the previous month or quarter.

Dan Kaplan engages the hearts and minds of his employees and involves them deeply in the process of improving the company. He exemplifies the contemporary leadership characteristics of respecting employees and giving them a sense of purpose and loyalty to the company, yet not shirking his own obligations as the leader who projects the vision and sets the pace. If leadership can be defined as the force that makes the whole greater than the sum of the parts, then Dan Kaplan has proven to be an outstanding business leader. He values consistency, respect, attention to detail, high ethical standards, a concern for the environment and for the safety of all employees, a learning organization, and the satisfaction of devoting untiring effort to the task. In short, he provides an excellent management role model by demonstrating that service businesses, no less than manufacturing firms, can subject themselves to quality practices and disciplines with outstanding results.

One of Dan Kaplan's greatest contributions is his keen insight into both the potentials and the limitations inherent in the "management systems" under which organizations operate. He is aware that most behavior, be it effective, neutral, or dysfunctional, derives from the expectations set up by the systems that control the operations of an organization. The management system functions in an organization the way the nervous system functions in the body. That system is simply:

▶ The way information is collected and reported.

▶ How individual performance is measured, evaluated, and rewarded.

▶ The "signals" the bosses give off through their words and actions.

Dan Kaplan provides us with numerous samples of how HERC, in effect, got the management system out of its own way. He is one of the few CEOs able to stand back far enough to see objectively the system of which he is an integral part, and to change it—and his own behavior as well—when employee behavior or business results indicate a need for change.

In readable detail, Dan Kaplan describes the thought processes he went through as he helped to evolve the management tools that have worked effectively at HERC. And with equal candor, he also discusses the tools and procedures that failed to work. Although every industry and organization is different, the *methodologies* in this book (to use a favorite word of the author) are transferable to a host of operating issues not only in the service industry but also in other industries as well.

Students of business and practitioners of business likewise will benefit greatly from this recounting of management as it is lived and practiced by a dedicated professional. In the spring of 1992, when Dan Kaplan addressed the management students at Boston University's School of Management on the art of hitting 1,000 singles, the reception was uniformly enthusiastic. The business students saw in him a down-to-earth, unaffected executive who was passionate about excellence. Most importantly, they gained a new appreciation for constant, incremental improvement as a key to organizational success.

In writing this book, Dan Kaplan has done more than hit 1,000 singles. By sharing this level of practical, implementable detail about his real-world experience in transforming the culture, operations, results, and long-term health of his company, he has in fact hit one out of the park.

Louis E. Lataif, Dean
School of Management
Boston University

Contents

Introduction:
Make Tomorrow
Better Than Today

Service Success! Lessons from a Leader on How to Turn Around a Service Business offers a set of simple methods that will enable managers to become more effective and productive. Based on my experience at Hertz Equipment Rental Corporation (HERC), I show how basic concepts, applied consistently and across the board, can turn any service business into a leader and convert quality from a concept into a reality.

This book is not a panacea; it is a road map that enables business decision makers to move into the quality environment that is much talked about today but seldom achieved. It does not matter whether you have been in business for many years or are just starting out: Service Success! is intended to help service managers make tomorrow better than today. The basic premise of this book is that you need to stay with the same philosophy and work for constant improvement, day by day, on an ongoing basis.

That sounds like a simple idea, and it is. My approach is easy to keep in focus, and it gives you daily markers for measuring progress. The challenge lies in first identifying the problems that stand in the way of improved performance; then, in breaking them down into components; next, in quantifying these activities wherever possible; and finally, in getting commitment from the team that must implement the hundreds of small improvements needed.

Because of this focus on continuous improvement, my approach to managing my business relies on *hitting 1,000 singles*. In baseball, sluggers often clean up the bases with home runs that may win the game; they are great to watch and provide some exciting moments. But the players that keep the team in the game and win pennants are the ones who go after the base hits and bring their teammates across the plate inning after inning. They are the vital team players, who know how to execute a winning play that will bring in yet another run. They understand the strategy, they know how to place hits. They're looking to score, not to break up the game. *Hitting 1,000 singles* means to achieve continuous improvement by taking small steps every day over an extended period of time toward a well-defined goal. It is a business philosophy that has proven successful to me at HERC, and throughout this book, I describe how I've implemented it.

▶ *Turning Around a Losing Company by Asking the Right Questions*

This book was written from my experience running an enterprise that has become a recognized success story in the service field. HERC wasn't always a success. In the early 1980s, HERC had all the signs of a loser. It was by far the biggest equipment rental firm, supplying everything from bulldozers to pneumatic drills, mainly to the construction trades and industry. But it was being eaten alive in price wars, its locations and inventory had deteriorated, and it was losing money.

HERC turned around within a few years to become the industry pacesetter in quality and efficiency. It showed profits even during the severe recession of the early 1990s. Today, it is the only truly national enterprise in the equipment rental business and has also moved abroad. How this happened provides the material for this book. The story told here emphasizes these lessons so that others can experience the same success.

The methodologies in this book have all been tested under fire and have proven to be realistic and workable. I am a practical manager, not an academic or a consultant. My background is in purchasing, and everything I know about managing a service business, I learned firsthand, out of necessity. I took over the operation of a service business with few preconceived ideas about the art of managing, and I had to learn on the job. My task was to turn around a loser. Fortunately, I was backed by the considerable resources and prestige of the Hertz Corporation, the parent company of HERC. There was a great deal I did not know about my assignment, so I had to ask a lot of questions as I pursued my own form of on-the-job training.

The simplest and most basic of all methodologies is asking the right questions. I am totally unabashed about asking questions; the art is to ask them in the right order and to find the right people to ask. The core of the HERC mode of operation is derived from asking many questions again and again—always seeking clearer answers so that performance can be defined and quantified ever more precisely. This can be done more readily if individual failures or mishaps are perceived not as situations requiring disciplinary action (though that may also be warranted), but as opportunities to improve the system.

▶ *Measure Performance and Progress against a Plan*

Quality in the service business is the product you have at the end of the day. And a very long day it is in the service business. At HERC, we are on call 24 hours a day, thanks to the customer's ability to summon us via telephone answering systems and beepers. At that time, some harassed repairperson may be paying for someone else's mistake or slipshod handling at any point along a trail that extends back weeks, perhaps months, maybe even a couple of years. Getting any service or product to the starting line, to the customer, is a long and arduous task. The person who happens to be at the front desk, behind the sales counter, in the showroom, on the phone, or on the service call almost invariably gets the blame when something goes wrong—maybe rightly so in some instances. Nevertheless, when something goes wrong, you had best look back along the whole spectrum of myriad activities to find the systemic flaw or weakness that may have caused the specific failure.

  "Quality of service" to me means "quality of system." My definition of "system" is an inclusive one. It embraces not only "outputs" such as customer satisfaction, but "inputs" such as capital expenditures on the equipment we rent, plus our expenditures on maintenance and service. We are trying to measure all those inputs and outputs at HERC so that we can establish relationships between them and then tie them all together in a meaningful way to monitor "quality."

  Managing a business effectively today is possible only if you can measure performance and progress against a plan. At the center of our management system is a mass of complex data that we call "rental revenue analysis." This is the statistical heart of HERC, tying together and monitoring the quality, productivity, and profitability of its operations, which would otherwise be uncoordinated and unrelated. To take just one important example, we know at all times the age of our rental fleet and we can relate this to:

▶ The rates we are getting for rental.

▶ The return on our investment.

▶ The tradeoffs in terms of increased or reduced service costs.

▶ The capital investment needed to alter the ratio.

I believe rental revenue analysis is HERC's unique contribution to the management of a service business. To my knowledge, there is nothing comparable to our measurement system in terms of its coherence, unity, depth, and coverage. Our system continuously and instantaneously reveals to us a wealth of vital information about our business, all of which—in one way or another—bears on quality of service and customer satisfaction.

▶ A Statistical Model That Triggers Action

Rental revenue analysis not only yields invaluable comparative data but also triggers the actions within the company that bring about the results we want to achieve.

From our database, we derive "peer performance measurement." This is a management tool of exceptional value. It translates an abstract statistical model into a guide for action. It tells managers throughout our service network just how well they are managing the key activities that make for success or failure in serving our customers while at the same time making a profit. For example, it reveals whether managers are:

▶ Maintaining the rental equipment in good repair.

▶ Delivering equipment on time to the customer.

▶ Keeping overtime pay in line.

▶ Retiring old equipment on schedule.

▶ Keeping their rental fleet balanced.

▶ Charging appropriate rental rates.

Peer measurement has a built-in response element that ensures the performance we are seeking. There is an important moral here that applies not just to our service business but to all kinds of businesses: *Any effective monitoring system must not only flag exceptional situations to managers but require that they carry out the needed corrective actions.*

I encourage people not to copy our measurement system, but to *adapt* the concept to their own use. Our system has been developed to serve the specific needs of our particular business; it is unlikely that it will exactly fit your needs, which may be very different. But this book will show you how to apply methodologies that will help you design your own coherent and unified system. Not by following some theoretical design, but by using practical methods that worked for one successful company. Not by looking for breakthroughs, but by seeking to improve what you already have but are not employing properly. Not by changing the rules of the game, but by improving them.

▶ *Raising Service Standards by Continuously Redefining Them*

Managers have a responsibility to see that systems do not become mindless tyrants, but instead free us from irksome and repetitive work. Systems should make people available so they can relate productively and creatively to their customers, suppliers, and fellow employees. We can accomplish this by constantly improving the system, which is another major theme of this book. We make improvements by carefully noting our mistakes so that we can fine-tune our system to be more responsive to the human needs and the realities of the marketplace and larger economic conditions.

The challenge of defining terms with precision, clarity, and specificity is a main thrust of this book. *If you can't define actions and procedures precisely, the whole statistical approach to controlling the quality of service can't possibly work.* In other words, we are constantly concerned with standards: with defining them, raising them, holding people to them.

One thing I find appealing about the *kaizen* principle of management is that the concept of standards is central in its scheme of things. In his authoritative book *Kaizen: The Key to Japan's Competitive Success,* Masaaki Imai says that the "Japanese perception of management boils down to one precept: maintain and improve standards."[1] This means continuously reviewing standards, always seeking yet higher standards. His advice is to never rest on the status quo; he goes on to say, "Once the standard has been established, management must make sure all employees observe it strictly. That is people management. If management cannot get people to follow the established rules and standards, nothing else it does will matter."

These remarks state succinctly the management philosophy that we independently evolved at HERC in our struggles to turn the company around. The early years in particular were a constant daily battle to raise all the standards we live by. This effort included standards for:

[1] Masaaki Imai, *Kaizen: The Key to Japan's Competitive Success,* New York: McGraw-Hill, 1986.

- ▶ Buying equipment from suppliers.
- ▶ Maintaining our equipment.
- ▶ Reporting inventory status.
- ▶ Answering the telephone.
- ▶ Punching in orders.
- ▶ Ensuring safety and environmental protection.
- ▶ Locating new stores.
- ▶ Pricing our products.

After identifying these and other key standards, we then had to convince people to observe them—which is another story. But first we had to reach general agreement on what the standards should be and then get them down on paper in clear and precise form. This is why I put so much emphasis on asking the right questions. *To get people to observe standards, you must state them so unequivocally that there can be no question about what is meant.* That is the big challenge in the service business, where activities often can't be measured with the precision of a caliper.

▶ How to Keep People Saying "Yes" to Change

"The message of *kaizen* strategy," says Masaaki Imai, "is that not a day should go by without some kind of improvement being made in the company." I practice this credo, too, but I have my own way of stating it: *Make tomorrow better than today.* I look for small gains—one here, one there—and I am satisfied with gains that to others seem almost trivial.

Sheer necessity taught me to respect this mode of management. When I took over HERC, there was no other way for me to proceed; to take any major steps toward improvement, which the situation cried for, would have been folly. The company would have imploded, I along with it. The structure—in terms of communications, facilities, people, and expectations—didn't exist for putting large-scale reforms into being. The results that we finally achieved by the less dramatic process of making steady progress day by day—hitting 1,000 singles—confirmed my gut instinct that this was the way to manage companies and people successfully. From the beginning, I did not have a clear idea of the goals that had to be achieved, but I cast these expectations in realistic bites that people could accept and handle realizing that constant improvement would produce results.

I have come across another name for this concept: "small wins." This phrase was coined by two West Coast business teachers and consultants, James M. Kouzes and Barry Z. Posner, who have evolved a change process built around what they call "incremental commitment."[2] They note that people can be overwhelmed by problems too grandly or broadly conceived; no one can get a handle on them, much less act on them. According to the authors, the most effective change processes are incremental: "[B]reak down big problems into small doable steps," they advise, "and get a person to say *yes* numerous times, not just once." Small wins raise people's confidence and reinforce their wish for success, hence increasing their willingness to go along with the leader the next time. By deliberately employing a policy of small wins, leaders are able to bring people along with them as they challenge the process and move beyond the status quo.

Kouzes and Posner make another vital point that is fundamental to success: People must remain committed to the new course of action. They recommend accomplishing this with "mechanisms" in the form of systems and structures.

In effect, Kouzes and Posner are describing what I have tried to do at HERC, by focusing on peer performance measurement. In the aggregate, such measurement reflects the dynamism of the business and our continuous, day-by-day effort to raise and redefine our standards. It is my experience that new standards aren't created; in an organization open to new learning, they evolve through the accretion of experience. Peer measurement is a mechanism designed to:

▶ Incorporate the new efficiencies that have been built into the system, along with new expectations for the quality of the company's services and the level of business volume.

▶ Make it possible for each manager and supervisor to see their own contribution to this new base and their own progress in meeting the new incremental goals.

▶ Commit people to the new standards that have accreted, a day at a time, through continuous upward revisions and clarifications on the basis of new experience and greater capability.

In any dynamic business, people are always aiming at a moving target. The trick is to make success possible by raising the sights incrementally.

[2]James M. Kouzes and Barry Z. Posner, *The Leadership Challenge: How to Get Extraordinary Things Done in Organizations,* San Francisco: Jossey-Bass, 1988, p. 219.

▶ *Five Ways for a Leader to Win People's Trust*

But what about the commitment of the leader to the employees? The answer to this question is simple: Without sensing the strong commitment of the leader, employees will feel no commitment of any real value.

There are many books about mutual trust, a vitally important and often missing social attribute in our times. It isn't necessary to elaborate on the idea here beyond quoting a brief statement that speaks to my own style of leadership. It is from a book co-authored by Warren L. Bennis, whose writings on leadership are among the contemporary classics in the field.

> We know when [trust] is present and we know when it's not, and we cannot say much more about it except for its essentiality and that is based in predictability. The truth is that we trust people whose positions are known and who keep at it; leaders who are trusted make themselves known, make their positions clear.[3]

This very nearly defines for me what leadership is, or at least how I try to practice it. My philosophy can be summed up in these brief aphorisms borrowed from Bennis:

1. Be predictable.

2. Make yourself available to people.

3. Be willing to take firm positions.

4. Be clear about your positions.

5. Keep talking, keep working at it.

I realize it is unusual to begin a book on the quality of service with a discussion of trust, especially trust between the leader of the company and the employees. When trust is seen as an issue in the service business, it is often defined primarily as a problem of customer *mistrust*. The focus is usually on building trust between customer and employee—and this is certainly a serious problem in this country today. But before we can bring about trust between employees and customers, something has to be present— namely, *trust between the leaders of companies and the employees*.

There is nothing theoretical about this concept for me. My understanding of the crucial importance of trust arises directly out of my experiences at HERC starting very nearly with my first day on the job.

[3] Warren L. Bennis and Burt Nanus, *Leaders: The Strategies for Taking Charge*, New York: Harper & Row, 1985, p. 44.

Part One

The Art of the Turnaround

Building Trust through Commitment

I t was the fall of 1982. I had just been appointed general manager of the Hertz Equipment Rental Corporation and was making one of the first of those innumerable field trips that already marked my style of management. I was on a swing through the Sun Belt, where most of our stores were then located, and was sitting in the office of a regional manager. He was one of the best of them, an old-timer who was very good at his job and who knew infinitely more about the rental business than I did. I had just been telling him about some of the problems I was finding and some of the hopes I had for HERC when he leaned toward me a little in his chair, looked me squarely in the eyes, and said quietly and evenly, "I've seen 15 general managers come and go, and I'll see you go, too."

When I tell the story, people invariably ask whether I got angry and fired him. The answer is no. Instead, I told him that I appreciated his candor, which was quite true. It taught me something important that I needed to know: I realized this able employee was reflecting an attitude of cynicism, skepticism, and doubt that was prevalent throughout the company after years of false hopes and failed promises. He was really putting it to me point-blank. In effect, he was saying, "Sure, you're full of enthusiasm now. But will you stick with it? Are you really committed?"

As I walked out of his office, I knew that I had to get a message across to everyone in the company, and I knew that I had to find a way to say it loudly and unequivocally. The message was: *I care; I am committed; I will be here tomorrow; you can trust me. Together we will succeed.* As I went about my travels, I began to develop this insight into a working philosophy that took into account what people expected of the company and what role the leader played in this.

Creating trust is where all management wisdom begins. It is fundamental to any lasting business success, and so it is also where this book begins. In this chapter, I describe the personal style that grew out of that realization. Mine is an activist, engaged style. I try to be with people where they are, to understand their issues, and to help them solve their problems. This style demands a great deal of others and myself. Wherever I go, I poke into every detail of the business, and I tell people frankly about my findings. I hold everyone, including myself, to standards. I make decisions on the spot when issues arise. Above all, I am always aware that I am setting an example wherever I go and to whomever I speak.

▶ *Build Credibility the Best Way You Know How*

What I soon realized was that people wanted to know that the company had plans for growth and expansion, and that they would have a future in it. Mechanics, coordinators, drivers, secretaries, dispatchers—all were looking for an environment in which they could be secure and could earn a living for their families until they retired. They wanted to hear that the company was happy with this operation in their city, that we supported it, that we wanted it to prosper and grow. They were looking for words of encouragement that allowed them to feel secure. Managers were looking for opportunities to accept greater challenges and achieve more significant roles in the company.

My job was to show people that I believed in them so that each one would come out looking and feeling stronger. I had to let people know that I was listening to them in order to understand their operation better so that I could support it more effectively. In other words, people wanted to hear that this company was committed to tomorrow—to making tomorrow better than today.

Consistency builds trust. Peter Drucker points out that leaders do not necessarily earn trust by being liked or by always getting people to agree with them. Good leaders are not permissive; they are willing to make tough decisions, and when things go wrong they accept the buck themselves. According to Drucker, trust comes about when people become convinced that the leader means what he or she says because every statement is backed up by a record of consistency. I wholeheartedly agree with him that leadership "is not based on being clever; it is based primarily on being consistent."[1]

That ultimately was my answer to that hard-eyed regional manager sitting across from me back in 1982. You can win trust even from the skeptics if:

▶ You are willing to work at it a step at a time.

▶ You say what you mean.

▶ You deliver on it.

People must get to know you, and they do not get to know you if you sit in a corner office and issue pronouncements. I call this approach the "corner-office mentality." From my experience in turning around HERC, I have learned that the essence of trust building is to get fully immersed in the details of the business—not only the financial details but the human and physical details. Immersing yourself in everything, asking employees all the questions you can think of, and showing that you are paying attention to their answers—all these actions not only build your credibility, they also keep you in touch with what is happening out there in the world.

What I practiced from the beginning goes by different names. "Managing by walking around" is a phrase we often hear nowadays. The term I use is "touching the iron," which comes from my own industry; it is a variant of "touching metal," the term used in the automotive industry. It simply means:

▶ You have been on location, whatever or wherever that may be.

▶ You have seen whatever there is to be seen with your own eyes.

▶ You have asked some questions if what you have seen doesn't seem to add up, is in the wrong place, or isn't there.

Touching the iron is more than just a metaphor to me; I literally touch the equipment, climb onto it, poke under the hood, and sometimes get under it. Walking around discovering, touching the iron—it all comes to the same thing. I just happen to make my discoveries by poking about more than most other top executives do.

This is simply my personal style, which probably can be applied to any management task in any industry. You may be more comfortable with

[1] Peter F. Drucker, *Managing for the Future: The 1960s and Beyond,* New York: Dutton, p. 122.

another management style, but the moral remains the same: *Build credibility the best way you know how.*

▶ *A Switch in Career Paths Led Me to HERC*

I evolved my style of hands-on, incremental, day-at-a-time management out of sheer necessity when I was rather unexpectedly switched out of a staff job into operations as head of HERC in 1982. Considering my lack of preparation for an operations job, I had to get to know the business—and fast. My experiences in doing this can provide useful insight for many people: those just getting started in their careers; those who may be about to move into some new industry or job; or those who feel dissatisfied with their present methods and need a new way of going at their work.

When that switch occurred in 1982, I was on quite another career path: purchasing management. I had joined the Hertz Corporation four years before as director of purchasing and had become staff vice president of materials and support services a year later. I had gained a reputation as a troubleshooter, and this brought me a short assignment helping the HERC subsidiary straighten out some tangled logistical problems that afflicted its fleet of rental equipment.

The long and short of this task was that HERC was losing money, and the fleet was too large to support the small revenue base. Nobody knew which type of equipment in the fleet was surplus and which was readily rentable, so I began by identifying the excess equipment in each of the six regions of the company. I put together and consolidated a list pricing out the total value of surplus by category. With this list, I contacted wholesale auctioneers for estimates of the value the equipment would bring if we liquidated it through auction. The preliminary bids were so drastically low and the resulting loss would have been so severe that, to minimize the loss, I recommended either disposing of the excess units one piece at a time or redistributing them throughout our branches.

All of this helps to explain why Frank A. Olson, the chairman and chief executive officer of Hertz, called me into his office in September 1982 and told me that he wanted me to take over as general manager of HERC. I tried to gain a little time to think it over. I had developed a niche that I enjoyed and that suited perfectly my temperament and capabilities. Materials and numbers I knew I could manage—but what about managing people? And how about managing them in the context of an industry and products that I knew nothing about? It quickly got through to me, however, that the chairman was indeed serious about my taking the job. He promised that the parent corporation would give me full support and the resources to do the job properly, which helped ease some of my misgivings.

In October 1982, I duly became vice president and general manager of a business that I knew nothing about except for that short logistical task some months earlier. I was about to get not only a total immersion in this new world but a crash course in management training as well.

▶ *The Idea Behind HERC Was Diversification*

When people hear that we are in the equipment rental business they often think of those rental service stores or centers in almost every town in the country where you can obtain a vast assortment of household items, from hand tools to furniture. Equipment rental businesses, on the other hand, handle machines used in construction and materials handling; you will find our kind of stores in industrial areas and along strip centers on major highways. There are about six thousand of them in the country, mainly mom-and-pop enterprises. You may have driven by many of them without ever taking particular notice. What you see is a low building that looks something like a service station sitting in the middle of a lot perhaps surrounded (if it is a HERC site it is certain to be) by a chain-link fence. In that lot will be bulldozers, front-end loaders, dump trucks, water trucks, trenchers, compressors, and aerial equipment such as mobile platforms and telescopic booms. The smallest pieces of equipment we generally carry are things like pumps, air compressors, and generators.

When the Hertz Corporation got into the equipment rental business in 1966, it looked like a good way to diversify its car rental business. The Hertz name had a high public recognition value that would inevitably spill over into the new rental field. Hertz, as the pioneer in car rental, also expected its expertise to transfer over into the new business and yield useful synergies. Hertz started out by buying a half-dozen small regional companies mainly located in the Sun Belt and also in Massachusetts and California. There were no national rental equipment companies, so that HERC, with the 62 stores it eventually acquired or built itself, became the dominating concern in the equipment rental industry even though its national coverage was spotty. However, sticking mainly to the Sun Belt had the compensation of making it possible to do business 12 months of the year.

▶ *The Harsh Reality: Instability in Revenue and Profits*

HERC's seeming geographic advantage proved in the end to be illusory, however, because the equipment rental business was tied tightly to the highly volatile and cyclical construction industry. The result was that HERC's revenues spiked up and down in a way that no corporation can tolerate. The whole point in diversifying is to get away from the troughs and valleys and to assure an even flow of revenue. You can give up dramatic growth if you can stay stable and profitable, but you can't take the spikes. In addition, some of the expected synergies between the auto rental and the equipment rental businesses did not eventuate because of many fundamental differences.

My first year was particularly difficult. The one word that describes it best is "survival." I did not have much time to think about quality, just surviving. We had all the symptoms of a loser, and in fact we literally were losing money—big-time losses of millions a year on sales of $58 million. Here is just a short list of our problems:

▶ Facilities were rundown and inadequate.

▶ Pricing was not centrally controlled.

▶ Employees were insufficiently trained.

▶ Morale was poor.

▶ We still had millions of dollars of surplus equipment in the wrong places.

▶ Twenty percent of our fleet was broken.

▶ We had no standardization in the equipment we offered from one city to another.

▶ We didn't know who our customers were, and our problems hampered our ability to fulfill their needs.

▶ We were constantly caught up in price wars where all we could offer was lower prices, not added value, quality, or service.

In fact, our future viability as an equipment rental company was in question.

We had to take some truly draconian measures before the whole HERC operation could be turned around. This included not only shifting equipment around once again but also selling some and actually closing locations. I had to shrink the company. I couldn't manage it; there were too many problems. So we closed the worst stores, took the equipment out, and in some cases just parked it for a year while we concentrated on the 53 stores that I figured could be saved. On that basis, we had about $25 million excess equipment (the details of the disposal of this equipment and the renewal of the fleet are described in Chapter 7). These emergency measures went on through all of 1983, and it was during this period that I formed my basic style of management.

▶ How Your Appearance Sends a Signal to Employees

We have a place near the New Orleans airport, and I was there shortly after taking over my job inspecting the equipment with corporate and branch representatives. I happened to see a truck in the lot that looked as if it had been in the same place a long time. I could see weeds growing up through the bottom of it, and it was obvious that it had not been moved in quite a while. I unlatched the hood and threw it open, and exposed the damnedest hornets' nest I have ever seen. Out poured the hornets, mad as hell, and we started running like maniacs. It was the office manager, the regional vice president, the hornets, and I for 50 yards. A scary experience—but that was what it took to get that truck into shape and make it operational.

Our locations in the South can be very hot, and there are often sudden rainstorms in the late afternoons. When I visit these places on such occasions, the tendency of everyone is to walk to the edge of the garage and look at the equipment lying out there in the rain and mud. Now, what you have to do is walk to the equipment whether or not you have a raincoat; you don't acknowledge the weather—you're committed. You don't look at the equipment from the edge of the building protecting you. You visualize the sun shining and a dry field, and you go out there. You go out and walk through the mud intentionally, and you know everybody is going to follow along because you are doing it.

I don't care what you are wearing. I have ruined some good clothes; there was a fabulous pair of Gucci loafers that my wife is still annoyed about. I lead them straight out to the equipment. What I'm doing is showing that I care more about what I'm doing than about the weather, my clothes, or my personal comfort. *If you want people to go beyond the safe and usual, you must demonstrate that you are committed to a degree that goes beyond the safe and usual.* This applies not only to the industry I am in; it is a universal precept.

More than ever, I am conscious of the message I bring in my appearance. When I go into field operations, I represent the company, just as I do when I am chairing a meeting in my own office or visiting a major corporate customer. I have two sets of clothes, one for the office and one for travel. The only difference is that the travel clothes are a little older than the office clothes—a year-old suit rather than a new one because it is going to take more punishment. I visit a field office wearing well-shined shoes, a fresh white shirt, and generally a dark suit. And when I walk into the yard, I forget what I am wearing. I can't tell you how many hotel towels I have destroyed getting the mud off my shoes at night.

I have a message to deliver to the people in the field, and it starts with my appearance from the moment I step out of the car at the site. The message is a constant one: I honor and respect them in the same way that I honor and respect my peers in management, our suppliers, and our customers.

▶ *Never Pull Surprises on Your Employees*

When I go out in the field, I have two operating axioms that are applicable not only to our own service business but to virtually all businesses with dispersed operations.

Axiom 1: *When you find situations that need to be corrected, you must take immediate action.*

You can't turn a blind side; people will know you are aware of the problem and will be watching you carefully to see how you respond. Your actions will reinforce the messages you are trying to convey. You cannot get away with going back to that corner office and thinking it over. You have to respond on the spot or lose credibility.

Axiom 2: *It is perfectly all right to cut through lines of communication if you do it sensitively.*

I often go out into the field with regional managers and other regional officers; in the Louisiana hornet episode, for example, I was accompanied by a retinue of people representing various levels of authority. Likewise, I also travel by myself, and I am often with the people who report to the managers who report to me. This kind of interaction will not undercut the authority of senior managers if you handle sensitively and if there is a feeling of mutual trust. You have to work on this: Your managers must feel confident that you are not on location to cut them down or weaken employees' respect for them, that your purpose is to learn, teach, and communicate.

The basic rule is, *Never surprise anyone.* Don't drop in on a location unexpectedly. Let the people at the next higher level of command know your plans so they don't get nervous.

Well in advance of your arrival, inform the people at the location that you are coming. Sure, that gives them time to get busy and make the place all clean and tidy, but if that is what it takes, well, fine! The last thing I want my trips to be are white-glove inspections. I want people to accept these visits as my modus operandi, just as everybody expects Bill Marriott to show up at his locations to look over the whole place and meet people. Nobody in the company appreciates having the president pay surprise visits to an operation by dropping on the roof in a helicopter. People don't take it seriously; they know it's just a stunt.

By going out on the road, I am trying to say to people, "You are my staff; I believe in you. I am here to look around. I am here to talk with you and help you. I am here to learn. When I walk around and see something I don't like, I will tell you so: I'm not just on a public relations junket. You tell me what you think, too. This is a give-and-take proposition." I try to give them my vision and tell them where the company is headed. I want the people I have met to say, "Well, I know what is going on. I talked to Dan Kaplan. He knows what is going on, he's president of the company."

The only difference between one business and another is people. *The closer you can get to people and show them personally that you are committed to them, the greater your chances are of success.* I am trying to tell each employee I meet that there is no such thing as "'the company': *You* are the company." In a service business, it is all people, and if you do not relate to people and overcome what I call "the people problem," who on earth is going to do it for you?

▸ *The Practiced Eye and Touch: Evaluating Your Operations Personally*

When I visit our locations, I usually begin out in the yard to see if anything jumps out at me. Is the ground around the fuel pumps clean? Are the chain-link fences tight and secure? Is there junk around? Is the equipment clean and lined up in a uniform fashion? Is the place generally orderly? These seemingly small but crucial details tell me a lot about morale and the way the place is being managed.

If you are in the manufacturing business and find a mess on the floor of a factory, it may indicate something basic is wrong in that location and needs attention, but your customers are unlikely to see it. In the service business, however, you are constantly exposed to the public. Appearance is everything in a service business like ours: It reassures customers that the place observes good safety practices and is well managed. It indicates that the people running the business care enough to show it off to the customers. It also says that people who take such good care of the place must likewise give superior service.

I want everyone who works for us to know that appearance matters a great deal to me personally. Keeping at this is time consuming and often tedious, but if you are the head of a service business and want to maintain a high level of quality, you have to make the effort.

A practiced eye can detect pretty much what is going on with a business and how well it is serving its customers—even something about the state of the local economy—just by looking at the store and lot. If it is a HERC location and a few dozen pieces of equipment are lined up neatly on the lot, Dan Kaplan is going to be pleased going in because the place seems to be well tended and guarded and the inventory looks lean and balanced; things are on rental and producing income. Some excess inventory in certain things is all right; air compressors, for example, are in high demand almost everywhere and have a high turnover. But I am alert for problems if the yard is filled with big equipment scattered around and seemingly in need of cleaning and attention.

Here are some tips I have learned over the years that help me make the most effective use of inspection trips:

1. Take Pictures of Problem Areas. From the very beginning, I have taken a camera with me on my field trips. At a typical location we will have anywhere from 200 to 400 pieces of equipment, and in the early days, as I have already indicated, 20 percent of them were apt to have serious problems. So I would always ask the manager what he or she was going to do, to remedy the situation, and I would get a plan in response; but I still took a picture of the broken equipment. Taking the picture showed that I cared when I saw a bad piece of equipment. When I went back to the office, I would mail the manager a picture of the equipment and ask its status. Sending the picture, let the manager know I was serious.

I still carry a camera and use it to make points. When I was in Spain not long ago visiting one of our locations, I happened to look in the alley behind the shop, and there the mechanics had dumped every conceivable piece of junk: old wire, beat-up carburetors, boxes, scrap metal, you name it. I sent the manager a picture of the heap, and the next time I was there I took another shot and sent that to him, too. What an improvement!

I always take a picture of the whole facility and put it in an album showing every one of our operations—a sort of family album that I keep in my office. It helps me visualize all our locations. These are not abstract businesses run by robots; they are real places with real live people. The pictures of the facilities and the employees remind me of the reality of the situation. When somebody comes in to see me and we talk about HERC, I bring out the album and start flipping through it with pride. This simple act conveys an important message: *This guy cares; he's talking about these places and these people as if they're family.*

2. Keep Your Visibility High. I like to have the manager and the maintenance supervisor with me when I do these tours of the yard and facilities. I will climb up into the seat of a roller and check to see if it starts. Then I will look at the hour meter, and if I see that it is a couple of years old and has had only 300 hours of use, I know that machine is not being utilized a lot. I check the blade of the bulldozer that is next in line. If the cutting edge is too rough and worn, it means we have to replace it before the whole blade is destroyed, which is a costly repair job. Sometimes I don't have to say anything. The people with me know perfectly well what I am looking for as I poke around, and they make a mental note to get that gizmo fixed.

3. Don't Be Afraid to Get into a Dialogue. When I inspect tracked vehicles, I always check the wear on the tracks to see if they are being properly maintained—they cost $5,000 apiece. I may see that the tracks sag a little too much, but the manager may disagree with me and point out that if they are too tight there will be too much friction. That is perfectly all right, because I have shown that I know my job, am alert to everything that is going on, and am willing to get into an open give-and-take on the question. My purpose in all these encounters is to set up a dialogue in which a mutual learning experience will emerge.

A visitor who accompanied me on a yard visit asked the manager who was with us whether he didn't feel under surveillance on these tours with the top boss. The manager's reply was, "No," explaining that his background was in service, and in this business everyone is comfortable with people who know what they are talking about. "Take Jerry here, my service manager," he added. "I instructed him years ago on this equipment. He knows he can't give me any bull." This rough-and-ready interchange is essential in our business, probably in any service business. The decisions that have to be made involve calls that equally well-informed people often can make one way or the other. Don't be afraid of dialogue. In my experience, people rarely confront you with questions that are really too tough to answer or that will embarrass you. Moreover, you can learn a lot of valuable information and tips through dialoguing.

4. When You Pick up New Ideas, Give Generous Recognition. We had a problem in HERC with overloaded trucks; the equipment would protrude, and occasionally a truck would hit a bridge. We probably hit five bridges a year. We would wreck the truck, wreck the equipment we were delivering, and damage the bridge; altogether, it would cost us a quarter million dollars. When I was in Houston, I once noticed that someone had put up two posts across the exit to the yard with a chain hanging between them. The idea was simply that if a truck was overloaded it would rip down the chain. I now call that our "low bridge device," otherwise known as "LBD." I said to the supervisor who devised it, "I am going to make you famous," and I took some pictures of that prototype LBD. I sent them to every HERC location in the country with a note that explained, "Call John in Houston if you want advice on how to put it up, but I want everybody in the country to have one." Ever since we put those LBDs up, we have not hit a single bridge. Five bridges, five trucks a year; one person can make a big difference.

▶ Always Offer Your Hand to Your Employees

When I walk into the workshop and see mechanics at work, I always go up to them and shake hands. Usually, they don't want to shake hands with me because I am in a suit, my hands are clean, and the mechanics are dirty and grimy. My advice to anyone who wants to be effective when walking about and discovering: *Shake hands every time.* It shows that you are committed, that you and the other person are in this thing together.

I always ask people about the equipment and what problems they are having. I not only want to know what is going on, but I want to learn more about that particular piece of equipment so I can be smarter the next time I meet up with it. I also want the mechanics to know that I care about what they are doing, that it matters to me. And I want my managers to be with me there, too, asking the same questions, sharing the same interest and commitment. I am not saying you have to walk to the far end of the yard to find people, but if they are across the room, go over and shake their hands. *It is important to affirm people.*

Once when I was doing the rounds in a shop, I inadvertently passed by a mechanic who was standing right there; I simply failed to see him. The next time I was there, he said, "Mr. Kaplan, are you mad at me? I was upset for six months because you didn't come over to me and say hello." You cannot know the hidden value in these encounters. What does it mean in my life as an executive to walk over and say to the man or woman, "Hello, my name is Dan Kaplan. What are you doing here? How are you?" The significance of that action to others may be immeasurable—just to have the president walk a little out of the way to say "Hello." Not enough managers and executives do that, and I wonder why not. That person is working for you, you are paying him or her, and here you have taken the time to go all that distance to get to the location in the first place. What more does it cost to walk over and say hello? Ten seconds of your time?

Are you familiar with those enormous red toolboxes that mechanics have, the kind you can buy at Sears? They are great big boxes that sit on wheels and come up to about eye level. The mechanic owns that box and the tools inside: it is to the worker what my office is to me. Inside, you will find shelf after shelf of tools, and on top is usually a family photograph. I always comment on what a beautiful toolbox it is and what an investment in tools it represents; almost every time, the mechanic will open it up proudly and say, "Look at this new tool I just bought." Or, when I see a truck driver who keeps a clean truck, I always commend the person. I am trying to relate to the driver, to provide assurance that his or her job is important, that as president of the company *I see what the person is doing and care about it.* Then I go on to ask the employee for any comments or any ideas.

In Baltimore, I once noticed that a mechanic seemed to be having a lot of difficulty working under a bulldozer, so I got down on my hands and knees with him to take a look. I understood only part of what he was pointing out to me, but enough to see that this was a major repair job that probably required more information than he had available in the field. So I crawled back out, went to the phone in the office, called company headquarters in New Jersey to get some technical advice, and then crawled back under the bulldozer to tell the mechanic what I had learned. I wanted the mechanic to know that the president of the company thought that the job he was doing was important, that there were no lengths to which I wouldn't go to see he received all the help he needed.

That to me is the essence of the leader's job. The horizon tends to close in on people when they are under a boom wrestling with a wrench and a rusty bolt. People need a vision to find meaning in their work, as well as the tools to implement that vision. A leader is responsible for supplying people with whatever they need to get the job done properly. At the same time, the leader must keep the vision alive by demonstrating total commitment to it. I can't think of a better, more tangible way of expressing this commitment than by showing that you ask of your employees no more than you ask of yourself.

▸ *How Many Days Are Enough to Spend on Location?*

During my first years with HERC, I had to spend as much as 200 days a year on the road. When we had about 53 locations, that meant I was getting around to some of them several times a year. However, as the number grew to 85 locations in the United States, plus another 10 abroad, my appearances began to thin out. I still spend a great deal of time on the road, although perhaps not 200 days a year, because I have many other important responsibilities at Hertz headquarters office in northern New Jersey. The development of our powerful electronic information network keeps me in continuous and instant touch with what is happening everywhere in the system. Nevertheless, *touching the iron* remains an essential part of my personal management style. Both figuratively and literally, it is my style.

I give great credit to Sam Walton. He had too many stores to visit all of them, yet he visited enough of them to build and hold his credibility. The operation he left behind is immense compared with mine (there are nearly 2,000 Wal-Mart stores), yet he was able to show his genuine interest and remain in touch with the business. He was respected by his peers and employees because he showed he cared; he proved his commitment to the business and won people's trust. Walton liked to think back to the early 1960s when he managed his nine stores by flying to each store once a week in his Tri-Pacer. Walton eventually had to bring a lot of other people into his peripatetic act. Just before his death in 1992, he said the company's 18 regional vice presidents were now doing the job he had managed alone 30 years earlier. He simply made it a condition of employment for both regional vice presidents and buyers that they spend at least the first half of each week out on the road. "We've drummed into their heads," he said, "the belief that they should come back with at least one idea that will pay for the trip."[2]

Like Sam Walton, I insist that my then-six, now-seven regional managers get out constantly and touch iron, too. Nowadays, I would guess that I average about $1^1/2$ visits to each of our stores during a year, and I confess to showing a certain favoritism in picking the locations to visit. Most often, I choose stores that are either doing very well or are in trouble. The stars teach me a great deal that I can carry elsewhere. I also have an opportunity—which I value greatly—to tell them they are doing a superb job. As for the losers (or the ones on their way there), they obviously require a lot of instruction, coaching, morale building, and just plain close attention and Dutch uncling—along with lots of praise when they earn it. So no one gets a lot of my time any more, and some admittedly get shorted.

▶ *No Matter How Much Time You Give, People Will Still Want More*

Regardless of how much time you spend at a site, the people there will always feel it isn't enough. After all, they may be spending a lifetime in that city, and you are there for an hour, two hours, half a day. The problem for local management is whether you can grasp all you need to know in such a short time. My managers don't always understand that I've been doing this for a long time; I know what to look for. They want to know, "Why are you leaving so soon?" Meanwhile, I'm thinking that I have to get around to 95 locations a year, plus do a lot of other things. As they see it, I'm leaving forever, and they are worried about being short-changed.

It is critical to realize that if you don't leave your people "up," you will have a real problem. You may not be back again for six months, maybe even a year, so if you are going to knock heads together, you had better be sure to get back to them on a more positive note before you leave. I'm not saying you shouldn't knock heads together, just that you had better figure out how to do it without creating a lot of damage.

The value of these visits for you and your employees depends on the spirit in which you make them and what happens afterward. I have learned two essential rules:

[2] Sam Walton with John Huey, *Sam Walton: Made in America: My Story*, New York: Doubleday, 1982, pp. 224–225.

1. If you visit locations for show—just grandstanding—or if you don't exactly know what you are after, you are likely to gain very little from your field trips. Worse yet, people will quickly pick up on your posturing or indecision, and reactions to that perception will surface after you leave. You will succeed in leaving only a feeling of indifference and cynicism behind you. *If you show your employees something less than total commitment, they, too, are going to give the workplace something less than that.*

2. There has to be a follow-up after you have gone, something tangible to show conclusively that you were there and meant what you said. In my early months at HERC, it was when the employees saw new equipment arriving at our locations, facilities being improved, and sales and marketing programs being implemented, that morale began to skyrocket. People listened to me, but until something actually happened, no one was really sure I was trustworthy. These concrete signs of improvement, displayed in small increments day by day, demonstrated the reality of the commitment and the concern from the top. With improved morale, we had increased dedication to the task, which led little by little to improved operating results that turned a loser company into a winner.

Because HERC is a division of a larger corporation, I had to think not only of employees but also senior management. By showing firm commitment, we were also able to get senior management to buy into what we were doing. I took members of the chairman's staff, as well as the chairman himself, on some of my touching-the-iron trips so that they could see firsthand all those myriad independent actions that we were taking to improve the company's results and the quality of its service. Setting as your initial goal a better tomorrow, no big promises, buys time while you're getting your priorities in order and raising your sights for the long haul. Show people steady progress as evidence that your ideas are indeed taking hold. It enhances your credibility, and meanwhile your bosses will have greater patience as you develop your detailed plans for the big step ahead.

A better tomorrow is just about the right time frame to think about if you want to get into the twenty-first century intact. I recommend it as a good working principle; at least it has worked for me.

WRAP-UP
A Primer on Touching the Iron

"Touching the iron" is a variant of "management by walking around." The style is similarly involved but is adapted to a rough-and-ready scene like equipment rental, which often requires climbing into, on, and under large machines. The human principles, however, are the same:

▶ On a site visit, your basic job is to create trust, to show that you believe in people, so each one will come out looking and feeling stronger.

▶ Don't be afraid to get into dialogue. People will rarely embarrass you with questions too tough to answer.

▶ If you want people to go beyond the safe and usual, you must demonstrate that you are committed to the same degree—which can get your Guccis muddy and ruin a good suit.

▶ If you find something wrong, you can't turn a blind side: You have seen it, you have to do something about it.

▶ In the beginning, you may have to spend 200 days out of the year in the field. Touching the iron is not a drop-in-drop-out affair. It demands commitment. You have to make sure it is the style for you.

▶ A basic rule: "No surprises." Never drop in on a location unexpectedly. Always let the branch—and the regional office—know ahead of time that you are coming and when.

▶ Let people know that you regard them as your staff, and that you are there to look around, talk with them, learn from them, help them. And also to be candid with them if you find things you don't like. Stress that this is not a public relations trip.

▶ If you do have to find fault, first figure out a way to leave them on an upbeat note, otherwise you can create damage.

▶ Go out of your way to walk up to people in the shop and shake hands. You don't know the hidden value in these encounters. What is 10 seconds out of your day?

▶ Another basic rule: There should be a follow-up after your visit— some tangible result—to show that you were there and meant what you said.

2

Start with Simple Methodologies

I define a methodology as *a standardized approach across an entire system* ensuring that everybody is working toward the same objective and being measured on the same basis. When you deal with multiple locations, as we do in the service business, there can be as many different ways of performing any given action, or of submitting a report, as there are locations. You need to arrive at just one way of doing it that everyone can understand and be held accountable for.

This chapter describes how we developed two related methodologies:

1. How to evaluate locations.

2. How to analyze the customer base.

Because a lot of trial and error went into getting these methodologies right for our purposes, others may be able to benefit from our experience in shaping their own approaches and in setting up similar evaluation and measurement techniques.

▶ *Methodology 1: How to Evaluate Locations*

The scene was Shreveport, Louisiana; the year was 1984. We were having a grand opening for a state-of-the-art Hertz Equipment Rental facility on the outskirts of town. There were balloons and ribbons, the band was playing, and the crowd was about to sit down to a big Louisiana dinner of ribs and crawfish. The mayor was there to cut the ribbon, and I got a nice photo of him as he was finishing some appropriate welcoming remarks and was handing me the key to the town. Then, as we sat down to talk, he said to me, "Whatever do you know that we don't know that brought you here to Shreveport, Louisiana?" I can still feel my blood draining into the soles of my feet as he said that. The one thought that filled my mind was, "Now we've really done it: There's nothing here." And there wasn't. I was too embarrassed to give up right away, but in the end, there was no way to make a go of it; we closed the branch about two years after we opened it.

The trail that led to this fiasco began back in my earliest days with HERC. From the moment I joined the company, I was eager to start doing positive things that would make the company grow again. I wanted to see some evidence, and so did my corporate bosses, that HERC was beginning to turn around. Even as we were going about closing stores in those early days, I was thinking about how to start opening new stores. My desire for action got the upper hand, and I went ahead with planning my first new store without asking those careful and probing questions that need to be answered before starting a new venture. My error was in assuming that there was more accumulated expertise in HERC than in truth existed at that time. I did not stop to consider that if so many of our stores were in trouble, didn't that say something about the staff's ability to locate stores in the first place? I simply failed to realize that I was unwittingly becoming captive to the prevailing mentality of the equipment rental business as it was reflected in HERC through its origins.

Don't Take Anything for Granted

Mom-and-pop businesses are by definition scaled to a locality and have very different economics than that used by the kind of national business HERC was aspiring to become. The criteria for locating mom-and-pop sites—and how long to stick in there if things don't go well—are entirely subjective. Where to locate such a business is primarily a matter of where the would-be owners happen to live, their personal knowledge of the town and its people, and other adventitious factors. The mom-and-pops often persist against an adverse local economic tide because they are willing to take less profit and to suffer erosion of capital. They are your toughest competition, because their only alternative is to go out of business. Therefore, they will go to any lengths in pricing before they make that final choice.

The equipment rental industry simply had never matured to the point where there was any felt need for highly complex models to determine store location demographically and geographically. The great national supermarket, merchandising, motel, car rental, and other chains had all reached that phase decades ago. The largest operations in the equipment rental business were still regional in size, and even at HERC, the giant in the field, the thinking hadn't reached this stage at the time I entered the picture. Nor was there enough competition within the industry to force HERC or anyone else into more professional and aggressive techniques for locating units.

The Wrong Method for Finding a New Location

Here is how they went about finding new locations at HERC when I arrived there: Headquarters would call one of the regional vice presidents and ask for a recommendation on where to open a new operation in that area. The regional vice presidents were familiar with the economic activity in their territories just from making their ceaseless rounds. They could hardly help noticing a strip center going up here, a mall being built there, a factory or some other kind of facility under construction over there. They were also in touch with friends and business associates all over the region. So when they got our call, they would put all this visual and anecdotal information together and say to themselves, "Well, right here is a very good place for us to expand." They had no definable basis for what was "good," but they did have a natural desire to offer some plausible suggestion to headquarters in order to expand the branch operations in their particular region.

The final step in this process therefore was to go to the local chamber of commerce to get some corroborative evidence that would sustain the vice president's seat-of-the-pants recommendation. Now, I don't care where you go in the United States, the local chamber of commerce will always give you a glowing report indicating that their economy is booming or is on the edge of a big wave of activity. There is always something encouraging to point out—a couple of new industrial plants, housing starts, construction spending, something. And sometimes there is indeed a burst of development, but it may only be short lived. Nevertheless, the regional vice president would use these soft data to support the eyeballing technique, and about two weeks after our initial inquiry, we would have a firm recommendation for a site for a new HERC store. And that is how we wound up in Shreveport.

Moral: *When you are in a new situation, don't take anything for granted, especially your own judgment.*

The Right Method for Finding a New Location

I knew there had to be a better methodology for locating sites for new stores. I was aware that every service business has unique dynamic socioeconomic factors—age of population, per capita income, and so forth—that determine where it will locate its outlets. It doesn't matter whether you are a Wal-Mart, a Home Depot, a McDonald's, or a HERC, you have to find the key drivers for your business. So we decided to build our own model for locating units nationally.

It took us some time and a good deal of experimentation to get the model just right for our purposes, and that, too, was an important part of the exercise. For all of us at HERC, it became a learning experience that helped raise the standards of the entire organization. Because we are a very cost-conscious company, we did not hire in expensive outside marketing consultants, nor did we set up a formal unit within the company to manage the study. Instead, we handled it informally out of headquarters, assigning people to the task as they were available; we also called on people in the branches and units to provide their input and ideas.

We sent people to the library to study the possible factors that could be influential in determining success in the construction equipment business. They spent some months on this problem, and what they eventually came up with was nothing revolutionary or unique—simply what a group of bright and inquisitive MBAs could achieve given good information and some time. What they developed was a basic model for predicting potential markets for equipment rental based on the government's *Standard Statistical Measured Areas (SSMAs)* adjusted to the particular characteristics of our industry.

Seven Weighted Characteristics

We started this process by conceptualizing the local construction cycle. We saw this cycle as starting in any locality with new houses and roads and going on to a strip shopping and service center. Typically, the strip center will attract a light office building, followed perhaps by a light industrial area; eventually there may be a water slide and an industrial plant. What we needed to know was where a given community was in the cycle to see if it was ready to support an equipment rental facility, and if so, what the potential size of the market would be. We therefore needed to know a number of things about that community.

After some study, we assembled the following list of seven characteristics that would provide the information we needed to rank each SSMA in the order of its potential for our business. The factors were all readily definable; that is, you could look up the hard data in available statistical sources:

1. *Present Population*—A determining factor in deciding whether a locality had the primary resources to support a facility large enough to be profitable.

2. *Population Projection Five Years From Now*—Rapidity of growth could put a very different light on a given market's potential for our business.

3. *Population Growth Rank*—The anticipated percentage increase over the next five years. Any area with a high growth rate was one that should receive careful attention.

4. *Industrial Rank*—The dollar volume of goods and services for the area.

5. *Total Spending on Residential and Nonresidential Construction*—Key in ranking an area for the purposes of an equipment rental company.

6. *Growth Rank in Residential and Nonresidential Construction*—Another ranking that should flag attention.

7. *Construction Growth per Capita*—Key to the wealth of the area.

If you were involved in some other service business, you would undoubtedly pick other criteria. Changes in the aging of the population, for instance, would be important to you if you were in the homebuilding supply business, because it would tell you something about the potential size

Table 2.1. "Weed-and-Feed" strategy highest and lowest scores in 1987 (projections to 1992).

	City, State	Current Population (1987)	Future Population (1992)	Population Growth (1987–1992)
1	Los Angeles, CA	1	1	67
2	New York, NY	2	2	204
3	Riverside, CA	14	17	8
⋮	⋮	⋮	⋮	⋮
317	Pine Bluff, AR	308	307	300
318	Grand Forks, ND	317	318	206
319	Casper, WY	318	317	318

of the remodeling market. These were the seven factors that seemed germane to our business.

The only problem we had with them was deciding their *relative* ranking in our model. How were we going to determine which of these factors was of greater importance when compared with others? Here are the kinds of questions we wrestled with:

▶ Was future population or per capita spending the more significant factor in determining the potential for us in that market?

▶ How about industrial activity? And how about industrial activity as compared with, say, construction?

We simply didn't know the definitive answers to these questions, but we did know that we had to put a relative weight on each factor and that they were all close calls.

In the end, we took a chance on our own imperfect judgment and simply made arbitrary decisions in weighting each factor. We then fed our data into a computer, ranking each of the SSMAs in our model according to the seven weighted characteristics. Using a scale of zero to a hundred percent, we scored each SSMA the way you do in golf: the lower the city's score, the higher its rank in our scale of desirable markets.

Table 2.1 shows a sampling of cities at the top and the bottom of the scoring for the year 1987. The best score of the 319 cities in our model is 22, and at the other end of the spectrum, the worst shows a value of 308. As might be expected, Los Angeles and New York come out at the top of the list by sheer weight of population; the cities at the bottom are in thinly populated areas where growth is slow. The high position of Riverside, California, by contrast, shows how fast growth, a significant factor in our

Industrial Goods/ Services (1987)	Residential/ Nonresidential Construction (1987)	Construction Growth (1987–1992)	Construction Growth Per Capita (1987–1992)	Strategic Score
2	1	144	117	22.1
1	3	32	161	25.4
43	4	174	6	30.3
⋮	⋮	⋮	⋮	⋮
294	312	265	306	302.2
313	311	311	287	302.6
312	315	241	302	308.4

weighting, can influence ranking. There are many surprises throughout the list that cannot be revealed because of the data's proprietary nature; my intent here is simply to provide enough information for others to develop their own methodology.

Convincing People That Your Formula Works

To find out whether this scoring really was valid, we decided to play a strategy game with it. We said, "Now, here are some cities with certain kinds of characteristics; if we open stores in them, what chances of success do we have?" We then looked at other cities that showed similar characteristics and that we knew about firsthand because we had stores there. Lo and behold, it worked out on paper the way it had worked out in our actual experience! The cities with poor (high) scores were the very ones giving us the most trouble. One thing was certain: Had we developed our methodology earlier, we would never have opened in Shreveport; its high score would have warned us off after a single glance.

The new methodology met its first real-life test in Ventura, California, a low-scoring city that immediately attracted our attention at headquarters as having a wonderful potential for a HERC facility. Ventura, which is about 60 miles north of Los Angeles and 25 miles south of Santa Barbara, appeared to be in the middle of a construction cycle, and there were still a lot of homes to be built. That was the first piece of good news; the second was that there were offshore oil wells; the third was that there was a lot of agricultural activity. Further investigation also showed that rental rates were strong in Ventura, a positive and welcome signal. To our way of thinking, we couldn't find a better test case, and we told the regional office to go ahead with a branch in Ventura.

But the regional people balked. They could not, it appeared, help thinking of Ventura as really a part of Santa Barbara, which was fixed in their minds as merely a quaint and sleepy place. We argued otherwise on the strength of our data, but they kept dragging their feet. They had no faith whatsoever that Ventura could be successful, and they said so in a most decided way. I finally became annoyed. "Look, open in Ventura, don't even question what we are telling you," I told them. "The report says do it, so do it." I had so much faith in that study that I was willing to go for broke on Ventura without feeling that I was seriously risking my reputation and prestige. I didn't even bother with a single; I decided to point to the bleachers and swing.

Well, it worked. We opened in Ventura, and in the first year we made a million dollars. Our study was now validated by the acid test of experience, and we knew that we had found the methodology that would open up our business. And I went back to hitting singles once more.

How to Use a Weed-and-Feed Strategy for Growth

At the time we built the branch in Ventura, we were still in the process of closing the weak branches that we could not successfully rehabilitate and make profitable. Closing the first dozen or so losers in the HERC system was a depressing task, but accomplishing it hardly required any theoretical background in the distribution and service industries. The history of persistent, continuing losses year after year was right there in the books, and it took only a few touching-the-iron visits to these locations to confirm the financial diagnoses. Some locations were so far gone and so hopeless that there was no doubt about what we had to do at that point of lingering crisis in HERC's history: Close them.

Our store in St. Louis offers a good example of the intractable situations we faced. This location had originally been opened to supply equipment for the construction of a new General Motors assembly plant. The branch stocked up on the sophisticated, scissors-and-boom aerial equipment needed for that job. It was specialized, high-tech equipment, and when the contract ended, the equipment came back to the branch. Because management was weak, the branch had failed to diversify its customer base. We were therefore stuck with an inventory no one wanted, in addition to which a great deal of broken equipment had been allowed to accumulate. Another difficulty was that the St. Louis branch was distant from other stores in our network, so we could not give it logistical support.

The problems in St. Louis were thus simply too large for us to fix along with all the other problems we had to deal with at that time. So we closed the place and put the inventory in storage in Charlotte, North Carolina, where we had a large lot that we were using for this purpose as we shut down other branches.

Cases like this were clear-cut. *Radical surgery was the only sensible solution.* This is often a regrettable but inevitable aspect of turning around losing businesses to make them into healthy enterprises. Eventually, by a process of triage, we had eliminated the hopeless cases and were getting the ones that seemed sound back on their feet.

About the time we opened Ventura, we had gotten rid of most of the dogs and were down to marginal cases, where the available evidence did not indicate clearly whether it would be worthwhile to make the effort to save them. One of the first uses to which we put our new evaluation technique was in determining which of these locations had potential and were worth trying to save and which were candidates for elimination. We therefore called our evaluation project "weed-and-feed," borrowed from the vocabulary of lawn care: *weed out the poor growth, feed the good grass.* It told us when to close out stores that were no longer economically viable; and when we were ready to open new stores, it told us where the potentially good markets were.

Keep Your Methodology Up to Date

I always preach the value of consistency, of staying with your methodology: Improve it, yes, but stay with it. We have stayed with our weed-and-feed methodology for nearly a decade now. Its function is tactical rather than strategic. The advance information from weed-and-feed tells us where exactly we should pinpoint our locations in implementing an overall strategy for expansion. Various considerations have played a role in developing our strategy, one major factor being the needs of our major national customers and another being competitive pressures. Logistics have also played a vital role, since the location of new stores has to take into account the support that the rest of the network can give them. Now that we have developed an overall strategy for expansion, weed-and-feed provides us with the value of each square (SSMA) on the chessboard. The way in which we have developed our strategic and logistical plan is described in Chapter 6.

We keep watching and carefully revising the weed-and-feed data. Local economies can be volatile and are continuously changing either for the better or worse from HERC's standpoint. Our criteria change therefore as local economies move through cycles of development or are affected by outside economic forces. The economic climate in Ventura, for example, has become less favorable than it was when we moved there, and we have to struggle harder to hold our position in that market. On the other hand, St. Louis has moved up in our strategic ranking, and we recently returned there with a new store. We have been careful, however, to diversify our customer base in St. Louis so that we don't repeat our earlier debacle by relying wholly on a single big construction project.

Our methodology of weighted strategic scoring for SSMAs has thus become our basic means of keeping our distribution network attuned to changing economic reality.

▸ *Methodology 2: How to Analyze the Customer Base*

We knew that collectively our stores were serving about 17,000 customers ranging from contractors and construction companies to warehouses, chemical and oil companies, utilities, and golf courses. But just what categories were responsible for generating precisely what proportions of our business was a deep and troubling mystery. We urgently needed to have this information if we were ever to stabilize our business and break out of those rental demand cycles that drove our volume up and down in spikes. We needed to track and monitor the sources of our business and to begin to cultivate the kinds of businesses that would give us new earning potential and help to even out those peaks and valleys in revenues and profits.

This seemed so rudimentary that I knew finding the answers had to have a high priority if HERC was to become a viable company with any kind of future. I could not detect in this 15-year-old company any grasp of the basic concept that shapes every successful business: *It's your choice what markets you want to be in.* If you can't make those choices, you will have no control over your fate and you will be a set-up for whatever economic trend happens along. This is a basic premise of survival and growth.

How to Start Measuring When There Are No Guidelines

In this case, I was aware that I could take nothing for granted. I knew from just a few trips around our sites that the managers had only the vaguest ideas about their customer base. In April 1983, we decided to send out a questionnaire to all the managers to see if we could get them to think a little harder about the markets they were selling to. Since we had little or no guidance on how to proceed, we simply started out with six broad categories of customers:

1. Residential building.
2. Nonresidential construction.
3. Government.
4. Lease.

5. Agriculture.

6. Industrial.

These categories were crude, but at that stage of the learning process, it was the best we could achieve in defining our business segments. My premise in trying to measure any activity is simply to begin somewhere—anywhere—in the view that even poor data are better than none at all; at least you have something tangible to improve on. As it turned out, the answers simply confirmed my original impression about the managers' lack of knowledge about market segmentation. Here are some examples:

▸ One manager said that 20 percent of his business was in residential construction, whereas another reported that this category accounted for only 4 percent. You couldn't begin to average such figures sensibly or get a median. Besides which, I knew from my travels that HERC wasn't doing even a percentile of its overall business in homebuilding.

▸ Another manager reported that he was doing 26 percent of his business in nonresidential construction, when I knew from my own observation that the figure had to be closer to 85 percent—we were that dependent on nonresidential business.

▸ Still another estimate put industrial business at 13 percent of the branch's total revenue. If we had been able to make a showing like that anywhere in the country, we would already have had the key to the diversification we so badly needed to balance our business. In those days, the best any branch could do in industrial business was 1 or 2 percent of its total business.

Accountability Starts with a Definition

Here was yet another systems failure, though of a different kind from that which I was then confronting in trying to find a rationale for locating stores. In the latter case, some semblance of a method, however inadequate, at least passed for a "system," which in itself was recognition that there was some problem that had to be addressed. In the case of the customer base, however, there was not only an absence of any system at all, but no seeming recognition that a need for one even existed.

Actually, a well-entrenched nonsystem of this sort functions as a kind of powerful *unseen* system perpetuating local control versus centralized control. In this case, it enabled the managers pretty much to run their stores as they pleased without having to be accountable for the kinds of customers and businesses they went after—or failed to go after. There was nothing against which to judge their performance, no way to set goals. This is the Achilles heel of the services industry: accountability. *Without precise accountability for performance, there is no way to ensure uniform quality of product.*

In seeking a methodology to select sites for our stores, we had turned to a standard governmental source (SSMAs) as our gold standard against which all would be measured. In seeking a consistent way to identify and categorize our customers, we now chose an equally familiar and accessible government measurement: *the Standard Industrial Codes (SICs).* There are about 10,000 SIC codes, most of which we could eliminate instantly. By careful sifting, we finally worked down to 39 that seemed to catch almost all current HERC customers at that time or any potential customers we could think of. We then printed a special box on our rental agreements that had to show a HERC Revenue Code identifying precisely the category of the customer who was renting from us. Some examples:

▶ HRC 09—roofing and sheet metal contractors.

▶ HRC 08—schools and colleges.

▶ HRC 41—heavy construction.

▶ HRC 79—entertainment.

Very quickly, we started to get anguished calls from the field asking for help in sorting out the following kinds of confusion:

▶ A HERC location was renting a diesel air compressor to an electrical contractor doing some work in an oil refinery. How should they write this up? Would that be scored HRC 07 for "electrical contractor" or HRC 36 for "refineries"?

▶ How about a painting contractor renting a manlift for work on a residence? Would you score that HRC 14 for "specialty contractor" or HRC 01 for "residential construction"?

We solved this problem by declaring that what determined the coding was the identity of the contractor or the business that actually signed the rental agreement and took delivery of the equipment no matter what the setting was. For instance, if the renter was a sandblasting contractor (HRC 18) working on a railroad bridge, the contractor and not the railroad (HRC 23) was to be credited with this rental. In other words, we made another arbitrary decision, like the arbitrary weighting of criteria described earlier in this chapter.

These examples emphasize that when you are trying to assign numbers to things in the services field many decisions have to be made this way. The real world out there is not very symmetrical, and you are apt to wind up with somewhat hybrid structures. In this case, we were having to decide whether to give the weight to the "trade" or the "market," and we gave it to the trade. But this is not a perfect world: *Running a service business is an art not a science.* The main thing is to get a definition down on paper so that you have something tangible to measure. You can improve the definition as you go to make it increasingly accurate.

The Minute Details Make the Difference

Now came the real work, first of redefining the wording of each of the codes so that it worked for HERC and then of developing a more sophisticated model of our market segmentation. This effort went on for about a year and virtually made us all into economists as we talked back and forth between regions, branches, and headquarters. As new questions would crop up, we would amend the language to eliminate ambiguities. We wanted to make sure that every branch slotted customers where they belonged, so that at headquarters we could use the data with confidence, knowing that everyone was talking the same language.

This exercise proved to be another invaluable educational experience for the organization. As we struggled with the numbers and the definitions, we developed a clearer understanding of just *who* our customers were, *how much business* each accounted for, and *what the real structure* of our marketplace was.

My first rough cut at market segmentation using six components did not adequately characterize the cross section of the business. We therefore selected 39 segments, as described earlier, which did adequately characterize the business but were difficult to conceptualize and unwieldy to use. So we grouped these 39 components under the following three major market segments:

1. *Construction,* including both residential and nonresidential construction and ancillary trades.

2. *Industrial,* which ranged from mining and railroads to manufacturing and oil refineries.

3. *Fragmented,* which was the name we gave the remaining mixed bag of markets from warehouses to agriculture.

This was not only a simpler but also a more dynamic way to view our business. It dramatized where we were and where we wanted to go to stabilize our revenues: out of construction and into industrial and other markets.

The care we took is illustrated by the description of "HRC 41," which is the code we gave the heavy construction category. We define the operatives in this category as follows:

General contractors who engage in the structural construction, fabrication, and assembly of large and/or complex industrial plants and facilities (unlike those that are coded under HRC 02). Examples would include chemical, power generating, oil refinery, automotive assembly, steel mills, pulp/paper mills, etc.

This example emphasizes the extreme need to consider minute detail in the service business. That is the other name of the game: 1,000 small details. Just to make as certain as possible that no sales coordinator would make a mistake when keying in the code on a sales agreement, we stuck in that parenthetical reference to "HRC 02." This category is nonresidential construction, which includes all kinds of commercial building, motels, hospitals, and other institutional building. We wanted to ensure that there was no confusion between the two fields, one being identified in our book with the industrial field, the other with construction.

Applying the Results

Finally, we knew just where our business was coming from, and we had a pretty clear idea of where we ought to direct it. By shifting our sales emphasis little by little, a day at a time, we managed not only to quadruple our total business volume but completely transform its character. This dramatic change can be seen in Table 2.2. When we did our first crude market segmentation in 1983, HERC was doing about 90 percent of its business in the construction field. A decade later, the construction and industrial segments of the market had drawn about even in size and were each contributing about 45 percent of our vastly expanded volume.

Table 2.2 shows how small changes can radically transform an entire enterprise. The market shares of most of the trades in the industrial sector

Table 2.2. Market segmentation.

Construction			Industrial			Fragmented		
Year-to-Date	1983	1992	Year-to-Date	1983	1992	Year-to-Date	1983	1992
Residential	19.0	0.7	Water Sewer & Utility		2.5	Warehouses		0.5
Nonresidential	48.0	28.2	Special Trade Contractors		6.5	Schools, Colleges		0.4
Highway & Street	12.0	2.4	Mining		1.4	Building Materials		0.3
Plumbing & Heating		1.5	Chemical Companies		3.0	Trucking & Terminal		0.3
Electrical Work		3.4	Painting		0.8	Terminal Facilities		0.2
Roofing, Sheet Metal		0.7	Maintenance Services		3.5	Airport Terminal Services		0.2
Concrete & Masonry		1.9	Railroads		3.9	Agriculture		1.1
Structural Steel Erection		1.4	Paper Mills		1.5	Landscaping/Nursery		1.6
Glass, Glazing Work		0.2	Shipbuilding & Repair		1.4	Golf Course Construction & Maintenance		0.2
Excavating/Foundation		3.4	Manufacturers		4.4	Hazardous Waste Contractors		0.3
Plastering/Drywall		0.3	Refineries		4.9	Other	5.0	6.3
Wrecking Demolition		0.4	Oil, Gas Field		3.5			
Heavy Construction		0.2	Municipality Government	5.0	6.5			
Miscellaneous	11.0	0.0	Underground Utility Construction		.1			
Totals	90.0	44.7	Totals	5.0	43.9	Totals	5.0	11.4

are only a fractional part of our total revenues, but in the aggregate they now account for nearly half the total. And the way we made this vast change was by hitting 1,000 singles and paying attention to 1,000 small details. Not least important, the HERC revenue code was a vital building block of the massive statistical base that eventually became the core for our peer performance review.

WRAP-UP

Getting Everyone to Speak the Same Language

To measure a service business, or any business for that matter, people must speak the same language and use precisely the same terms. A methodology is a standardized approach across an entire system so that everybody is working toward the same objective and being measured on the same basis. To get the building blocks for such a system in place, you don't need elaborate models or high-priced consultants. Figure out what you want to measure by asking the right questions, then turn a few of your MBAs loose in the library. Here are two useful suggestions that will keep them busy:

1. *If your problem is developing a methodology for locating stores where they ought to go, see that everyone learns the vocabulary of "SSMA"* (Standard Statistical Measured Areas). You will need to adapt the SSMA vocabulary to your particular needs, but all that requires is patience, care, and a little ingenuity. With some knowledge of such terms as "local construction cycles," "per capita rankings," "strategic scores," and other useful terms extrapolated from the SSMA matrix, you won't repeat the Shreveport fiasco by locating a big new facility where only the local chamber of commerce can detect any economic bustle.

2. *If your problem is finding out who your customers are, make sure that your people learn to speak "SIC"* (Standard Industrial Codes). These codes offer rich vocabulary of 10,000 terms, and your MBAs' big job will be to see which ones specifically fit your customers. If your researchers work hard enough at this job of tailoring, the results will make it easy for you to distinguish between a customer who is an "HRC 02" and one who is really an "HRC 41." Knowing the difference is the kind of all-important small detail that keeps companies heading steadily toward their goal.

Hitting 1,000 singles; coping with 1,000 petty details—these are much the same thing.

3

Finding the Core of Your Business

I n my early days at HERC, I employed a simple and direct method for tracking current revenues and projections. Once a week, I would call each manager and ask how the business was doing and what the prospects were for the week ahead. I would jot down all the figures in long columns, and these big sheets were my database for tracking current revenues and forecasting the level of revenue just ahead. It took time, but it was still possible for me to do this kind of thing when we had fewer stores, and it was an effective way to keep in touch personally with every manager in the chain. The only problem was that the exercise did not really accomplish what I intended. Instead, I was continuously getting misleading signals about the trends in revenues.

The difficulty was not basically with the reporting system itself, primitive as it was, but with *the system's inability to screen out the short-term variables in our business,* especially changes in the weather, which greatly affect rental volume from day to day. These unpredictable fluctuations made it impossible to draw a trend line and to get accurate appraisals of how things really stood and where they were going. As a result, I was unable to develop reasonable business commitments and hold people to them.

This started me off on a search for what I have since come to call the "core" of the business. *The core is that segment of your business which yields steady revenues year after year.* It is the bread and butter of your business, the dependable and consistent performer every enterprise needs to be successful. The core is also that unique feature of your business which defines and differentiates it from other companies in your industry.

The story of how we located the core of our business at HERC can be helpful to other companies, not only in our industry, but also in other service industries. This chapter first describes the instability in revenues that was built into HERC when I arrived there, and how we identified the stable core of our business. Next, it tells how we institutionalized what we call our "monthly revenue base." Finally, it outlines a formula for stability that other service businesses can adapt to fit their own needs.

▶ The Inherent Instability of the Equipment Rental Business

To some degree, the equipment rental business always has been and always will be dependent on the weather. The weather is a basic fact about our industry in the same way that holiday surges in traffic are a basic condition of the airline industry, or that low-occupancy rates over the weekends tend to be a basic condition in the hotel and motel industry.

The Multiplier Effect of Rates on Revenue

When it is a nice, dry sunny day, we will obviously attract a lot more business coming in off the street than when it is raining and muddy and the equipment is liable to get bogged down. We may even experience an extra spurt of daily rental business because the weather forecast indicates rain the day after tomorrow; contractors rush in to rent bulldozers to get their jobs done in a hurry to beat the rain. Or if a long stretch of inclement weather is developing, the people who have equipment out on short-term rent will start returning it because they don't want to have an idle piece of equipment running up a daily rent of, say, $80.

The weather therefore can escalate daily revenues rapidly and can deescalate them equally sharply, typically creating numerous spikes in the rental revenue. Because of the rate structure of our industry, changes in the weather tend to have a multiplier effect on daily revenues. Daily rentals, which command the most profitable rates, are affected more by weather changes than are weekly and monthly rentals. This tended to distort further the projections my managers gave me each week. If they had just had a run of nice weather in their part of the country, that showed up as a nice sharp spike in last week's revenues as against the previous week, when the weather was rainy. If they looked out the window and saw blue skies, and if the local weather reports seemed favorable, their favorable expectations would go up for the daily rental business that would come in off the street the following week.

Many one-time bonanzas were also built into our short-term revenue figures. The classic case was the strip-center developer who moved into town followed by a dozen or so subcontractors, provided good revenues for eight months or so, finished the job, and moved on. There were many similar mini-boom-and-bust cycles, such as the so-called turnarounds of oil refineries, chemical plants, and other industrial operations, which require them to shut down for regular periods of maintenance and refitting. While these procedures were in progress, there would be calls for generators, light towers, welders, cranes, and a lot of other sometimes specialized equipment. All lucrative work—but lasting only a few weeks.

Our business is thus inherently volatile, and our day-to-day, week-to-week revenues naturally tend to bob up and down even under the most favorable conditions. I had to find some way to locate *a stable center* in the business that was insulated against these rapid and unpredictable swings. Until I could do this, our business would remain unstable, and I would continue to get misleading signals that could further destabilize it because of the overreaction that almost inevitably occurred.

The Key to Stability: Equipment Utilization

No guidance in this search could be found anywhere in the equipment rental industry at large, which was as yet an immature industry with no sophistication in theoretical marketing problems of this kind. I therefore had to find the answer on my own by studying the patterns that developed in those monthly revenue reports. As it turned out, the key to our core business was staring me in the face, right there in our *three-tiered price structure.*

As throughout our industry, HERC's three rates, daily, weekly, and monthly, are set so that the monthly rate commands a fairly heavy discount. The general rule is that three days at the daily rate is equal to the weekly rental, and three weeks at the weekly rate is equivalent to the monthly rate. Putting it another way, there are 22 work days in a typical month, and if we rent a piece of equipment to a customer for 9 to 12 working days, we will get as much revenue as from renting it for the full month. Although we do very well when we rent equipment out at the daily rate, we have persuasive reasons for preferring to rent it on a longer-term basis.

When we rent on a monthly basis, we go through only one cycle of delivery, pickup, cleaning, inspection, servicing, and billing as against several cycles when we rent the piece on a daily or weekly basis. Our expenses are therefore less, in addition to which we know the equipment will stay out on rental even if there is a stretch of bad weather. Furthermore, unless that particular piece of equipment is a high-turnover item in continuous short-term demand, such as our welders, it is unlikely to go out often enough, even at daily rates, to make up for the dead times when it is in the lot earning nothing. When it is out on monthly rental, I therefore know that I am likely to wind up with better profitability.

The key was utilization. The daily rate could be very profitable—when we could get it. But sustaining profitability over the long term could be accomplished only by keeping utilization at a high level, even if the rates were lower.

A piece of equipment not out on rental, but just sitting in the yard, is losing money. It is like the empty airline seat, or the unoccupied hotel room that is depreciating in value and eating up interest costs and other charges. The driving concern in our business is to get equipment out on rental and keep it out there in use as continuously as possible. *Equipment utilization* therefore had to be the key to opening the door to our core business, whatever configuration it would finally take.

It took only a little study of the revenue and expense figures yielded by the three different rates to confirm these general premises. They proved conclusively that the long-term rentals, accounting at that time for about 40 percent of our total rental revenue, would give us a deep-core reading of what was really going on in the business.

▶ *HERC's Answer to the Problem: The Monthly Revenue Base*

We now needed to translate these findings into a workable set of definitions so managers could break down their revenue reports in a way that would give us that deep-core reading.

Watching for Warning Signals

In defining "long-term" rental, we made an arbitrary decision and said it would be anything out on rent for 30 days or more. We called this the "monthly revenue base." All the other business, the daily and weekly rentals, we simply called the "daily average." Together, the monthly revenue base and the daily average added up to net rental, which is the key figure in any operating statement. But it was the monthly revenue base that gave us the day-to-day signals indicating:

▶ The direction of the business.
▶ How we were really doing against the business plan.
▶ How we compared to previous years and seasons.

Once again, I found that my enthusiasm ran up against the mind-set of a whole industry. Our managers had great difficulty believing it was not the weather that drove our business, but rather these unexciting long-term rentals that were relatively impervious to the sun, rain, and mud. I had to pound home, over and over again, that the critical sales job was not to increase the daily business, but to raise little by little the level of the long-term business. That was the way we were going to build HERC, I kept telling them, by lifting the monthly revenue base. As teacher and evangelist, I hammered away at this message day after day on my travels from location to location.

The monthly revenue base became my point of reference. I went over the figures with great care every month, actually writing them down in pencil on a big sheet of paper in order to fix them in my mind for future comparisons. I still do this, and if the monthly base seems suspiciously out of line in any of the branches, I am on top of it.

When Virginia Beach's monthly revenue base dropped suddenly by $50,000, I was on the phone immediately asking why. The answer was that we had rented a number of big air compressors on ships that were being refitted in the shipyards and the work had been completed. Another time,

Table 3.1. Monthly revenue base, 1990.

		1/1	2/1	3/1	4/1	5/1
Cleveland	$ 43	$ 31	$ 35	$ 32	$ 33	$ 53
Detroit	171	144	116	163	172	158
Indianapolis	115	104	95	90	98	116
Chicago			6	11	12	46
Nashville	182	173	156	148	161	194
Memphis	130	111	90	110	107	96
Louisville	55	63	60	54	53	63
Cincinnati	108	55	60	67	105	126
Kansas City	73	60	83	85	85	96
St. Louis	82	75	85	100	99	136
Division	$959	$816	$786	$860	$925	$1,078

Boston's monthly revenue base dipped from $178,000 to $148,000. It turned out that the snow in Vermont was great and the ski slopes were returning the air compressors that powered the snowblowers. So there was nothing abnormal about these events—certainly nothing that indicated any threat to the health of the long-term core business. But I had received a warning signal of something out of the ordinary occurring, and I needed to know whether or not I had a real problem.

Knowing Seasonal Patterns Gives You Control

The movement of the monthly revenue base over the course of a year is closely tied to the calendar and the seasons (see Table 3.1). Historically, the equipment rental business begins to recover from the winter doldrums in January and under ordinary conditions grows stronger each month through October. In our industry, we bill on a monthly basis, and the billings follow this upward curve faithfully, growing steadily each month with one aberrancy: February. Because it is a short month, with fewer working days to bill for rental, there is a technical decline in billings during February even though business is improving each week. Once past February, the monthly revenue base resumes its interrupted climb until November, when it stops abruptly with the onset of winter. It isn't only the cold weather: Users also want to save money over the holidays, so they return the equipment they have out on rental, short- or long-term.

No one knows a way to flatten out that seasonal curve: *You simply can't make the business grow in November or December.* We have seen it happen in one year only: 1989. That was the year of Hurricane Hugo and the earthquake in California. The cleanup following these natural catastrophes

6/1	7/1	8/1	9/1	10/1	11/1	12/1
$ 63	$ 68	$ 75	$ 83	$ 86	$ 76	$ 66
174	190	213	210	220	181	146
135	150	163	155	155	148	105
52	80	132	120	130	140	104
189	197	199	215	198	182	174
96	107	123	118	135	135	129
64	86	59	74	82	95	70
137	144	156	164	151	144	100
102	111	115	105	112	99	90
142	151	175	175	170	160	138
$1,154	$1,284	$1,410	$1,419	$1,439	$1,360	$1,116

created a sudden demand for all kinds of earthmoving and other equipment. Aside from such unexpected events, however, the equipment rental business performs pretty much as I have described. Like the seasonal patterns in airline traffic, it is something we have to adjust to.

Knowing about these patterns precisely is what gives you some control over your business. If you are going to grow steadily in the equipment rental business, your objective will be to build that long-term core business a little higher each month. When you tail off in November, you want your monthly revenue base to be a little higher than it was when business wound down last November. And when business comes to life in January, you want it to take off at a slightly higher level than the start-up a year ago. You have to know exactly where you stand at every point in the cycle, which is impossible if your index is cluttered up with daily spikes from short-term jobs or the weather.

We never look for big movement in the monthly revenue base. It is exactly what the term implies: the base on which our business is built. You don't raise a base by big heaves; you do it by increments. By focusing on the base, HERC keeps centered on steady growth through continuous improvement.

Let's say we would like some branch to develop a tidy base of around $150,000. I am not looking for it to jump $25,000 but rather for it to show incremental gains of up to $4,000 or $5,000 for at least several months of the year. If you are reaching for a $125,000 base and you suddenly get an increase of $25,000: beware. You have to know that a big project must have just come in and that your revenues will soon drop back by $25,000—so don't build that spike into your projections.

In the equipment rental business, we know that if we have a low monthly revenue base compared with a high daily average, something is wrong. It is a warning sign that we are in trouble. We have a lot of difficulty with our European businesses, much of it attributable to their failure to establish a solid monthly base; the business can dry up overnight. We will look at this problem in Chapter 14.

We have worked hard at developing our monthly base a day at a time, and today it accounts for about 50 percent of our net revenues and 60 percent of our total earnings. It is thus a more stabilizing element in our business than ever before.

Our move into the industrial marketplace, noted in Chapter 2, has added even greater stability, because it is driven by the overall economy and is there 12 months of the year. Individual industrial accounts tend not to be as big as those in the construction sector, but whatever their size,

$5,000 or $50,000 a month, they are more stable from month to month. The interruptions for maintenance or other reasons are usually of short duration, and when the factory gets back on stream, the business is there waiting for us. Industrial business therefore leads into our monthly revenue base and is a major factor in our core business. We explore this at length in Chapter 4.

▶ *A Formula for Stabilizing Your Business*

It is difficult to think of a business that in some degree cannot gain stability by recognizing and developing its core business in the way that we have done at HERC. Nor are we by any means unique in our emphasis on the importance of core business, even though I am proud to think that we are among the leaders in this field. "Core" business is defined differently in different industries:

- ▶ In the hotel and motel industry, the business traveler provides the core business, which is likely to be the high occupancy experienced between Tuesday and Thursday nights. For airlines, likewise heavily dependent on business travelers, the core business falls into much the same weekly time frame.

- ▶ In a fast-food chain, the core business may be the luncheon trade between 11 A.M. and 2 P.M. If you are in this business and have a firm handle on your luncheon trade, you can afford to guess at the numbers coming in during other times of the day. You may get a lot of opportunity business at those times and can enjoy the boom while it lasts, just as we do when the sun shines or a new construction project gets under way. But you won't make false moves because of misleading estimates. Your core business is your reality check.

- ▶ At Wal-Mart, the core business is called "item promotion," an innovative concept that originally made Sam Walton's dramatic style of merchandising famous. Walton liked to purchase an enormous quantity of some item of merchandise, price it specially, and promote it heavily. These displays of "volume-producing items" (VPIs), are still a hallmark of Wal-Mart stores and indeed are embedded in the company's way of doing business, which has always remained merchandise-driven. David Glass, who became president of the chain in 1987, says the philosophy behind VPI merchandising rests on the idea that the stores are full of items that can "explode" into big volume and big profits; managers are encouraged to identify and promote them. He says that Walton's "item promotion mania" is "the heart of what creates our extraordinary high sales per square foot, which enables us to dominate the competition."[1]

A service company's core business can thus show up in a variety of configurations, depending on what drives the business. The preceding examples demonstrate that it can be defined by these parameters:

1. A retailer (Wal-Mart) may define its core business in terms of a *promotional and pricing formula.*
2. Hotels and airlines define their core business in terms of *time frames.*

Pricing and time frame are two dimensions that define the core business of all industries, but a third dimension is also crucial to the core's function as a stabilizer of revenues: *a high and steadily maintained rate of productivity measured against the standard of productivity used in a specific industry.* We have mentioned three examples of such standard measures:

1. *Occupancy* in the hotel business.
2. *Sales per square foot* in the retail business.
3. *Utilization* in the rental equipment business.

Based on our experience in the rental business, identifying a core business in the service industry is essentially an effort to bring together three crucial factors in determining that base:

1. *The base will be a time frame that conforms to the customers' convenience or preference.* Ours happens to be a monthly time frame; yours perhaps could be derived from heavy traffic patterns at certain hours during the day. The time frame, whatever it happens to be, is the *volume* or *flow* dimension.

---

[1] Sam Walton with John Huey, *Sam Walton: Made in America: My Story,* New York: Doubleday, 1982, pp. 61–62.

2. *There must be some measure of efficiency or productivity appropriate for the specific trade or industry.* We employ the concept of utilization in our industry; elsewhere the term may be occupancy, and so forth. This in a sense measures the *velocity* of the flow, which in turn emphasizes the steadiness and reliability of the flow—these qualities count for everything.

3. *You must establish a price or rate to charge for the service, which in turn determines profitability.* We have a three-tier pricing structure in our industry, and it is the long-term (low) rate that works for us, giving optimum utilization, productivity, and profit. But the configuration is different in other industries and could be different in yours, too.

If you get these three factors together, you will have located your core business. Keep your eye on it.

WRAP-UP

Profitability = Rate × Time Frame × Efficiency

This formula will help you to identify your *core business,* which can be defined as:

▶ The steady, dependable segment of your trade that, from month to month and year to year, yields consistent profits and assures the survival of your business.

▶ The index that you follow with special attention because it is free of temporary distortions and gives you a reliable trend line for your revenues.

▶ The special characteristic of your business that differentiates your particular enterprise from the competitors.

The nature of the core business varies widely from industry to industry. In the equipment rental industry, the core business is the revenue from rentals contracted for 30 days or more. As long as the critically important "monthly revenue base" is performing satisfactorily, the enterprise is fundamentally in good shape.

Every core business represents the optimization of three congruent factors:

1. A *time frame* that is meaningful to the customers who account for your steady trade—the people who like to come into your restaurant for lunch, who want to fly your airline weekdays, or who prefer to rent equipment from you on a monthly basis.

2. A generally accepted *measure of efficiency* that is used by your industry (e.g., utilization, occupancy, sales per square foot).

3. The *price* or *rate* that the service commands.

The combination of these three factors will determine the profitability of the business. Thus, profitability (P) is a function of rate (R), time frame (T), and efficiency (E).

The shorthand way of stating this: $P = RTE$.

It's a useful formula. Try working with it: It can lead you to your core business.

4

Creating a Customer Base

As I traveled around the branches in those early days, I was dismayed by the lack of revenue support the local managers' sales efforts received from either the parent company or the regional offices. These managers and their tiny sales forces of two or three people had to fend for themselves to bring in revenue. They were dependent entirely on their own skills, ingenuity, and resources in finding new customers and getting those increases in local revenue that we were pressing them for. This was tough on the local people, and not good for HERC. It contributed to our chronic instability in revenue flow and pushed managers hard to perform without their having the resources to do this effectively.

Coming into this situation with fresh enthusiasm, other experiences, and new insights, I saw some possibilities that others who had been raised in the rental equipment business overlooked. This is the valuable advantage that the outsider always has: *the gift of seeing hidden assets.* Thanks to my experience as a purchasing agent on the staff of the parent company, which was one of the world's great corporations, I detected two hidden assets that were pure gold if the Hertz Equipment Rental Company chose to exploit them effectively:

▶ The first was the name *Hertz* itself, a trade name known throughout the world.

▶ The second was *the company's distribution network,* the most extensive in our industry.

Put these attributes together, and to me they spell "national accounts." These simply did not exist in HERC at that time, and I knew from experience as a purchasing agent the advantages that national accounts can yield, not only for the buyer but also the seller. This chapter describes how we combined these two attributes to develop a new marketing program that helped to transform HERC from a local company operating at most on a regional basis into a nationally driven company with an important corporate and industrial clientele.

▶ The Advantages of Building National Accounts

The people in our company had always known the local value of the familiar yellow and black Hertz logo that adorned all our shops. That logo drew potential customers off the highway. It attracted the eye in ads. It had a *high recognition value* when our salespeople called on some contractor who had just opened up a trailer office somewhere in town. That contractor may well have done business with HERC in some other town, but if not, he certainly knew about Hertz Rent-a-Car. So the name rubbed off on us and helped to open doors. But we were not using that name to its fullest potential—and the potential was growing as Hertz developed its international business in the 1980s. I had a gut feeling that the prestige of the name "Hertz" could give us a sales entree to the top level of the corporate world.

Because I was a purchasing-agent-turned-supplier, I could see the advantages of national accounts from both sides of the fence and therefore understood just what a potentially powerful package we could work up.

▶ If you are on the *purchasing side* of the national account, you can use your leverage to get the supplier to give you competitive prices, and consistent pricing, across the country. You are also dealing with only one source and can get a lot done with a single visit, fax message, or phone call. With one supplier, you can also can keep a close watch on performance.

▶ If you are on the *supply side,* you trade off price to get privileged access to a customer and can lock in a guarantee of a minimum level of annual purchases at agreed-on prices. There are many variants to this basic concept—and we were missing them all.

HERC possessed the crucial advantage that could make this vision into a reality: We were the only company in the equipment rental industry with enough locations around the country to make these kinds of deals and deliver on them. We could offer to supply the big corporation's need for identical industrial and construction equipment at a number of its operations throughout the country. This could have a great attraction for corporations with multiple sites by giving them a guarantee of being able to have the equipment they needed when they needed it at a distant point and at the same time reducing their clerical costs.

So in 1983, we linked up our two powerful but unused marketing tools by setting up a national account purchasing program. We hired a director and began writing national account agreements modeled on my experience as a purchasing agent on the other side of the bargaining table. In the first year or so, we did contracts with about a dozen national customers, most of them corporations whom we had already been serving locally somewhere in the country. These companies knew us and had some idea of what we could do. So we were up and running, although not very fast in the beginning.

▶ Breaking Out of the Cyclical Construction Sales Mode: Job Site Mentality

We were rather proud of our strategic vision and felt we had created a powerful tool for building revenue at the branch level. But the local managers emphatically did not see it this way. This was perhaps not surprising in view of the customary strong feelings of field staffs about local autonomy, which naturally colors their attitude toward any innovations initiated from above. Furthermore, the concept needed a lot of selling within the company because it cut across the experience, customs, and ingrained habits of an entire industry that I sum up as "job site mentality."

An Uneven Playing Field Tilted Our Way

The concept of selling in the equipment rental industry was adapted to the construction project. The contractor moved into town and raised a red flag beside the trailer office. Then a dozen or more subcontractors set up their trailers nearby, and the site was open for business. The equipment rental salespeople went from trailer to trailer, and the chances were that they would call back to the local HERC branch, which resulted in putting out pieces of equipment on rent. It was tough, competitive work, but it was the kind of challenge our people were used to, and they could see results the next day or week when the work started.

We were now asking our sales force to move into alien territory—the world of industrial customers and national accounts—and this called for another kind of selling. They now had to call on purchasing agents, who sat in an office, who had more sophistication about the equipment and the market than our previous customers, and who perhaps also had a network of suppliers already in place. It wasn't a matter of paying a quick call and writing up an order. Maybe they had to make many calls cultivating a purchasing agent before they got an order. They had to sell dependability, image, and quality, as well as price. So it could be a year perhaps before they saw results from their sales efforts.

Our local managers and sales staffs were already wrestling with the new challenge of industrial selling when we threw the national account concept at them. They had trouble grasping the long-term implications of what we were now trying to do and how it would eventually benefit them.

Since none of our competitors had national accounts, I wanted to use that precious advantage to create an uneven playing field. I wanted to provide our branches with revenue that would come in *automatically* because they were part of Hertz Equipment Rental. Not because they got into a car every day and went out to a site like every other equipment rental salesperson in the country. But the local people didn't see it that way. They said that all we were doing was converting our existing customer base into national accounts—in effect, cutting the rates, through a volume rebate, on business the branches already had. They said that I was not trying to hit singles and advance the runners around the bases, that I was trying to slam homers right over their heads.

They complained so bitterly that I had to go out there and sell them on the national account concept and what it would do for them when it took hold and was feeding business to them. I tried to show them that it would work if people would get behind it. And they still didn't see it and wouldn't buy it. As a result, revenue from the national account program merely trickled in at first because nobody wanted the damn thing. It was a kind of rerun of the weed-and-feed experiment, and in the end we had to become arbitrary once again. We had to tell them flatly that this was the way it was going to be, and then we held them to it. Little by little, one single at a time, the program took hold and worked.

Contracts with Firm Commitments

We continuously improved our product and made it more sophisticated. In the beginning, we just wrote "first call" agreements. These entailed no obligation on the customers other than giving us the key purchasing contacts throughout their organization and sending out letters of endorsement so the field locations would know us when our people called on them. A client would give us what we called an "implementation schedule," listing all the company's job sites and key decision makers. We would give that list to our sales force who would call on these job sites and ask the authorized personnel please to call on us first when they needed any equipment. In exchange for this, we agreed to consolidate the client's revenue into one account, so that the rentals from all the locations could qualify for a fixed rebate that varied from 1 to 5 percent of all the business based on volume. In other words, we got first crack at the business, and if we could work out a price at the going local competitive rates, good, we would get the business.

Soon we began to write firm-price contracts in which we traded price for guarantees of minimum volume. The client company committed itself to give us all its equipment rental business, and we not only offered a volume discount in return but also established a firm *national rate*. That gave the customers assurance that the equipment would be available whenever they needed it and at a price that would always be consistent. For us, it meant a *guaranteed volume* of business nationally at prices that were competitive but that we could live with and would give us a fair return. That enabled us to build realistic business plans based on a solid, steady underpinning of anticipated revenue.

▶ *How Tax Reform Facilitated Our New Marketing Strategy*

For the first few years, our national account program grew at pretty much the company's rate of growth; though encouraging, this still fell short of being the driver of our business that it was capable of becoming. The ratio hung in there at around 15 percent of our total rental revenues. Then suddenly it doubled in just two years thanks to an unexpected bonanza: the passage of the federal Tax Reform Act of 1986, which gave a major advantage to renting equipment as against owning it. The figures tell the story. National accounts as a share of our total rental business inched up from about 13.5 percent in 1984 to 16.5 percent in 1986. Then they shot up to 23 percent in 1987 and have been moving up ever since (see Figure 4.1). In 1993, just a decade after we inaugurated the national sales program, it accounted for a figure in excess of $100 million a year, nearly half of our total rental revenue.

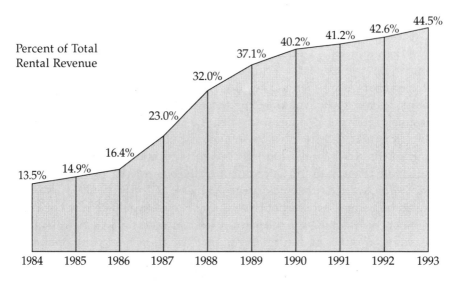

Figure 4.1. Tracking the National Account Rental Program (NARP).

An Opportunity to Get the Iron off the Books

Without question, the equipment rental industry owes a great deal of its impetus in recent years to the impact of the Tax Reform Act of 1986. By removing the 10 percent tax credit on capital equipment, the act had a profound effect on the investment policies of businesses, both large and small, throughout the country. This change in the tax laws was an entirely fortuitous occurrence. But when it happened, we at HERC were able to reap special benefits from the potentials it created, thanks to our initiative in setting up our national account program. If you develop a *versatile marketing structure,* it will catch the windfalls as they occur.

Prior to the tax reform, the ownership of metal tended to have emotional overtones beyond its economic significance. Entrepreneurial pride was involved. To have the company name on its own bulldozers, cranes, and rollers was visible evidence of success, the owner's solid assets made tangible. The new tax law suddenly focused attention on the economics of the matter and forced people to look at the real costs of maintenance and of depreciation, and to weigh carefully the costs of idle machinery. There were also the constructive things that owners could do to build their business with working capital released when their investment in metal was off the balance sheet. In this way, the Tax Reform Act changed entrepreneurial mores. It used to be that a business that owned a lot of iron was a success; now the criterion of success has become a good balance sheet.

Big corporations of the kind we were wooing were even more susceptible to unloading these burdensome costs. They had no vested interest in owning equipment that was entirely peripheral to their main lines of business, whether they were in transportation, warehousing, manufacturing, or whatever. Many of them didn't have repair facilities to handle the equipment, so there were interminable downtimes while the operators waited for pieces to come back from the company shops. Corporate managers were especially sensitive to the long periods of idle time between jobs when construction equipment just sat unproductively. These were only some of the headaches that could be eliminated by renting equipment from someone else who would take full responsibility for its ownership and maintenance and worry over full utilization. So when the economics tilted toward rental as opposed to ownership, many corporate finance officers began to look seriously at rental as a way of getting all this investment in dead metal off their books so they could put the capital to more productive use elsewhere in their business.

The Stability of National Business

Today, we have some 1,500 national accounts, many with a potential of from 50 to 75 locations that we are in a position to serve. There are some impressive names on our list of national accounts: Allied Signal, Ford, and General Motors to name just a few. We are also getting business from corporate and industrial customers that none of our competitors knows about, such as railroads, environmental companies, and fiber optics. We love this kind of business and aren't anxious to give away our customer list. When a fiber optics crew moves into a city to set up an installation, they automatically contact us to arrange for rentals of our equipment— and no one except our own field people even knows they are there. We have a lot of protected business of this kind. Our contracts with some customers give us business in as many as 30 cities simultaneously.

National business is stable business: It stays with us whether the national economic indexes go up or down, because these customers are dependent on us in ways I will shortly describe in more detail. Thus, more than 40 percent of our total rental business is being delivered into our stores without the sales staff having to go out there and beat the bushes for it. This is the responsibility of the national sales staff. There are national account directors and managers in each of our seven regional offices, who report to the director of national account sales at corporate headquarters in New Jersey. They are continuously at work generating and enlarging this stream of business to keep our stores busy. The branches no longer have to rely solely on cold calls by the salespeople, on advertising in the yellow pages, on tips from friends, or on the traffic that comes in off the road to develop a customer base. The business is already there for them, if they are willing to follow up the leads from our national sales force. It's manna from heaven, but they do have to go out and gather it.

▶ A Ready-Made Customer Base for Each of the Branches

Experience with national accounts differs from branch to branch, and attitudes of branch managers toward this business vary accordingly. Different parts of the country have different competition and cost structures, and there are problems sometimes when a purchasing agent or a decision maker for one of our national customers moves from one part of the country to another. For instance, there is a lower rate structure in Houston than in Boston, and in California it may even be higher. Our cost of operating in those cities is therefore different. If it is a first-call account, with some flexibility in the pricing, there may be haggling. But it can work the other way, too. The purchasing agent who moves from another city may like the service and will call HERC right away without question. That is more likely to be the situation than the other way, when they use competition against us.

Since that 40 percent-plus figure is our national average, the contribution of national account business to the revenues of any one store obviously can vary greatly. In Allentown, Pennsylvania, for instance, it accounts for about 30 percent of the revenues because it is a rural area that relies more on local customers such as the municipality and the public service company. But our branches in some western cities, such as Denver, Salt Lake City, and Portland, would be out of business without national accounts. In Denver, to name an outstanding case in point, they account for no less than 70 percent of the revenues. Actually, if it were not for the existence of our national accounts, we would never have gone into some cities.

One of the biggest benefits we have received from the national accounts program is the *ready-made customer-base* awaiting us when we move into a new location. This has given great flexibility to our expansion program. When we go into new areas, more likely than not we can come in with a substantial revenue base even before we open, thanks to the various units or projects of national accounts located in that area. We simply sweep these due bills in as we open our new shop and bring in our inventory. One of our new stores can therefore be turning a profit within its first year in business, which is a prodigal performance in our field. This makes us formidable competitors and gives us an enormous advantage over the mom-and-pops or our regional operators in almost any given city we choose to enter.

▶ *Educating the Customer*

When we first started calling on Fortune 500 companies and asked to talk to the purchasing agent who handled rentals, it turned out there was no one who answered to that description. Equipment rental was handled at the local plant or job site level by the guy who bought buckets and mops. They had no idea that there was a company like HERC that could work with them across their entire system and provide a professional, high-level service from region to region. Nor did they have any idea what such a national service could do for them. It was a new concept.

Today, when we call on a large corporation, we find a very different situation from that which existed less than a decade ago. Now, when we ask to see the purchasing agent in charge of rentals, they don't send us to the person who buys mops. We talk to a savvy professional who knows a great deal about *our* business, and who talks knowledgeably not only about volume discounts but also about utilization, imputed interest, and other highly technical matters. It puts us on our mettle. In fact, this new breed of corporate purchasing agents is giving us some tough bargaining when we go to the table to renew our contracts.

We have somewhat mixed feelings because we realize we were instrumental in helping to bring about this level of sophistication in the industry. Nevertheless, I remain convinced that increasingly this is the route by which true advances will be made in the quality of service throughout our entire service industry. It will come through shared development resulting from the interplay between suppliers of services and their customers.

Figuring Tradeoffs, Risks, and Advantages

A customer base by definition is that group of customers who in some way are committed enough to you or to your product or service to assure a certain level of revenue. Everyone who is in business has a customer base of *some* description, or they wouldn't be in business. It is your bedrock; you can count on it.

A customer base has three characteristics that should receive careful consideration:

1. *There is always some quid pro quo that cements the relationship—a tradeoff of some kind.*

   ▶ Usually that means a price concession in return for the customer's loyalty.

   ▶ It can be more binding. There can be a contractual agreement to guarantee a price for a guarantee of minimum volume.

   ▶ Or there can be a "first call" arrangement.

2. *There are always risks of some sort in building a customer base through contracts.*

   ▶ Generally, offering a price concession or other advantaged position favors one group over another.

   ▶ That means that another group of customers may be annoyed or that competitors can retaliate.

   ▶ Another likelihood is that it will create internal dissension because certain managers feel undercut.

   ▶ It might give the client an opening to twist your arm in negotiations.

3. *The advantages still make it worthwhile to cultivate your base through concessions and other ties.*

   ▶ It provides a group of customers on whom you can depend, which helps in developing realistic business projections.

   ▶ It creates an uneven playing field tilted in your direction.

   ▶ It establishes a firm base on which to expand your business.

   ▶ It helps to create customer dependency on the services provided by your firm.

5

What Happens When You Go National?

Our growing involvement with corporate and industrial clients worked some major changes throughout our entire organization. We encountered new expectations about the quality and meaning of service from these new and demanding customers, and we had to move to a new level of responsiveness. This chapter deals with these new pressures and how we responded to them: first, by providing new dimensions in the quality of service, and second, by expanding our distribution network and upgrading the quality of our locations.

▶ New Dimensions in the Quality of Service

By the early 1980s, we had become aware that we were not a very user-friendly company. Our equipment was aging and often in need of repair, many of our people lacked training, and our idea of serving the market was pretty much confined to matching the other guy's cut-rate pricing. We knew a lot of other things were wrong, too. As we began to shift equipment around and improve things little by little, we decided we needed to find out more about what our customers thought of us and how we could improve our service to meet their expectations. Like enterprises of all kinds in that era, we aspired to become *a customer-oriented company,* so we hired a marketing research consultant (at $75,000) and set up a focus group to see what we could learn.

We did learn something from this experience about building a quality image. It helped us relate better to our clients and in turn to keep our own people up to mark. Basically, we learned pretty much what any text-book on quality service will tell you; namely, that the customers wanted fair prices, equipment that was in good condition, fast repair service when something went wrong, and someone on the end of the phone line when they called. Most of all, they wanted to be treated like friends, politely and with respect; they wanted someone to listen to them—a cheerful voice at the other end of the line. (One of the customers in the focus group said what he really liked was friendly equipment rental locations where they passed out free six-packs of beer.)

There was nothing particularly surprising or insightful about any of this, and the reason for this was that we were talking to the wrong people: our old friends. Our managers picked candidates for the focus groups because they were basically comfortable with them; they had all grown up together in the equipment rental business—and therein lay the problem. This was a marketplace in which expectations were not very high. They were pretty much limited to the horizons of the mom-and-pops that dominated the industry. HERC was made in this image, too; we provided no more or no less than the traditional service offered by the industry, which wasn't too much. Mainly, as mentioned earlier, the industry competed on price, and on price alone.

A Closer Involvement in Plant Operations

Serving our new industrial business propelled our quality of service into a new dimension. For starters, there was the matter of round-the-clock service. In the construction business, our customers mostly worked from 8 A.M. to 5 P.M., Monday through Friday, and we were used to handling that. But now we had industrial accounts that operated around the clock seven days a week, and that was a different ball game entirely. They expected us to be in there with them or available around the clock. And there were many other services that we had to provide if we were going to keep their business.

Our involvement with these industrial clients therefore began to make some profound changes in our work style. Our managers and other key people began to wear beepers, and we arranged for 24-hour call-forwarding at all our locations so we could get crews together and send them out on emergency calls at any time of day or night. More calls around the clock put a strain on the fleet of service trucks that work out of our branches, so we had to add more trucks in a number of locations. These trucks are actually small repair shops on wheels; they are equipped to handle any kind of field repair from mending split air hoses to welding broken axles. They are also expensive: The price tag is around $35,000 apiece. Some of our larger sites have as many as 5 of these vehicles, and our national fleet now numbers around 200 full-service repair vehicles.

These moves represented only a few of the many we had to make to accommodate our national accounts and service them properly. In the long run, it meant a much closer involvement with the internal operations of the client corporation at the plant level. Here are two examples:

▶ Norshipco offers an example of how closely we work today with a national account. Our contract with the company requires us to supply all the equipment for the sandblasting and painting of the ships in dry dock. The shipyard does the work on contract, and the jobs last anywhere from three weeks to six months. When a ship comes in, we deliver the equipment and maintain it with mechanics on the site. The shipyard takes no responsibility for the maintenance of the equipment; if anything breaks, we provide new equipment. When the job is over, the equipment is shipped back to us. Norshipco neither owns the equipment nor lays out money not using it. The company orders it as needed, and it is up to our branch to have it in inventory or get it from another branch when the call comes in.

▶ Shell Oil provides an illustration of a still more involved relationship. We handle a number of Shell sites, including its drilling operations in the desert near Bakersfield, California. The company involves us in its actual production. We supply a great deal of equipment for drilling the wells, and we maintain it. We even supply special kinds of equipment, notably air-conditioned, four-wheel-drive, extend-a-hoe backhoes, which we don't stock anywhere else in our network of stores. In this case, however, we do it because the long-term economics work out favorably for us. *We are an integral part of our client's business.* We are involved not only in the drilling end of the business, but also in the refineries. We maintain equipment used in the production processes, and when the company does turnarounds, we bring in the extra equipment needed for that. And whenever the work slows down, the equipment is returned to us.

Bakersfield is only one of the Shell locations we serve. We also supply equipment to other Shell refineries and construction sites around the country. When Shell decides to build a facility anywhere in the country, the firm turns to us to provide the equipment to do the job. This underscores one of the important aspects of a national account for both parties to the contract. When Shell or any other national client has need for equipment in some location, it doesn't have to go to the expense and trouble of shipping its own earthmovers or other equipment across country. Corporate headquarters simply dials our "800" phone number and orders whatever equipment the operations people need, for as long as they need it, wherever they need it.

That shifts the whole logistical problem over to us, a job we are very willing to take on; we are equipped to handle it more effectively than the client.

How to Lose a Valuable Account

This kind of close working arrangement with an important customer obviously gives you, the supplier, many advantages—as long as you perform satisfactorily. The catch is that if something goes seriously wrong for some reason with your performance, it isn't like having a problem with a casual customer. To guarantee yourself an important learning experience, all you have to do is to let a major customer down through some kind of carelessness.

One day a few years ago, one of our repair crews rolled up to a customer's refinery on an emergency call and stepped out of the truck in their usual work clothes. They were not wearing helmets, fire-retardant suits, safety shoes, or goggles. In keeping with the somewhat casual style of the equipment rental industry at large, our people didn't pay too much attention to that sort of thing as long as the job got done on time. It so happened, however, that the owners of this particular refinery were quite serious about safety, and they didn't like our workers' appearance at all. The customer said we weren't a "safe" company, and suddenly we lost an account bringing in $1 million a year in revenue.

It was the most valuable lesson we ever had in learning to distinguish between mere image and real quality of service. Not only did that lesson stick with us; *it transformed the way we did business both internally and externally.* We were playing in the big leagues now, and the players were demanding a great deal more of us than we had ever had to deliver before.

Learn How to Turn Problems into Assets

That event was an eye-opener for us. When we took a look at our injury and accident statistics, and then took stock of the condition of our yards and stores, we were jolted by how deplorable our safety conditions really were. Our housekeeping and work habits were awful, and I immediately made a big issue of this throughout the company. I went into my pedagogical role about safety whenever I visited a site. I made a point of inquiring into every accident that had recently occurred to get at the cause and to show how seriously I treated each such event, no matter how minor. This remains a standard part of my repertoire when visiting locations.

We made a pledge to become the safest company in the industry:

▶ We hired a safety consultant and laid out an ambitious safety program that reached into all our facilities and activities.

▶ We ran training programs extending over months and including everyone in the company.

▶ We purchased safety apparel, and we insisted that it be worn at appropriate times and places.

▶ We revised all our repair shops to conform to strict safety standards. It was then that we installed ratchet binders on all our delivery trucks.

These are just a few of the scores and scores of similar small but significant actions we took.

By working doggedly, we dropped our accident rate by more than 50 percent in the first year. But the rate is still too high, so we are continuing to work at bringing it down. We go after the exceptions: *You need exception reports to keep an awareness of safety constantly with people.*

Safety is now a factor in peer measurement, and we are experimenting with more sophisticated ways of reporting statistically the safety component of our business. Eventually, we will know the direct costs of safety to the company in terms of training, equipment, and other expenses, as well as the offsets to this in terms of lower insurance premiums and other tangible benefits. As the data improve, we will have increasing control over both the costs and the effective performance of the service. In other words, we will better understand our productivity in "delivering" safety. It will take time to get these figures where they should be; they are still pretty crude. But the important thing is that we've made a start on measuring an important intangible—and that we will continue to improve on it one step at a time.

We also reaped another benefit from our new safety consciousness. We came to realize that our operations cover a wider spectrum of safety problems than most other companies. We are involved daily with safety problems in the workshop, on the highway, in construction sites, and in many other locations, under many different conditions, and with many different kinds of vehicles and equipment. As a result, we have more valid experience with the whole field of safety than most other companies. We therefore employed our new expertise to develop a training course in safety that we offer to any of our customers who feel they need help in this area. This has added a whole new dimension to the services we offer. What looked to be a drawback has thus turned out after all to be another of those hidden assets we talked about in Chapter 4.

How to Use Information Creatively

We look for new opportunities arising from our internal operations to move into closer relationships with our customers. There are always possibilities here for developing additional dimensions of service, but you have to be constantly on the alert for them or they can slip by unnoticed.

When we were expanding and improving our database, for example, we saw that a great deal of detailed customer information was automatically being cranked into the database every time a piece of equipment went out on rent and was billed. We realized that we were learning a great deal more about our customers' businesses than the customers knew about their own businesses. They would have had to go to inordinate effort to capture all the information we had about their use of rental equipment. Actually, they had no practical way of retrieving these data in the detail in which we showed it, much less with our accuracy and speed. That gave us a new reach in extending our services to large customers who have complex needs for construction and industrial equipment at many sites.

For example, take a railroad that has written a national sales contract with us to supply rental equipment along its right-of-way running across several states. We are able to tell the central office at any instant what kind of equipment each stationmaster has out on rental, and what its total expenditures are for dozens of locations. This greatly simplifies budgeting control and planning for the railroad, and we are thus able to go deeply into the client's daily operations and suggest greater efficiency. By providing one of our railroad clients with centralized billing, we actually enabled it to reduce the size of its accounting department by six people.

This major advance in the quality of our service is the result of once again using a latent asset. We had acquired a growing body of knowledge about computerization and how to apply it to our business; we then tapped this knowledge creatively by making it available to our clients to apply to their business, just as we did in the whole area of safety. *Borrowing Peter M. Senge's evocative phrase,* our latent asset here was actually our growing ability to perform as a "learning organization."[1]

▶ *Providing More and Better Stores Where the Customers Want Them*

When we first resumed expanding our network of stores, using the weed-and-feed methodology described in Chapter 2, we stayed pretty much in the Sun Belt. The economy was basically strong in the first half of the 1980s, and we expanded in the Sun Belt to the point of saturation. But we soon found ourselves under pressure to go beyond that area because of the needs of our national accounts. Allied Signal, General Electric, Ford, and other big industrial customers wanted coverage in the Rust Belt, especially in Chicago and Detroit, and we weren't in those places. They also wanted coverage in the Northeast, but we had only one store in Boston and then nothing down the East Coast until Norfolk, Virginia. Because of our saturation policy in the South, we had four places in Atlanta, so we really had to start moving northward.

What we were being asked in effect was to become a fully national company. There was no such thing in our industry; although we were the biggest company, we were still only regional. *To become national was a major strategy decision,* and since there were no models for this, we had to figure out how to do it by ourselves. We had to develop a system that could be supported logistically and that also would capitalize on any efficiencies of size that we already had. What we devised was a methodology I called "block and tackling," which I picked up from football: As you move ahead, you block behind you so you are secure.

The Importance of Logistics

Applied to the logistics of our business, block-and-tackling means that before we move into a new territory, we *make sure that we have supporting units firmly established behind us and that we are not moving beyond their range.* If we open an isolated store, we can't support it. We are then competing with the mom-and-pops and have none of the advantages of a big rental company

---

[1] Peter M. Senge, *The Fifth Discipline: The Art and Practice of the Learning Organization,* New York: Doubleday, 1990, p. 4.

with its ability to shift equipment around from one place to another to match shifts in local demand. Success in our business depends on the utilization of equipment, the key concept of the "core" business described in Chapter 3. If our utilization is weak in one of our branches, we transfer equipment somewhere else where we can rent it. The mom-and-pop has only has two choices: (1) sell it, which is tough to do, as we found out for ourselves when we were clearing out our surplus equipment; or (2) rent it at such a reduced rate that it could put the owner out of business.

When we started moving north and west, we were therefore careful to move in a sequence that we could support logistically and operationally. Our expansion program finally took hold in 1986, the first year that our openings exceeded our closings. ("Feed" finally exceeded "weed" by six stores to four stores that year.) For the next four years, until the recession began putting a frost on the growth in revenue and earnings in 1991, we were gaining a net of about 10 stores a year.

Table 5.1 shows all the stores that we closed or opened between 1982 and 1992, a total of 31 closings and 53 openings. After 1987, most of the openings were in the northern tier of states. We were in Newark, New Jersey, in 1987; Detroit in 1988; Cleveland in 1989; Chicago in 1990. We were able to open in Chicago because it is near Indianapolis and other cities where we

Table 5.1. HERC domestic locations—openings and closings.

	1982	1983	1984	1985	1986
Domestic Beg. Year	62	55	53	53	53
New Openings	1	0	2	3	6
Closings	−8	−2	−2	−3	−4
Domestic End Year	55	53	53	53	55
Openings	Clearwater, FL	None	Elmhurst, IL Shreveport, LA	Memphis, TN San Diego, CA Ventura, CA	Forestville, MD Kansas City, MO Jackson, MS Burbank, CA Sacramento, CA Huntsville, AL
⋮	⋮	⋮	⋮	⋮	⋮
Closings	Columbia, SC San Diego, CA Marietta, GA Everett, WA Hutchinson, TX Albuquerque, NM Carollton, TX Lafayette, LA	Portland, OR St. Louis, MO	Beaumont, TX E. Chicago, IL	Kenner, LA Elmhurst, IL W. Houston, TX	Shreveport, LA Arlington, TX Plano, TX Tulsa, OK

already had stores. We think we have even a better chance of success in Milwaukee than in Chicago, but we have to network ourselves there. This applies equally to Minneapolis, where we also want to be.

Some Basic Rules for Expansion

The basic rule is, *we can't afford to isolate our stores*. Although we are a national company who has recently become a fledgling multinational company, we still must compete on a local basis with the mom-and-pops. I like to describe our operating policy to business school students as "Economics 101": It is your typical demand-and-supply business. We compete city by city, market by market. Each of these branches is a profit center, and the manager has great autonomy. Each facility is capable of doing everything from minor mechanical work to major repair work, from managing a sales force to making buy-and-sell decisions; it is a profit center. What we are really saying to a manager is this:

> Here is a city. We're putting up $4 million to $6 million in capital. Run our rental equipment business there. These stores carry everything from pumps that cost $500 and rent for $30 a day to large hydraulic excavators that cost $150,000 and rent for $6,000 a month. We are going to empower you to run this business for us. We are making you an entrepreneur who is managing that facility with our capital.

1987	1988	1989	1990	1991	1992
55	64	74	84	90	86
11	10	11	9	0	0
−2	0	−1	−3	−4	−2
64	74	84	90	86	84
Richmond, VA	Hartford, CT	Reno, NV	Marietta, GA	None	None
Hopewell, VA	Allentown, PA	Lodi, NJ	Chicago, IL		
Fredericksburg, VA	Greer, SC	Portland, OR	Bakersfield, CA		
Chesapeake, VA	Wilmington, NC	Augusta, GA	Richmond, VA		
Baltimore, MD	Indianapolis, IN	Cleveland, OH	Salt Lake City, UT		
Las Vegas, NV	Louisville, KY	Palm Springs, CA	Port Arthur, TX		
Newark, NJ	Cincinnati, OH	Pittsburgh, PA	Lake Charles, LA		
Savannah, GA	Lancaster, CA	Kissimmee, FL	Denver, CO		
St. Louis, MO	Detroit, MI	Sterling, VA	City of Industry, CA		
Tucson, AZ	Newport News, VA	Woodbridge, NJ			
Northboro, MA		Jacksonville, FL			
⋮	⋮	⋮	⋮	⋮	⋮
Mobile, AL	None	Hartford, CT	Lodi, NJ	Newport News, VA	Kissimmee, FL
Chesapeake, VA			Woodbridge, NJ	Fredericksburg, VA	Hopewell, VA
			Northboro, MA	Louisville, KY	
				Sterling, VA	

All stores are more or less fixed-cost operations. The more you can grow the business on a *fixed-cost* basis, the more profitable you are going to be. Say you have a location with an inventory of $4 million to rent. If you can grow the business and the rates stay the same, you are going to be incrementally more profitable because your overhead stays the same. There is one real estate cost to cover and one manager to cover; your variable cost then is the equipment that is coming in, plus a minimal increase for drivers, mechanics, and so forth. When we can't grow any more in a given location, we open a substation 30 to 40 miles away under the same management, thus keeping down the overhead.

Volume gives us added efficiencies. Our rule of thumb is that we average one mechanic for every $1 million investment in equipment. If you have $2 million in equipment and two mechanics, they have to work hard to maintain that equipment. But if you have $8 million and eight mechanics, then you can hire mechanics who specialize in changing oil, say, or in handling electrical systems, and you can really begin to pick up incredible efficiencies.

To sum up our logistical approach, if we are going to move beyond the 30- or 40-mile satellite range and set up a free-standing store, we want to be sure of several things:

1. We have to know whether the city has a *potential economic base* that will support our facility. Weed-and-feed tells us this.

2. We look for the existence of a *customer base.* We can tell this from the presence of national accounts in that area, as discussed in Chapter 4.

3. We need to locate the new free-standing unit *no farther than 150 miles* from at least one other existing unit. If it is beyond this, swapping equipment between branches is no longer economically viable.

If these three key conditions are satisfied, we know we will be able to supply materiel efficiently to the facilities where it is needed. That frees us from the constrictions of competing on a strictly local basis—again, we want that uneven playing field tilted in our direction.

The Advantages of Starting Your Own Facilities

HERC had gotten into business by buying companies, and when I took over, we continued for a while to grow by acquisition. It seemed then a sensible way to induce fast growth. We acquired instant business by buying established companies in the area. We let it be known in the industry that we were looking for local equipment rental companies with an annual volume of $1.5 million. We applied our new expertise and bought companies in potentially strong markets applying the new tough criteria we had developed. But eventually we switched over to opening our own greenfield operations for a number of reasons.

To begin with, we found we had *problems of incompatibility.* HERC was making great strides toward standardizing its equipment and investing in a younger fleet, and the mom-and-fleet fleets we were picking up were generally a mixed bag of off-brand equipment that was anywhere from 60- to 72-months old. Right away, we incurred large capital costs to replace the fleet, as well as to rebuild the facilities, which usually were a mismatch with ours. Any computerization was always way behind our sophisticated system, so we had to scrap theirs at more cost. We also had to retrain people into our way of doing things, and that was another expense. In addition, we ran into a lot of hidden costs, such as the replacement parts they had on their books: A lot of these parts turned out to be for obsolete equipment, so we couldn't get the value back.

Whenever you buy another company, one of the big costs is goodwill; the better the company, the more you pay for the goodwill. That has to be earned back, of course. We soon found that we didn't need to burden ourselves with this cost. Thanks to our own homegrown methodologies and efficiencies, as well as our other advantages (e.g., our national customer base), we saw that we were actually better off starting from scratch. We could be profitable in a year's time and catch the competition within two years.

Provide the Same Services and Safety Everywhere

Building our own places from the ground up also gave us the opportunity to develop a prototype HERC store, with neat, clean lines—an efficient-looking and open place with the familiar Hertz logo highly visible. (See Figures 5.1 and 5.2.) You can see what we are selling as you pass by, and you can look into the shop and see what is going on. All our new stores look the same. There is a competitor I respect who has the opposite point of view. Every time I pass one of his new locations, I can see he has been personally involved. Each store is a new architectural feat—and it is a disaster. I don't want to redesign the wheel each time. *I have the wheel*—it is a cookie cutter.

Figure 5.1. Hertz prototype store.

All our stores are standardized; they look just the same wherever you go. (This is true in Europe as well as in this country, even though, as discussed in Chapter 14, the Europeans tend to have less enthusiasm than Americans about standardization.) We think it is important for HERC customers to realize that the amenities and services we offer are identical everywhere they go. Standardization also extends to our insistence that all our places must be secure, safe, and environmentally sound, a policy that we owe to the safety shock of losing that million-dollar customer. Every lot must be paved and each facility must have an alarm system and a tight chain-link fence around the lot—not to mention one of those "low-bridge devices" standing guard over every exit gate.

Thinking "safety" put us in a new mode of environmental awareness, and we also looked underground. Leaking fuel tanks are the bane of all service depots. Everyone in our industry has "leakers," which do a lot of damage through pollution, are costly to clean up, and generally give a shoddy image of an uncaring company. We decided to become the environmental leader in the industry by going over to state-of-the-art fuel storage and delivery systems in all our yards. That meant double wall fiberglass tanks with monitoring systems to detect leaks; each installation costs $55,000 to $65,000. We also took care of another problem resulting from our policy of washing all equipment when it is returned from rental. We now put the runoff through oil–water separators to make sure we don't contaminate the underground water supply.

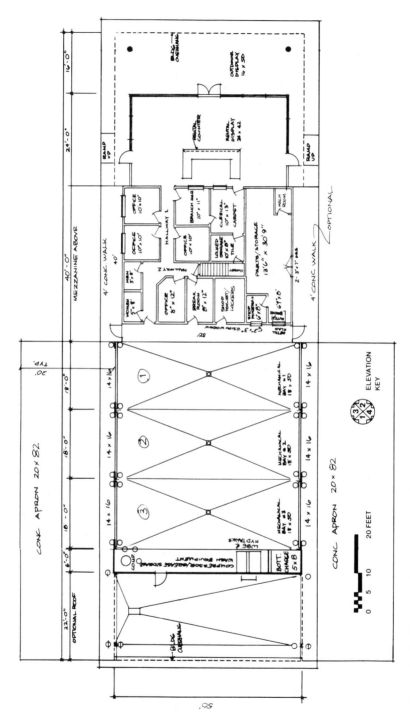

Figure 5.2. Hertz cookie cutter plan for its stores.

All of this has put us far ahead environmentally of any other company in our industry. We feel that it will take five years for any of them to catch up with us. The changes have been expensive, but they have made us a better corporate citizen and have helped to instill pride among our people. These improvements have also helped to make our customers aware of HERC as a truly mature, responsible national company.

WRAP-UP

How to Raise Expectations of Quality Service

Focus groups may not tell you what you need to know. Your customers themselves may not know what they really need or want, or what may be available to them. Their expectations may be low because no one has yet showed them what is possible. They may therefore just be recycling tired ideas.

This presents you with an opportunity and a challenge. Make it your job to raise new expectations about the meaning of quality service in your field.

Based on HERC's experience, here are some suggestions for doing this:

▶ Don't talk to your old friends: Listen to the newcomers who are giving you difficulties. They are the ones who can point you the way you should be going.

▶ Explore your organization carefully and with an open mind to see what hidden assets and capabilities you may have overlooked.

▶ Share the new learning experiences you have had within your company by putting your knowledge at the service of the customer.

▶ Help educate the customers. Encourage in every way you can the professional capacities of the people you deal with outside the company. It will reward you in the end by giving you more informed customers who understand your business.

▶ Be ready to change your work style drastically to meet the new demands you yourself may have helped foster.

Keep in mind that advances in the quality of service in your industry will come through *shared* development resulting from the interplay between suppliers of services and their customers.

6

Managing and Renewing
Your Stock of Goods

I n the rental business, the "product" we sell comprises a package of both services and goods, and the quality of that package depends on three things:

1. *How successful we are in satisfying the customers' need for service.* A variety of actions fall under this heading, from answering the telephone politely to washing the equipment before it goes back into the field.

2. *Our ability to get the equipment to the customers when and where they need it.* This involves the logistics of locating stores in strategic places and keeping them supplied.

3. *Our skill at managing the fleet renewal problems.* Successful management enables us to provide the customers with new and up-to-date equipment.

The first two topics were introduced in Chapter 5; this chapter looks at the third key ingredient in delivering a quality package of services and goods to the customer.

▶ The Third Ingredient of Quality Service:
The Youth of the Fleet

The newness of the rental equipment is critical in our business. It is key in keeping the customer satisfied, which gives us a competitive edge over the competitors, and in making us a profitable company. If we have a young fleet of equipment, the customer is assured of getting state-of-the-art machinery that has relatively few hours of use on it and therefore won't break down on the job and cause a lot of lost time and trouble. For the supplier, new equipment is a blessing because it requires less maintenance, fewer emergency repairs, and less parts cost, all major expense items. Fleet renewal is a complex subject that reaches all the way back to decisions on capital investment and all the way forward to the ultimate disposal of the machines. As with new-car dealers, who perforce are in the used-car business, we are also in the used-equipment business. And in both cases, clearing the market efficiently is essential to profitability at the same time that it makes way for bringing in new models either to rent or sell, as the case may be.

The need to find a rational way of renewing the stock is an endemic problem throughout most of the service industry. This is an imperative whether you are a merchandiser or a supplier of services, whether you are dealing with the replacement of a stock of consumer goods or a stock of capital goods:

▶ If you are the manager of a women's wear store, you worry about remaindering the winter dresses in order to bring in the spring and summer styles.

▶ If you are an airline operator, your concern is how to phase out your obsolescent fleet, which is eating up fuel and requiring ever-more-costly maintenance.

▶ If you are running a rental car business, you know you must sell off each rental car when it reaches, say, 15,000 miles.

▶ If you are in the office maintenance business, you know your people will do a poor cleaning job if you don't replace worn-out equipment regularly.

Each business has its own special characteristics, but in almost every case the important thing is to develop a system that brings together the logistics of the replacement program with the balance sheet and the operating statement.

HERC's experience in developing new approaches to this critically important task can provide useful guidelines for other service businesses.

▶ *How to Manage Surplus Inventory*

My education in fleet logistics began in the summer of 1982 while I was still running the purchasing department at Hertz headquarters and was asked to look into the affairs of the troubled HERC subsidiary.

One of the major causes of the red ink on the HERC books was the huge excess of idle equipment in its fleet, and my assignment was to see what could be done about it. I visited all six regions of HERC to define the surplus equipment so that we could put a plan together to dispose of it. We listed all the stores in each region, itemized the first cost of the inventory, and estimated how much appeared to be surplus; then we enumerated the monthly depreciation expense that we were incurring for that surplus equipment. This emphasized the point that this idle equipment was not merely failing to earn income, but was actually eating up income. This represented an attempt at an integrated approach correlating logistics and finances.

Table 6.1 shows the results for eight branches in various parts of the country, mainly in the South. In some of these branches, the surplus equipment was about 10 percent of the total value of the fleet. There was a total of $22 million surplus for the entire HERC fleet across the country. We then tested the used-equipment market to see what our surplus would fetch if we decided to sell it. I took the list with a description of each type of equipment and went to five national used-equipment auctioneers and asked for estimates on our likely receipts if we put this surplus into national or regional auctions. Their estimates indicated that we would incur significant losses, so the corporation decided to find other methods of somehow

Table 6.1. Surplus and deadlined equipment, Northeast Region, September 1982 (dollars).

Branch	Current Inventory	Total Deadline	Cost to Repair	Surplus Total	Monthly Depreciation
Norfolk, VA	4,473,200	347,400	29,550	520,829	6,162
Charlotte, NC	1,736,900	-0-	-0-	266,555	3,449
Greensboro, NC	2,116,300	36,500	4,540	273,244	3,740
Raleigh, NC	1,738,500	-0-	-0-	141,094	1,855
Winston-Salem, NC	2,116,300	-0-	-0-	-0-	-0-
Boston, MA	3,724,400	-0-	-0-	126,300	1,126
East Chicago, IL	3,897,700	9,200	2,800	106,350	1,560
Pennsauken, PA	3,945,800	-0-	-0-	167,916	2,358
Total	20,394,500	393,100	36,890	1,602,288	20,700

disposing of the surplus over a protracted period of time. In other words, much of the problem was waiting for me when I assumed management of HERC later that year.

Coping with a Deepening Inventory Problem

The situation actually had worsened because, by then, the full impact of the recession of 1981 was making itself felt, exacerbating HERC's other underlying logistical problems.

Just a few weeks of going around and touching the iron had taught me that no one really knew the extent of the problem. A lot of broken equipment was not being deadlined by the managers, so the numbers reported to us were no good, let alone our knowledge of what it would take to get the stuff back into use. Yet those same broken units were on the books costing us depreciation and interest, and no one had the foggiest notion how long it would be before they could be put back in service—or even if they could be put back in service. My best estimate was that out of our total fleet of about 30,000 pieces of equipment, as much as 20 percent was not operational for one reason or another. That translated into 4,000 or more units sitting somewhere on the lots and not earning anything because something was wrong with them, anything from a missing spark plug to a broken crankshaft.

But there were still worse aspects to the situation. Nobody in our distribution network understood the problems at other stores or had any sympathy for them. Each manager's goals were basically self-centered: to earn a profit and to hell with anyone else. So when managers had to ship a piece of equipment to someone else, they shipped anything they wanted to get rid of. If we opened a new location and brought in $2 million worth of equipment from other locations, we generally received $2 million worth of the oldest equipment in the fleet. And guess what? That operation failed. I knew of instances where vehicles had to be winched onto a truck because they could not move on their own and then had to be winched off when the truck delivered them to the unsuspecting branch to which they had been consigned.

Identifying the Underlying Distortions

These were only the most glaring problems. Underlying them were serious distortions having to do with the general condition and the balance of the fleet. Here are the major ones:

▶ *For lack of a replacement policy, we had an aging fleet on our hands.* This was putting an undue strain on the mechanics and the shops and likewise causing customer ill will because of recurrent break-downs. At that time, our fleet probably averaged 72 months in age—only a rough estimate since the ages of different pieces of equipment varied wildly. While that kind of profile was not un-usual in the mom-and-pop industry, we could not tolerate it if we were going to have a system that made sense logistically or that delivered quality service.

▶ *There was no standardization of the fleet at all from one city to another.* Like other companies in the equipment rental industry, we were buyers of opportunity, picking up what was priced attractively that season regardless of how it fit into an overall fleet profile. In any one location, we might be running as many as five or six dif-ferent brands of any one piece of equipment. The result was an-other headache for the mechanics; they simply were not trained or equipped to handle all those different models. In addition, we had an inventory problem trying to keep spare parts on hand for this jumble of equipment.

▶ *Much of our equipment was too specialized for the general run of con-struction or industrial use.* This had come about because managers prevailed on the purchasing department to stock special equip-ment for certain customers. If a customer wanted to rent a special-ity item, the manager put it in the inventory regardless of whether it was compatible with the rest of the fleet. Have you ever heard of gas chronomatographs? They measure gas pressure in the oil fields, and we had them as well as a lot of other highly specialized oil field equipment in Texas and Louisiana. Now, where are you going to transfer that kind of equipment when the oil business goes into a slump?

▶ *There was also equipment that was too highly technical for our trade.* The Fabtek manlifts that we had stockpiled in St. Louis were highly engineered and sophisticated; the construction people we catered to had a lot of trouble operating them. Here and there around the country were other clusters of equipment of this kind, machines that were in perfectly good shape but that could not be made rentable even if we swapped them around the system.

In short, I had a shambles on my hands.

▶ *The Solution: Rent It, Fix It, or Get Rid of It*

We decided to take a simplistic way out of this mess: Every piece of equipment either made a contribution by bringing in rent or had to be eliminated, thereby eliminating its expense. We established a kind of emergency triage: rent it, fix it, or get rid of it. As long as the unit could be made to work without too much difficulty and was rentable, we would keep it on the books, put it in condition, and get it out there into the customers' hands where it could earn rent. If it wasn't rentable, we would get it off the books as fast as possible, either by selling it or junking it, whichever was appropriate.

Using as an illustration a piece of equipment that originally cost $10,000 and was now "deadlined" for whatever cause, I reasoned this way:

▶ If we could fix up that broken piece of equipment through a reasonable investment in repairs, then we would gain the use of that asset nearly for free. That in turn would produce positive cash flow, revenue, and profits where there were none before.

▶ If we couldn't fix it and had to sell it or scrap it, we would take the hit once and would get it off our books, thereby saving, say, $138 in depreciation and $69 in interest each month thereafter. That may not sound like much, but eliminating the drain permanently added up to real money. I was not interested in showy, big-dollar fixes, which we didn't know how to do anyway. But I knew that we could do innumerable insignificant fixes of $138 or $69 or maybe even $39. If we made one fix at a time, eventually we could turn around millions of dollars.

A turnaround of the magnitude we faced takes time. We were trying to sort out an odd-jobs lot of 30,000 pieces of equipment, 4,000 of which weren't working at all and an untold number that were in various stages of disrepair. It took us at least two years, a step at a time, to get a real handle on our fleet problem, and it took another two years of hard work to get the fleet truly balanced out so that it reached a profitable level of utilization. But at least I was certain of where we were going during those years because we had a crude but workable plan of action. I knew we were doing the right thing every time we hired a mechanic and fixed another piece of equipment; shipped another piece to a location in the distribution network that could rent it; found a buyer somewhere for yet another. We did all those things simultaneously, but naturally it took longer to do some than others, a single at a time.

Shifting Inventories Where They Can Be Used

My tour a few months before coming to HERC had shown me how bad the maldistribution of the fleet was and what this did to our utilization, profits, and service. Doing something about this proved to be the quickest and easiest fix I made. It also provided the whole company with an effective object lesson in the logistics behind good utilization, not to mention a lesson in cooperation.

Over here in city X, say, was a lot full of unrented bulldozers or backhoes, while over there in city Y, they were crying for bulldozers and backhoes and had none available to rent. However, they had plenty of spare cranes on hand, which city Z was crying for because of the demand for cranes in that area. Faced with a big underutilized inventory that was creating expenses but no income, the managers in cities X and Y resorted to price cutting, as would many other entrepreneurs, while the manager in city Z had to report lost revenues. He was also hurting customer goodwill because he couldn't respond to orders for equipment that his branch was expected to handle, so the potential customers went elsewhere.

To shift those idle inventories around where they were needed and could satisfy demand, I gathered up the six regional vice presidents of HERC and put them on a plane. Together, we did a one-week whirlwind tour of our 20 worst cities. The regional vice presidents saw for themselves the problems we had to fix, which was highly educational for them; our regional people weren't accustomed to looking beyond their own borders.

When we got into a city, the scenario would go something like this:

First, we would get hold of the listings, and then we would go out and look at the equipment on the lot. We would see 20 idle but usable dump trucks and backhoes sitting there, and right on the spot we would hold an impromptu curb exchange. The regional managers would get on the phone back to the branches.

Pretty soon one of them would come back and say, "I can use six backhoes in Tampa."

Another man would say, "Give me three dump trucks for Atlanta."

I would jot all that down on a pad, and at the end of the trip we had a plan to straighten out the distribution of equipment throughout our system.

The follow-up was a $150,000 transportation bill as we physically swapped around equipment from branch to branch on low-boy trucks.

This was the crude beginning of what later became a well-orchestrated system for transferring equipment from location to location and even between regions.

The moral: Turn every possible occasion into a *multidisciplinary* event: Get something practical done, put a lesson across, plant the seed of future action.

The Easy Part: Selling Metal for Scrap

After "rent it" came "fix it," which I pursued in my usual style as I visited the locations. While I was touching the iron, I was also taking a lot of snapshots of wrecks and sending the pictures back to the managers to emphasize the seriousness of the problem. I leaned on everyone involved to get those pieces of deadlined equipment into the shops for repair. This got some immediate action, but more importantly it marked the beginning of a major company-wide effort to beef up the efficiency and quality of repair and maintenance. We hired new mechanics where needed, but mostly we concentrated on giving intensive training to the crews we had. We also improved their working conditions by rebuilding and/or refitting a number of the shops. In this way, we pushed through a vast amount of work, picking up speed and efficiency as we went.

It took us about a year all told to cull the wrecks and sell them for scrap metal, which turned out to be the easiest part of the whole job. It took longer to salvage the borderline cases and get them back onto the lots, where we had to decide whether to take them back into the rental fleet or try to sell them. This dilemma put us back into the bind we had encountered during our earlier attempt to auction off used equipment.

▸ *How to Establish a Market in Used Equipment*

We bypassed the auctions this time and tried alternate routes for unloading used equipment:

> ▸ We contacted *brokers* and asked them for prices on individual pieces. Where we received quotes that were in line with our book values, we sold the equipment a piece at a time. This was slower than auctioning off the equipment, but it did get rid of some surplus inventory.

▶ I went to our major *suppliers* and told them I had just taken over HERC and needed some help disposing of equipment. I pointed out that once the fleet had been balanced, we would again be in position to buy new equipment. To help out a (potentially) good customer, J.I. Case, Ingersoll-Rand, and Ford, among others, took equipment from us and disposed of it through their used equipment sales systems. In a few instances, where we felt we really needed to buy new equipment and could justify it, we "traded packages," to use the trade expression. For example, when we wanted to buy $100,000 in new earthmoving equipment, we prevailed on the manufacturer to take back $50,000 of our used equipment.

When You Are Forced to Take a Bolder Step

All these devices were useful, but they were merely makeshifts considering the volume of used equipment that HERC would feed into the market in the course of its regular business as it grew. We had to be bolder in our approach to the inventory disposal issue, which played such a key role in the larger issue of fleet renewal.

In the end, we established our own market by setting up a clearing house for used equipment in a rather innovative way. Our clearing house was a publication called *The Source* that listed and priced more than 30 categories of used equipment available for sale at all our yards. Most of the well-known trade names were there: John Deere, Ingersoll-Rand, Case, Bomag, Bobcat, Komatsu, Lull, and so on. We issued it three times a year; at first, we sent it to a few thousand end-users of equipment here and in Latin America; eventually, we increased the circulation to 50,000. *The Source* isn't just a price list; it is a magazine filled with information and color photographs of the actual equipment up for sale (see Figure 6.1).

By degrees, the publication not only began moving our backlog of idle units, but helped to stabilize the entire industry by establishing an orderly market for used equipment. We received a lot of praise for this from both the rental and the construction industries. Our publication was aptly named: It became *the* source to which the construction industry turned when it wanted to get a fix check on the prices of used equipment.

How to Stabilize the Market

In a typical issue, you will find about a thousand listings. The prices range from $3,500 for an Atlas-Copco air compressor to $53,000 for a

Figure 6.1. Cover page from *The Source,* a price list publication.

National truck crane. You are looking at perhaps $12 million or $13 million worth of equipment at resale value, representing a massive amount of iron being cleared through our market at any one time. The oldest units will be no more than five years old, and you will find precise information on the Hertz I.D. number, the model number and year, and the manufacturer's serial number (see Figure 6.2). I make a point of this because we set

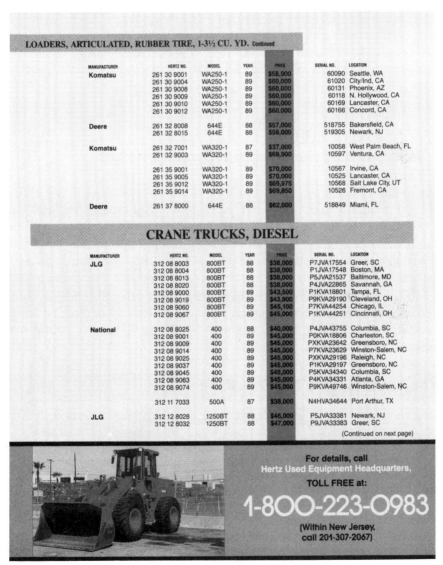

LOADERS, ARTICULATED, RUBBER TIRE, 1-3½ CU. YD. Continued

MANUFACTURER	HERTZ NO.	MODEL	YEAR	PRICE	SERIAL NO.	LOCATION
Komatsu	261 30 9001	WA250-1	89	$58,900	60090	Seattle, WA
	261 30 9004	WA250-1	89	$60,000	61020	City/Ind, CA
	261 30 9008	WA250-1	89	$60,000	60131	Phoenix, AZ
	261 30 9009	WA250-1	89	$60,000	60118	N. Hollywood, CA
	261 30 9010	WA250-1	89	$60,000	60169	Lancaster, CA
	261 30 9012	WA250-1	89	$60,000	60166	Concord, CA
Deere	261 32 8008	644E	88	$57,000	518755	Bakersfield, CA
	261 32 8015	644E	88	$59,000	519305	Newark, NJ
Komatsu	261 32 7001	WA320-1	87	$37,000	10058	West Palm Beach, FL
	261 32 9003	WA320-1	89	$69,900	10597	Ventura, CA
	261 35 9001	WA320-1	89	$70,000	10567	Irvine, CA
	261 35 9005	WA320-1	89	$70,000	10525	Lancaster, CA
	261 35 9012	WA320-1	89	$69,975	10568	Salt Lake City, UT
	261 35 9014	WA320-1	89	$69,850	10526	Fremont, CA
Deere	261 37 8000	644E	88	$62,000	518849	Miami, FL

CRANE TRUCKS, DIESEL

MANUFACTURER	HERTZ NO.	MODEL	YEAR	PRICE	SERIAL NO.	LOCATION
JLG	312 08 8003	800BT	88	$38,000	P7JVA17554	Greer, SC
	312 08 8004	800BT	88	$38,000	P1JVA17548	Boston, MA
	312 08 8013	800BT	88	$38,000	P5JVA21537	Baltimore, MD
	312 08 8020	800BT	88	$38,000	P4JVA22865	Savannah, GA
	312 08 9000	800BT	89	$43,500	P1KVA18801	Tampa, FL
	312 08 9019	800BT	89	$43,800	P9KVA29190	Cleveland, OH
	312 08 9060	800BT	89	$45,100	P7KVA44254	Chicago, IL
	312 08 9067	800BT	89	$45,000	P1KVA44251	Cincinnati, OH
National	312 08 8025	400	88	$40,000	P4JVA43755	Columbia, SC
	312 08 9001	400	89	$45,000	P0KVA18806	Charleston, SC
	312 08 9009	400	89	$45,000	PXKVA23642	Greensboro, NC
	312 08 9014	400	89	$45,000	P7KVA23629	Winston-Salem, NC
	312 08 9025	400	89	$45,000	PXKVA29196	Raleigh, NC
	312 08 9037	400	89	$46,000	P1KVA29197	Greensboro, NC
	312 08 9045	400	89	$45,000	P5KVA34340	Columbia, SC
	312 08 9063	400	89	$45,000	P4KVA34331	Atlanta, GA
	312 08 9074	400	89	$45,000	P9KVA49746	Winston-Salem, NC
	312 11 7033	500A	87	$38,000	N4HVA34644	Port Arthur, TX
JLG	312 12 8028	1250BT	88	$46,900	P5JVA33381	Newark, NJ
	312 12 8032	1250BT	88	$47,000	P9JVA33383	Greer, SC

(Continued on next page)

For details, call
Hertz Used Equipment Headquarters,
TOLL FREE at:
1-800-223-0983
(Within New Jersey, call 201-307-2067)

Figure 6.2. Sample page from *The Source.*

a high standard in our industry for accurate record keeping. Not all equipment rental companies have such records. The dealer who originally sold a particular unit to a small service company may have had it in stock for a year or more; so it may not really be the 1990 unit that the rental company thinks it is but a 1988 unit. We guarantee that the buyer of one of our used pieces of equipment gets what is represented.

One of the side benefits from our role as a used equipment dealer is that we can keep tabs on who is buying our equipment and where it is going. We take some pains to cultivate the Latin American market, for example, because it siphons our used equipment out of the domestic market—we prefer, if possible, not to have our own used equipment return to our backyard to compete with us.

▶ Putting Fleet Renewal on a Systematic and Flexible Basis

As we gradually unclogged our pipeline of used equipment, and had money available for capital investment, we went to the equipment manufacturers once again and began renewing our aging fleet with new and updated equipment. One of my first discoveries was that there was not a firm bottom on the price you paid for new equipment: How good a price you were quoted depended on the quantity you ordered. Since we were the biggest buyers in the industry, we had a great deal of clout—and we used it, with the result that we began to rebuild our stock with brand-new models at good prices.

The Reasons for a Two-Brand Policy

I was determined that we were not going to fall back into that hodgepodge of models and makes that had given our mechanics and customers so much trouble in the past. The new policy was that there would be just two sources, a prime source and a secondary source, for each line of equipment. The only exceptions to the two-brand policy were in deference to regional preferences; we can't buck strong customer preferences, nor would we want to. For example, our two chosen brands in backhoes are John Deere and Case, but it so happens that there are strong regional preferences for Ford backhoes in certain parts of the country. So we carry Ford backhoes along with the two chosen brands in those places. We have a few other exceptions, but otherwise we stick to the two-supplier policy, which greatly simplifies our logistical problems, yet gives the customers top-value brands that have wide acceptance.

There are important benefits to this policy:

▶ We have a benchmark that encourages both suppliers to stay on their toes and give us their best prices and service.

▶ Because we are a good customer, the suppliers are eager to maintain close ties with us and cooperate in arranging intensive training programs at their facilities for our employees and in offering other kinds of support.

Controlling the Age of the Fleet

Of crucial importance in our overall scheme was the orderly procedure we adopted for selling off equipment in order to control tightly the average age of the fleet. The newness of the stock is not only a vital key to the quality of our "product" but also a sensitive figure in managing our capital budget. Everything in this chapter up to this point has therefore been a prelude to this issue.

Age of the fleet is the point at which the logistics of fleet management tie in with the ultimate quality of service as well as the economics of our business. Age determines the amount of expense that we will have in maintaining, repairing, and buying parts for the equipment. We have hundreds of millions invested in equipment, and our *return on this investment* therefore depends on how well we can control these costs by holding down the age of the equipment.

There are no absolutes in this business; instead there are tradeoffs. These vary with the level of revenue and how much we can afford to plow back into capital investment in light of the economic forecasts affecting our business. The end goal is always to provide quality service for the customer, and to sustain this under certain circumstances, we may have to absorb higher labor and maintenance costs in order to reduce capital costs. The whole point is to be in control and know where you are at all times so that you can make rational choices. You have to remain highly flexible at all times, and the specific disciplines you use for control must be adjustable to a changing situation.

How to Adjust the Tradeoffs

When we began our fleet renewal program by going back into the equipment market, we established a rule that we would sell off units when they reached 36 months in age. By selling off everything over that age, we were able gradually to reduce the average age of the fleet until it reached 18 months in 1989. Such a youthful fleet was unprecedented in our industry, and for a short period, everyone in the company and all our customers enjoyed the benefits of this in terms of trouble-free operating conditions. But then during the recession of 1991–1992, we had to let the age of the fleet drift upward again because of the economic pressures we were feeling.

When you go into a recession and your business begins to slide, you are obviously in a poor position if new equipment is still coming in. By 1991, we knew we were in a recession, so rather than committing ourselves to spending $150 million in new equipment as planned, we stopped ordering. We normally order equipment in October with a six-month lead time so that manufacturers can establish production schedules. In our effort to weight the fleet mix more toward our new industrial customers, we had been buying a great deal of new equipment. We therefore had a large inventory from the good years, and under recession conditions, we no longer needed to build the fleet. Nor was there any other way we could justify buying, even to keep down the fleet age.

We adjusted our strategy therefore by slowing the flow of new equipment coming in and increasing the disposal of the used equipment to get the fleet in balance with demand. That's the safe way to do it. Otherwise, if new equipment is coming in because of the long lead time, you have excess depreciation and interest—and then you have a real problem.

As a consequence, the fleet age grew in a year and a half from 18 months to 29 months. Because the people we were competing against were running fleets aged 60 to 72 months, we were still way ahead competitively. But our maintenance cost rose because it takes more mechanics to keep a 29-month-old fleet going than an 18-month-old fleet. It also costs more for parts. At the end of 1992, we ran up some numbers for future planning purposes to see how parts expense rises as fleet age moves from new to six years old. This dramatic effect is seen in Table 6.2, which treats parts cost as a percentage of the original cost of the equipment.

This was part of the price we paid to keep down the surplus inventory in our yards and keep utilization high. We planned this to happen. We have a computer system that can calculate our average fleet age down to one-hundredth of a percentage point, so we knew at all times what we

Table 6.2. Parts expense as a percentage of acquisition cost.

Fleet Age	Percentage
Less than 1 Year	0.16
1 Year	0.92
2 Years	1.23
3 Years	1.68
4 Years	1.75
5 Years	1.80
6 Years	2.37

were doing. We were able to calculate just how much this upward age drift was going to cost us in running expenses. At the same time, we also knew that we still were maintaining a healthy margin of quality versus the competition.

WRAP-UP

There Is No Easy Formula for Achieving Quality

The concept of quality is an elusive one in the service business. It is a bundle of incommensurables, among them:

1. *Behavior.* Judged subjectively by the customer when someone on the other end of the telephone in one of our branches takes an order.
2. *Time.* Measured by how close we get to delivering the backhoe at the hour that the customer specified.
3. *Appearance.* Depends on whether the backhoe looks beat-up and dirty when it arrives, or is in reasonably good shape.
4. *Performance.* Whether the backhoe breaks down or runs smoothly while the customer is using it.
5. *Accuracy.* Has to do with billing and follow-up.

On most of these matters, there isn't much question about the standards as far as the customers are concerned: The delivery either is on time or it isn't, the equipment is either clean or dirty, the machine keeps running or it breaks down, and so forth.

It is when you are on the other side of the fence that the ambiguity sets in. From the supplier's perspective, quality is often achieved by a set of *tradeoffs* that involve complex calculations.

The results for the customer are (presumably) the same in terms of quality of service as judged by the preceding five tests. But the results for the supplier can be very different in terms of return on investment.

More often than not, tradeoffs are posed in terms of *capital investment versus operating costs*. The following examples demonstrate this principle:

▶ In getting closer to the market, the supplier can—

1. Extend the distribution network by putting a fixed investment in stores and other facilities.

2. Accept longer hauls by truck to reach the customers' locations, thereby increasing operating costs.

▶ In providing customers with serviceable equipment that operates reliably, the supplier can—

1. Put enough capital investment in the fleet to keep its average age low.

2. Compensate for the aging of the fleet by incurring more operating expense through higher maintenance, repairs, and parts costs.

In reality, any service business at any given moment represents an amalgam of tradeoffs like these at different levels and in many areas. Flexibility is the name of the game. The important goals are:

▶ Have a policy you are working toward.

▶ Know just where you are in the business cycle.

▶ Have complete control so that you can shift policy immediately when conditions change.

Part Two

How to Measure
Performance

7

Numbers Are
the Core of the
Management System

With Part Two, we have arrived at the heart of the system required to deliver a package of quality services and goods to the customer. It comprises a complex spectrum of interrelated activities around a statistical core that measures and controls these activities and causes them to function as a whole. I could not agree more with Peter Senge when he describes systems thinking in his book *The Fifth Discipline: The Art and Practice of the Learning Organization* as "a discipline for seeing wholes"[1]. That is the theme of this chapter:

▶ It first describes the systems model we follow at HERC to discipline ourselves to bring all the pieces of the delivery system together and fuse them into a workable whole.

▶ Then it sets the stage for the discussion of the statistics that are the keys to regulating the operation of the system.

▶ *A Three-Dimensional Model of Delivery*

Table 7.1 is based on the flow of key activities as it typically occurs in any service business, whether it is delivering transportation, goods, rental equipment, or some other form of service or combination of goods and

[1] Peter M. Senge, *The Fifth Discipline: The Art and Practice of the Learning Organization*, New York: Doubleday, 1990, p. 68.

Table 7.1. Three-dimensional model for delivery of quality services.

Phase 1. *Preparation* (capital input and overhead)

    Overall business plan

    Store location, staffing, and maintenance

    Capital budget for new equipment

    Selection of supplier

    Timing of equipment ordering

    Depreciation allowance

    Replacement schedule

    Training of crews

    Balancing of inventory for customer availability

Phase 2. *Transaction (the "service encounter")*

    Regular contacts by salesperson

    Processing of rental contract by phone

    Operational check of equipment before rental

    Dispatch of equipment by truck

    On-site service calls (24-hour readiness)

    Backup units available if needed

    Pickup of returning equipment

    Billing of customer

    Computerized data reported to national customers

Phase 3. *Aftercare*

    Washing and servicing of returned equipment

    Routine checkup and maintenance

    Repairs and/or new parts

    Utilization report

    Status report ("deadlined" etc.)

    Return to line for recycling back through Phase 2 (or sale if unit has reached fleet age limit)

services. This particular version of the model is specific to our business, but with appropriate adjustments in terminology, the model will also serve other industries.

Phase 1, "Preparation," comprises the basic strategy and planning activities that must take place to get ready to bring services to the customers. In our business, this preparatory stage is heavily weighted toward store location, fleet planning for new equipment, selection of equipment and suppliers, and balancing of inventory so that the equipment is available to the customer. Part One of this book dwells in detail on these vital logistical functions to prepare the way for discussing the other two phases of delivery.

Phase 2, "Transaction," encompasses all the encounters and interchanges between our people and the customers. In the earlier chapters of this book, we touched on some of these functions, such as on-site service calls, operational check of equipment, and the reporting of computerized data to national accounts. As is immediately obvious, there is an overlap between what goes on during this phase of the delivery system and what goes on at the other stages. The interrelatedness of any system in our highly technological era is such that there is *continuous interplay* between the various parts of the system. I therefore have put off a fuller discussion of the transaction phase until the reader has a better comprehension of how this phase is impacted not only by the preparatory phase but also by the final phase.

Phase 3, "Aftercare," includes all the crucial activities that take place from the time the equipment is returned to our lots until it is either recycled back into Phase 2 of the system and is ready to go on rental again, or is earmarked for sale in the used-equipment marketplace if it has reached the mandatory retirement age under the fleet renewal program (see Chapter 6).

Aftercare embraces not only the maintenance and repair services necessary to keep the fleet running, but also such statistical activities as:

▶ Evaluating the information that feeds into the control system.

▶ Developing status reports (showing deadlined equipment, etc.).

▶ Preparing the utilization report, based on each day's activities, that keeps us in constant touch with our business.

Thus, the statistical information generated in Phase 3 recycles through the entire system, continuously adjusting the control systems in Phase 1.

▶ *Each Integrated System Is Weighted Differently*

"Quality of service" to me means "quality of system." This concept receives too little attention in the torrent of literature being produced today about the quality of service in the United States.

A great deal of the current literature deals with the mass-consumption industries, especially with retail distribution; the emphasis is therefore largely on what is called by some the "service encounter," which is the personal interplay between the salesperson and the customer. As a result, the measurement of "quality" tends to be examined in terms of how "the service team is performing in the eyes of the customer,"[2] to quote one writer. In this view, service quality measurement (SQM) is essentially a statistical profile of customer assessments. This approach, while useful, is inadequate because it is merely a one-dimensional model of quality measurement and takes into account only one level of the overall system.

This approach ignores Peter Senge's warning about keeping focused on the *whole*, which is why we have developed our own three-dimensional model. Any system for the delivery of service, whether the "product" is transportation, food, health care, or clothing, breaks down into the three phases outlined in Table 7.1. Depending on the business you are in, however, these three phases assume very different significance and weight.

In the retail food business, for example, the preparation time (stocking up primarily) would be foreshortened and aftercare (returned goods) would be minimal. Logistics would be of great importance, but transactions with the customers would occupy the center of concern.

In an industrial business such as ours, we deal with large pieces of equipment that entail considerable capital outlays. A great deal of planning and care go into the purchase of equipment and into the logistics needed to get the product to the customer; in addition, we must keep that equipment in running shape when the customer is using it. This totally shifts the emphasis on the different phases.

Transactions with the customer are important to us and have increasing significance as we develop national customers who are sophisticated buyers. But we are still handling relatively few customers through our 85 locations in this country as compared with mass-consumer services of various kinds that deal with myriad customers in hundreds and even thousands of locations. In our business, what commands our attention are the activities of the preparatory and follow-through stages, which guarantee that we get the right equipment where and when the customer needs it, in the right condition, and at the right price. All three stages—preparation, transaction, aftercare—are interlocked in one system, and this is true in any service business. Each business simply emphasizes a different phase of the system.

My definition of "system" is an inclusive one. To borrow language from the economists, it embraces not only "outputs" such as customer

---

[2] Karl Albrecht. *At America's Service: How Your Company Can Join the Customer Service Revolution,* New York: Warner Books, 1988, p. 218.

satisfaction, but "inputs" such as capital expenditures on the rental equipment, plus expenditures on maintenance and service. We are continuously trying to measure all those inputs and outputs so that we can establish relationships and tie them together meaningfully to monitor "quality."

It is encouraging to observe that the integrated systems approach suggested by Table 7.1 is beginning to take hold in the service business. An illustration of this is the recently published book *Service Breakthroughs: Changing the Rules of the Game*, a theoretical approach based on the experiences of 15 major national and international service firms. The intent of the book, according to its authors, is to take the reader "to the very core of the service firm, to its human, technological, and financial resources and the way they are marshaled and brought to bear on delivering a service concept."[3] The authors stress the importance of measurement and devote several chapters to exploring the relationships between productivity, costs, and quality of service. This approach strongly supports the whole thrust of *Service Success!*, which adds definitions, numbers, and specifics to the conceptualizations in *Service Breakthroughs*.

The service business, although a people business, is also a numbers game. Without the right numbers, quality service is impossible.

▶ *Keeping an Eye on Crucial Reports*

The earlier chapters of this book focus primarily on how numbers are developed to support a services delivery system. Collecting and defining numbers can be both difficult and tedious; furthermore, if you develop the wrong criteria, you often end up with a nice system but the wrong results. Nor can you ever be certain that the system you are measuring today is going to be the system you will need to measure tomorrow. My response to all of that is, Don't worry, go ahead and put numbers to things anyway. To gain an understanding of something, *try to define and to measure it*, even if you start by measuring the wrong thing. Eventually, you will start to measure the right thing if you keep redefining the criteria to meet the desired results.

This chapter and the next three chapters therefore describe the essence of our system as of a certain date in the early 1990s, just that. It is

---

[3] James L. Heskett, W. Earl Sasser, Jr., and Christopher W.L. Hart, *Service Breakthroughs: Changing the Rules of the Game,* New York: The Free Press, 1990, p. vii.

subject to continuing change as events warrant or as we discover imperfections. It will inevitably change as we come under new business challenges and the power of computerization grows exponentially, giving us more capability of gathering and analyzing data.

Information from Thirty-Nine Reports

The need to secure vital information about the business caused me to develop and refine various key indicators such as:

▶ Utilization of equipment.

▶ Monthly base and daily average.

▶ The business accounted for by national accounts.

▶ Age of fleet.

These represent actually only a handful of the statistics that we collect daily, weekly, and monthly, and that are processed by our computers. Table 7.2 lists 39 series of figures selected from the wealth and variety of statistical reports HERC gathers. This gives some idea of the fine detail required for us to comprehend the big picture, know what is happening at the crucial points, and most important of all, get people to take those thousands of actions that keep customers happy and make a company successful.

Some of these 39 reports are generic, that is, they are familiar to all businesses and require no discussion here. There are no surprises to be found in, say, our use of an operating statement, nor is it particularly germane to the issue of quality service; neither do I claim any special expertise in accountancy. Certain other reports, such as salespersons' revenue and equipment thefts, are self-evident and do not require explanation.

Nine Key Reports

For the purposes of discussion in Chapters 8, 9, and 10, I have selected nine key reports, either because they are essential in our business operations or because they illustrate some important principle regarding the development of effective measurement and control techniques. These nine are:

▶ Rental revenue analysis, which is discussed in Chapter 8.

▶ Slow rent, deadline, overtime, active accounts, preventive maintenance, delivery cost, and safety, which are discussed in Chapter 9.

▶ Utilization, which is discussed in Chapter 10.

Table 7.2. Thirty-nine selected HERC statistical reports.

Accident and safety rates	Net write-off rankings
Accounts receivable by age ban	New accounts opened by location per month
Amount of rental revenue being generated monthly	Number of active accounts vs. year earlier
Capital spending report daily average	Overtime as a percentage of total time worked
Credit applications by region	Pretax rankings
Comparative database report	Preventive maintenance
Comparative fleet/revenue/pretax	Rental revenue analysis
Comparative work injuries	Return on investment of each piece of equipment
Complete operating statement	Salespersons' revenue vs. quota
Deadline (percentage of fleet not operational for 7 days)	SIC code by location
Delivery charge as percentage of revenue	Slow rent
Dollar utilization of equipment	Ten largest receivable accounts over 60 days
Equipment not returned in 90 days	Thirteen-month trial balance
Equipment thefts	Time utilization by class of each piece of equipment in the fleet
Inventory aging	Top 15 accounts
Involuntary turnover of employees	Travel and entertainment report
Loss and damage waiver as percentage of revenue	Used equipment sales as percentage of first cost
Monthly base	Warranty claims
Monthly market segmentation	
Monthly status of o/s purchase orders	
National accounts vs. revenue	

While some of the data are unique to our kind of business, and therefore are not directly applicable to other industries, these reports may help others discover dynamic ways to measure, control, and improve any business.

▶ What You Can Learn from Baseball Statistics

The statistics we gather at HERC have for me a dynamic and living quality; the primary reason for collecting them is not merely for analytical purposes but to lead to action. Our statistics serve us in much the same way that they further the strategy in major league baseball, and I try to model our own use of statistics on the infinitely flexible purposes they accomplish in baseball.

A Statistical Approach to the Quality of the Game

Every day during the official baseball season, a mass of statistics is generated to comprise the database of the game. It is made up of thousands of individual actions on the diamond: balls, strikes, fouls, hits, runs, putouts, stolen bases, and so forth. All these actions become instant statistics that pour into many formats: box scores, indexes, reports, rankings, listings, and whatever. They are aggregated and then disaggregated as they are peeled off at different levels of inclusiveness and complexity to satisfy various purposes:

▶ In its most highly aggregated form, the great baseball database appears as the team standings in the two leagues and their divisions. This is roughly equivalent to a corporate operating statement; it shows wins, losses, percentages—a kind of bottom line for each team.

▶ In its disaggregated form, the same information emerges as the daily box scores of games, showing a great deal more detail on just what happened to the players in that day's games.

As the baseball season continues, the increasingly voluminous data are churned into all kinds of rankings at several different levels of inclusiveness and detail. There are rankings of team and individual performance in terms of batting, pitching, stolen bases, fielding, and so forth. There are rankings showing performance according to classification by position: one for pitchers, another for basemen, another for fielders; and so it goes, until you get down to the micro level of baseball cards showing lifetime performances statistically for each player.

The data are infinitely useful and flexible and can be used to reconstruct exact situations on a certain diamond as of a certain day, hour, and minute. Or you can get an overall view at the macro level of exactly where the great national (now international) pastime stands at any given moment. By historical extrapolation, you can even see the effects of major strategic decisions such as, for example, giving pitchers an advantage over sluggers by raising the pitching mound a little. Or of introducing the designated batter into the batting lineup to even up the playing field a little and liven up the game once again with more hitting. This is an approach to a *statistical control over the quality of the game* not unlike the statistical control we are trying to achieve at HERC over quality in a service industry.

When to Aggregate Up and Disaggregate Down

Baseball has an advantage that I greatly envy: There is virtually no action of any significance that cannot be impaled by a statistic, which is quite different from the real-life situation in my industry. Nevertheless, we are trying to move as far as we can in this direction, and HERC is making a pretty good showing.

In our equivalent to the great baseball database, the players are the pieces of equipment in inventory for rental at any given time. Our fleet totals approximately 30,000 units, and we keep close tabs on everything that happens to these "players" from the moment we take delivery of them to the moment we sell them in the used equipment market. Our livelihoods depend on this information in as detailed a form as we can manage to record and tabulate, and our means of capturing this detail are becoming increasingly refined as we go along. It is through the information we collect on these individual players in our service game that we construct many of the reports and analyses that are vital to the efficient and profitable pursuit of our business and to providing our customers with satisfactory service.

While our tabulations are expressed not in terms of hits or errors but in dollars and percentages, they are no means merely financial abstractions. They represent a myriad of specific, definable, and concrete actions that go on in our shops and on our lots, from filling a tank with gas to logging in a needed repair job. When we aggregate these millions of figures, we get a *panoramic view* of just what is going on nationally in our business, so that headquarters can derive *policy* and *strategy decisions.* This is the rule we follow throughout our use of statistics: Go *upward* to aggregate in order to find signals for policy decisions; go *downward* to disaggregate in order to find signals for action at the local level.

When we go deep down into the disaggregated detail, we can spot a deadlined bulldozer in Newark, New Jersey, that is overdue for repair. I say "we" can spot, but I mean the *system* can, because we have the computer programmed to flag the need for action at the local level—for something urgent to happen out there on the playing field, one single at a time.

WRAP-UP

Getting into the Feedback Loop

Turn back for a moment to Table 7.1 and look again at the three-dimensional model for quality measurement. If you tick off the topics discussed thus far in the book, you will see that we have covered many of the activities listed there, especially those occurring in Phases 1 and 2—the *preparatory* and *transactional* stages—of the process involved in delivering quality services. In the next three chapters of the book, we will look at various aspects of Phase 3, the *aftercare* stage of quality control.

The last item in aftercare provides for the return of the equipment to the line for rental, unless it has reached the age limit that was originally set in the preparatory phase of strategy and planning. In that case, the unit is earmarked for sale in the used-equipment market. The logistics of fleet age were described in Chapter 6, where the critical importance of fleet age is spelled out.

Other businesses have similarly critical factors in the delivery system that impact in some way other aspects of the system. In our industry, equipment age is such a factor. It has a profound relationship to return on investment and planning because of its key influence on a whole complex of factors from labor and parts cost to utilization, not to mention customer satisfaction.

Aftercare in our definition therefore not only has a vital *maintenance function* (in the operational sense of taking physical care of the equipment) but also an equally important informational *feedback function*.

Aftercare includes such key functions as evaluation of information and reporting on utilization and status of the equipment as the maintenance proceeds. These in turn loop back into the pricing function and the control systems associated with Phase 1. Fleet age is an illustration of how this works.

Once again we can see the need, in thinking about quality of service, to keep an eye on the *whole* system, as Peter Senge advises.

8

How to Interpret the Key Numbers That Reveal Company Performance

The most significant and comprehensive of all the reports from our database is the revenue rental analysis. It is the guts of the system. One of the keys to being a good manager at HERC is to use this analytical report effectively.

This one report contains all the information relative to the assets and their cost. *Revenue analysis* is ultimately the key to profitability. You can go to business school and get a degree, but with this series of numbers you can become an astute manager in the rental business. The report enables you to become a knowledgeable manager. Are the assets profitable? Are the assets breaking down? Do you have too many assets? Rental revenue analysis answers these questions and many more by revealing:

▶ The value of the equipment we have available to rent.

▶ The amount of revenue we are deriving on a monthly and yearly basis.

▶ The expenses incurred by each piece of equipment.

The report also analyzes these costs versus the revenue and gives us the return on investment and the time utilization of the equipment. The information from this report lets us know:

▶ When to buy equipment.

▶ How to price it.

▶ When to transfer it.

▶ When to sell it.

Everyone has access to these figures. All managers in the company receive the same data in a form appropriate to their operations and profit centers. In other words, we are all working out of the same data at different levels. Each manager receives his or her rental revenue analysis each month. The people in the regional offices receive it for every branch in their region. The people in division receive it for all the regions. We are happy to share this and other data with any manager who feels the need for it. The same open door policy applies to the peer measurement reports that we will discuss in the next chapter. These reports show branch managers and regional officers where they stand vis-à-vis all the other branches and regions in the company.

▶ Examining in Detail a Single Piece of Equipment

Rental revenue analysis describes every piece of equipment in our entire fleet of approximately 30,000 units. Through it, we can track a single piece of equipment through different levels of reporting for different purposes. We will be examining this process in detail because this is the heart—the very heartbeat—of the HERC system of asset quality control.

Figure 8.1 shows a portion of the rental revenue analysis report for the branch in Baton Rouge, Louisiana, for August 1993. The highlighted portion describes the 12-ton diesel truck cranes in the branch's inventory at that time. Baton Rouge had three units of this category of equipment; we will follow the underlined unit, identified as number 312-12-9146. Right under this entry are the words "size total," which sums up the various statistics for all three of these units in Baton Rouge.

On Figure 8.2, we can again pick up number 312-12-9146 (underlined), only this time we are looking at it in the context of the entire company report on 12-ton diesel truck cranes. As of fall 1993, HERC owned 270 of these big rigs, and the summary for this entire category of units appears at the bottom of the extract under "class total."

Figure 8.2 expands the data. We are looking at an extract of the companywide report for all diesel truck cranes. The rental revenue data is uniformly displayed in 17 columns; for your convenience, each column has been numbered above the heading across the top of the page. In the next section, we will identify these components and explain their significance.

HEIN4470-01
RUN DATE 09/08/93
FICHE INDEX - AREA-9440.CL-308

HERTZ EQUIPMENT RENTAL CORPORATION
RENTAL REVENUE ANALYSIS BY BRANCH
9440 - BATON ROUGE LA

AS OF AUG 31, 1993   PAGE 910

IC NUMBER	MO AV	CUR MO BOOK VALUE	CUR MO REVENUE	REVENUE	YIELD	ROLLING-12 DEPR EX	PARTS	MONTH LABOR	INT	C.M.	ROI	CUR RNTL DAYS	CUR RNTL %	ROLLING-12 RNTL DAYS	RNTL %	LAST RENT/ #UNIT
CARRY DECK CRA DSL 7																
308-07-0002	12	36,900	270	11,406	951	4,615	285	818	3,277	2,411	6.5	1	5	81	31	08-93
308-07-0005	12	37,627	270	5,820	485	4,610	191	526	3,338	2,845-	7.6-	1	5	49	19	08-93
308-07-0007	12	40,270	260-	7,856	655	4,883	411	671	3,570	1,679-	4.2-	1-	5-	69	26	06-93
SIZE TOTAL		114,796	280	25,082	2,090	14,108	887	2,015	10,185	2,113-	1.8-	1	2	199	25	3
CUR MO YIELD = 93 ANNUALIZED YIELD = 697																
CLASS TOTAL		114,796	280	25,082	2,090	14,108	887	2,015	10,185	2,113-	1.8-	1	2	199	25	3
TRUCK CRANE DSL 12 T																
312-12-0113	12	48,450	790	22,114	1,843	5,540	70	90	4,283	12,131	25.0	2	9	133	50	08-93
312-12-0115	12	48,908	2,190	29,875	2,490	5,539	28	135	4,321	19,851	40.6	6	27	138	52	08-93
312-12-9146	12	28,091	2,500	31,750	2,646	8,539	470	495	2,680	19,766	70.4	20	100	253	96	08-93
SIZE TOTAL		125,450	5,480	83,739	6,978	19,418	568	720	11,285	51,747	41.2	28	45	524	66	3
CUR MO YIELD = 1,827 ANNUALIZED YIELD = 2,326																
TRUCK CRANE DSL 15T																
312-15-3010	02	66,399	4,000	4,000	2,000	481			933	2,586	23.4	22	100	22	50	08-93
SIZE TOTAL		66,399	4,000	4,000	2,000	481			933	2,586	23.4	22	100	22	50	1
CUR MO YIELD = 4,000 ANNUALIZED YIELD = 2,000																
CLASS TOTAL		191,849	9,480	87,739	8,978	19,900	568	720	12,218	54,333	35.8	50	59	546	62	4
CRANES		306,645	9,760	112,821	11,068	34,008	1,455	2,735	22,403	52,220	19.3	51	34	745	46	7

Figure 8.1. Rental revenue analysis of truck cranes, Baton Rouge, LA, Branch, September 1993.

HEIN4470-05
RUN DATE 09/08/93
FICHE INDEX - IC-312-12-9130

HERTZ EQUIPMENT RENTAL CORPORATION
RENTAL REVENUE ANALYSIS BY COMPANY
COMPANY REPORT

312-12   TRUCK CRANE DSL 12 T

IC NUMBER (1)	MO AV (2)	CUR MO BOOK VALUE (3)	CUR MO REVENUE (4)	REVENUE (5)	YIELD (6)	ROLLING DEPR EX (7)	PARTS (8)	LABOR (9)	MONTH INT (10)	C.M. (11)	ROI (12)	CUR RNTL DAYS (13)	CUR RNTL % (14)	ROLLING-12 RNTL DAYS (15)	RNTL % (16)	LAST RENT/#UNIT (17)
9564	12	28,622	3,265	33,624	2.802	8,497	856	920	2,731	20,621	72.0	21	100	204	77	08-93
9643	12	30,104	2,135	25,620	2.135	9,006	267	1,490	2,892	11,964	39.5	22	100	258	98	08-93
9463	12	28,136	2,200	30,552	2.544	8,352	85	723	2,685	18,687	66.4	20	100	162	61	08-93
9631	12	28,220	3,000	31,199	2.600	8,377	534	993	2,693	18,602	65.9	22	100	205	78	08-93
9639	12	28,881		31,184	1.765	8,553	828	1,038	2,751	8,015	27.8	1	5	197	75	08-93
9333	12	28,143	1,320	20,433	1.703	8,354	265	1,866	2,685	7,262	25.8	8	36	133	50	08-93
9724	12	29,250		19,866	1.656	8,473	69	175	2,783	8,366	28.6			135	51	08-93
9643	12	31,998	2,400	30,480	2.540	9,049	362	1,250	3,033	16,786	52.5	22	100	258	98	08-93
9641	12	28,829	160	33,301	2.775	8,538	557	1,557	2,746	19,904	69.0			181	68	08-93
9638	12	30,377	6,200	17,545	1.462	9,026	166	585	2,899	4,868	16.0	36	164	92	35	08-93
9440	12	28,091	2,820	31,750	2.646	8,339	470	495	2,680	19,766	70.4	20	100	253	96	08-93
9326	12	28,218	2,820	18,227	1.519	8,377	259	508	2,692	6,391	22.7	23	100	114	43	08-93
9322	12	29,807	1,405	25,101	2.092	8,635	148	1,688	2,836	11,795	39.6	6	25	181	68	08-93
9169	12	28,888	2,380	26,914	2.243	8,368	522	391	2,748	14,883	51.5	15	68	194	73	08-93

SIZE TOTAL 11823,570   635,279   6604,539   575,494   1685,047   113,624   267,302   972,619   3565,947   32.0   4,038   70   43,945   64   270
CUR MO YIELD = 2.353   ANNUALIZED YIELD = 2.160

Figure 8.2. Rental revenue analysis of truck cranes by company, September 1993.

110

▶ *The 17 Components of Rental Revenue Analysis*

1. *Identification Number.* This is an internal company system for numbering each asset. At HERC, we call it an "IC number."

2. *Number of Months Averaged.* This shows whether the monthly averages shown are based on a full 12 months' experience, or whether the unit has only been put into service a few months before. Averages are on a 12-month "rolling" basis (i.e., they have been annualized by dropping the first month of each of the 12 months reported and picking up the latest month).

3. *Current Month Book Value.* The dollar value shown here is the acquisition cost of the asset minus accumulated depreciation calculated as of the current month.

4. *Current Month Revenue.* This shows how much rental revenue we were able to get from this piece of equipment during the past month.

5. *Revenue.* This is the total for the latest year. As the table heading indicates, this item and the next 7 items (through column 12) are on a "rolling 12-month" basis.

6. *Yield.* The average month revenue (e.g., the full year revenue divided by 12).

7. *Depreciation Expense.* Calculated by dividing the cost of the asset by the life of the asset.

8. *Parts Expense.* What was spent over 12 months for replacement parts such as carburetors, gears, and hydraulic fittings to keep the unit operational. This expense gets into the computer system through the shop repair order that the mechanic makes out when repairing a piece of equipment.

9. *Labor Expense.* Mechanics' salary cost pro rated.

10. *Interest Expense.* Cost of the interest we have to pay on our investment in the unit calculated on net book value.

11. *Cumulative Margin.* Revenue less depreciation, parts, interest, and labor.

12. *Return on Investment (ROI).* ROI is cumulative margin divided by net book value. This is the return from that piece of equipment based on the rental revenue received for the use of the equipment minus costs directly attributable to it and does not include overhead costs (e.g., management salary and store rent). If the unit has a zero ROI, it is not making money or losing money, but breaking even on the cost of that asset.

13. *Current Rental Days.* With this entry and the next, we are now back to actual monthly figures, not an annualized average. This figure tells us how many days that piece actually did bring in rental during the most recent month. However, it is subject to some aberrances. Our monthly billing cycle is 28 days, and it is possible for a unit to be billed on two cycles in the same month. This can happen if, say, the unit goes out in mid-October and comes in during early November, and then goes out again in November and comes back that month. It thus gets billed twice for that month. It is similarly possible for the unit to be rented during that month but not show up in the billing cycle. This is one reason that we also use a rolling 12-month average, which gets rid of these quirks.

14. *Current Rental Percentage.* The amount of days that the unit is on rental divided by 22. Because of the aberrances previously noted, a unit can rent for, say, 120 percent of the month.

15. *Total Rental Days for the Year.* Here and in the next column we switch back again to calculating on a rolling 12-month basis. This gives us a panoramic view of that unit's place in our fleet and a chance to compare its performance with other units in its class and in turn to review the performance of that model with that of other models in the same class.

16. *Rental Percentage for the Year.* The other name for this statistic is "time utilization." This critical figure is discussed in the following section of this chapter, along with ROI.

17. *Last Date Unit Was on Rental.* What you find here may cause you to check whether this unit has been deadlined for a protracted period and why, or whether there is some other reason for its not having been out on rental. Last-date-on-rental therefore provides an early warning signal of trouble.

Revenue analysis is studded with early warning signals of this kind. Parts expense (8) is another such signal we watch closely for trouble somewhere along the line. The following is a hypothetical case:

We are running two competing brands of the same piece of equipment from two manufacturers, and although we are having maintenance problems with one line, this hasn't surfaced as yet from our shop reports. The parts expense report will spit it out at us by showing that parts and maintenance costs went up sharply on various units, a finding that then sends us to the company-wide report for that model. From this, we see the collective behavior of that whole line of equipment. If it turns out that we have a lemon, or even if there is a minor product defect, we can go back to the manufacturer for parts or relief.

Rental revenue analysis therefore gives us the analytical data necessary to take actions that will make an asset profitable.

▶ The Two Key Indicators: ROI and Time Utilization

Return on investment (12) in tandem with time utilization (16) are the most powerful analytical tools at our disposal.

Each service industry has its own characteristic way of determining profitability and efficiency. In our industry, *ROI and time utilization* are the two key measures to look at when trying to determine what to do about assets. Together they tell us whether or not an asset is productive and help us determine what business strategy to pursue in dealing with such complex issues as pricing, repositioning, or selling the asset.

We can see how this works by taking a look first at the critical importance of ROI in terms of our competition. Mom-and-pop enterprises typically operate on a lower ROI than a big corporation because they have less overhead to cover. Big corporations most likely have a lower acquisition expense, depreciation is less, interest is less, and parts are cheaper because of economies of scale. But a big company still requires a higher ROI than the small local enterprise because of having greater overhead.

At HERC, we know exactly the point at which we are going to start making a profit after covering all our costs. The reason we are in business is to make money, and after using this report, we endeavor to get to levels that make satisfactory returns. Depending on the information from the key ROI indicator, we decide whether we are receiving satisfactory results. If, for example, the ROI is 50 percent, we are very pleased, because at that rate, it is covering all our expenses and throwing off a very good profit. In the case of truck crane number 312-12-9146, the ROI is 70.4 percent, which is quite satisfactory. But if the ROI had been 8 percent, say, we would not have been happy; although the equipment would have been paying for its costs, it would not have been covering its overhead.

Once we understand all the components of the ROI and know that there are no abnormalities (such as excessive repair costs that would indicate this model of equipment has some basic problems), then the ROI starts telling us things. We can look along the line to the column in our rental revenue analysis that gives us time utilization, and on the basis of this information, we can make some important strategy decisions. We have worked out the matrix described in the following section to help us with these decisions.

▶ *How to Use the ROI-Utilization Grid*

High time utilization and high ROI indicates that you have a winner: an item that your customers want and that rents at a good price. The 12-ton diesel truck crane that we have been following fits this criteria. As already noted, its ROI was 70 percent, and the other columns show that its time utilization over the previous 12 months was 96 percent. Truck cranes are a generally good item for HERC. They are in heavy demand and are rented out for long periods; and because they are a high-ticket item, we are one of the only equipment rental companies with sufficient assets to stock enough of them in the fleet. The only strategy questions raised here are whether the pricing might be increased and how many new assets to acquire.

High time utilization and low ROI signals that you may have one of two possible problems on your hands: (1) The machine may break down on the job, or (2) you have a rate problem. So you look along the rental revenue analysis to see the parts and labor expense, and if that is high and your time is high, you know it is a repair problem and may be a warning situation. If you don't have a repair problem, what you have is a rate situation, and you want to increase the rate you are getting. Start raising prices and watch time utilization. Do it in stages. Raise prices incrementally—and watch.

Low time utilization and high ROI tells you that it is a profitable asset and is used on a selective basis, such as a generator or a pump, which is used only for emergencies or infrequent situations. Seasonal items such as snowplows also fit into this category. That means you should not buy any more of the asset and that you might even consider deleting some assets. You should maintain or increase pricing.

Low time utilization and low ROI sends a short but loud message: Either get out of the asset or transfer it to a branch that can use it profitably. That asset is not making money, and drastic action has to be taken.

When I do a monthly meeting at a location, I take the latest rental revenue analysis with me, and with our grid in mind, we go over it item by item and category by category. We are working with a bulky document, as many as 40 pages for that location alone. As we run through it, we look for items that tell us we have a problem. When we spot a unit of equipment with a *negative ROI*, which means that it is not even covering its direct costs, we ask the manager why. If we find there is a problem, we look for an action plan to get that asset out. The reasoning behind hitting 1,000 singles has just one premise: getting action. If you can get rid of an asset with a bad return, you are hitting a single. The art of hitting 1,000 singles lies in knowing how to manage the rental revenue analysis.

Rental revenue analysis is our reference point in making hourly and daily decisions at all levels in the company. The managers refer to it at the branch level to see if they should transfer equipment, and I refer to it at a consolidated level every time they ask me to buy equipment. When an equipment request comes in, we look at our utilization of that equipment countrywide to see if there is a good return on asset. If it is showing a bad return on a consolidated basis, we are going to refuse that request. The report gives us a lot of other crucial information in determining our assets strategy. It tells us, for instance, the right timing for phasing any particular class of equipment out of the system. When we see mounting parts and labor expense, we know it is time to sell.

Rental revenue analysis is HERC's own homegrown course in Profitability 101. If you learn how to use this kind of report, adapted to your uses, you are going to have a profitable business.

WRAP-UP
You Don't Need a Mainframe to Run Your Numbers

To keep continuous track of 30,000 pieces of equipment, HERC requires a mainframe computer. This is not primarily because of the size of the fleet, but rather because of the complex data that the company cranks into the system to get a full picture of its assets and its operations in the desired detail.

This happens to be one way of doing business, and it may not be necessary or even suitable for other companies to be so elaborate. What you are trying to do is to find ways to measure, control, and improve your service business that take into full account its dynamic and changing nature. Once again, it is the *underlying methodology* that counts.

Here are some suggestions that may be useful in guiding you to find your own methodologies of measurement:

▶ Try to put a number on every significant action or procedure that can possibly be quantified.

▶ Don't worry if you don't get it right at first; you may have to experiment before you get the definitions right and identify just what you need to measure.

▶ Be consistent whatever else you do, so that you are measuring the same thing everywhere and in the same time frame.

▶ Design your data system so that you can view it on both macro and micro levels in order to yield policy decisions at the top and action at the bottom.

▶ Identify the most significant components of measurement and highlight them; one way to do this is to develop grids or formulas that will help people spot problems immediately and act on them.

▶ Never tire of going through the numbers in infinite detail with your managers—immerse yourself in the numbers and stay immersed on a daily basis.

Final thought: In developing a database for a service industry, there are many worse models to follow than major league baseball statistics.

9

Ranking and Improving through Peer Performance

This chapter details how to pinpoint individual responsibility for initiating actions that improve that the company's overall performance, a single at a time. To achieve this at HERC, we use a methodology called "peer performance measurement," which is embodied in company reports that tell managers how well they are handling crucial activities versus their counterparts.

Peer performance measurement is based on the concept that you cannot bring about lasting improvement in any activity in the service business unless you can measure it. Over time, we not only have improved our measurements but also have found new areas that we can measure with success. That progress in turn improves the quality and effectiveness of our performance as a company.

▶ *What Peer Performance Is and What It Does*

Peer performance measurement draws on the data in our basic rental revenue analysis and also taps those other 39 or more statistical reports described in Chapter 7. In addition, we develop new series of numbers when these are needed to accomplish some important goal or task, and we reformat these figures so they have an immediate and perceptible effect on performance. We then use the figures with the following purposes in mind:

1. To show people how the whole company is performing in some area of vital importance.

2. To put each manager and branch squarely into the big picture by bringing the numbers down to their level and ranking each person's performance against the performance of all other managers in the company.

3. To build an action element into the system.

These reports aren't issued so the front office can ponder and make pronouncements. Our intent is to get immediate action from the players on the field, who know that we want responses to these questions:

▶ What are you going to do about this?

▶ When?

▶ How much will it cost?

▶ How much will it reduce expenses?

It is the *response element* that is missing in many reporting systems. In the service business, it is especially needed because you often cannot tell whether some essential action has happened until somebody responsible signs a chit on the dotted line stating that it has and that chit gets into the reporting system and becomes a solid statistic.

Applying Pressure When It Is Needed

The seven reports discussed in this chapter are critically important in sustaining both the quality of service we provide the customers and our efficiency and profitability as a company. Some are concerned with just one of these aspects, but most look both ways at the same time: at our interest and the customer's interest. A good illustration of this dual interest is preventive maintenance: If the people in the shop don't do preventive maintenance on a regular basis and a piece of equipment breaks down on the job, it is costly for the customer and for us. We are looking here at the very heart of quality service—and of company profit.

Our peer performance reports provide a means to apply pressure at points where it is needed. What we decide to highlight depends on the issues that are confronting the company at any given time. We can use our data to provide, for example, a compelling lesson in profitability. When the situation demands it, we can spin off branch pretax earnings reports in which we rank each branch from worst to best. This particular form of peer measurement is a tough one, however, and we seldom use it.

Highlighting Both Good and Poor Results

Ranking individual performance is admittedly a delicate business, and when poorly handled, it can encourage too great a competitiveness among people generally, as well as be damaging to some people. Both are potential risks, and there indeed have been occasions when I chose not to disclose a ranking that might have had a hurtful effect on some managers and locations. Yes, these rankings do make people nervous at times. Despite these factors, however, it still has been our experience that most of our managers welcome the reports. In general, people like to know where they stand and how they are doing vis-à-vis their peers. Rankings of this kind give them a feel for what it is possible to do under a variety of circumstances, a sense of what they themselves might accomplish if others can do it, and even a chance to test their mettle against other players.

Some might call our system management by exception, but we prefer our term, "peer performance measurement," because it implies a more positive approach. *Our reports highlight both good results and poor results;* by learning how to interpret these signs in terms of their own operations, managers make their contribution to improving the whole system. Doing more of the right things is as important as doing less of the wrong things, and it is the first part of the syllogism that we try to emphasize.

Collectively, these reports, including rental revenue analysis, are the basis of our management training courses. From the moment they join the company, we educate people in the use of these reports. They learn how to manage a business by being alert when a report is telling them that some indicator is moving in a new direction. It is not critical for us that someone knows how the hydraulic system works on a backhoe or can explain the breakout force of a bucket hitting the ground. We have been successful because we take young people out of college and teach them how to manage a business using peer management reports.

The Principle of Selection

At any given time, we can locate many pressure points that need attention, but we have to be selective: *The human attention span is limited;* people can handle only so many urgent messages at one time before overload sets in. A wise leader respects this; peer measurement is a powerful tool that must be used with skill and discrimination. The seven pressure points discussed in this chapter are ones that we were focusing on when this book was being written. A year from now, we may be looking at a diffent mix; two years from now we may be looking at still a different one. For now, here are the seven areas HERC monitors: slow rent, broken equipment, overtime, preventive maintenance, delivery cost, active accounts, and safety.

▶ *The Slow Rent Report: Signals When Machines Are Idle*

The slow rent report tells us that a piece of equipment is idle and not making any money, and the report also leads us to the reason.

Slow rent is one of those points on which we keep constant pressure, month after month, year after year, and as far as we can see, this will continue indefinitely. The slow-rent indicator is like the fuel gauge on your car—it tells you whether your tank is full or you are running out of gas.

A piece of equipment becomes "slow rent" when it has not been rented in 90 days. Setting the cutoff at 90 was an arbitrary decision; we could have selected 30 or 50 days, or some other time frame. We picked 90 days because we thought that a piece of equipment being idle that long indicates a serious situation. An average location has 200 to 300 pieces of equipment in inventory, out of which typically 2 to 8 pieces will be on slow rent. In our national system, therefore, we may have the equivalent of two profit centers sitting idle at any given time.

Table 9.1 shows the slow-rent pattern for the whole company. It shows, first, that slow rent goes up seasonally in the wintertime, which correlates with our anticipated decline in rentals each year at this time. Second, it shows that we are making progress and that slow rent is gradually declining from one year to the next. The HERC fleet is worth more than $500 million, so if 1 percent is on slow rent that means $5 million worth of assets earning nothing; 2 percent gets us to $10 million wasted assets.

Table 9.1. Company report, slow rent percentage, 1988–1992 (over $5,000).

	Jan.	*Feb.*	*Mar.*	*Apr.*	*May*	*June*
1988	3.3	2.5	3.6	3.2	2.9	2.4
1989	2.7	2.8	3.7	3.3	2.3	1.9
1990	1.9	2.4	3.1	2.8	1.9	1.5
1991	1.6	2.8	2.9	2.2	1.6	1.2
1992	1.7	2.3	2.3	1.8	1.0	1.0

Our ultimate goal is to get slow rent down to zero days, but since that is impossible, we settle for a real-life goal of 1 percent. Whatever the figure, the point is that you can always drive the figure down to a still lower level. To do this, you have to understand why you are having slow rent problems. Is it due to some pattern? Is it accidental? Peer performance measurement is intended to smoke this out. There are several broad possible reasons for a slow rent signal:

▶ It may simply be that you are looking at a snowplow that doesn't rent during the summer months. Likewise, if it is a roller used for compacting pavement, and the branch is located in the Northeast, it is not going to rent during the wintertime. Or if it is a pump, it isn't going to rent when there is a drought.

▶ A more serious problem is that you may have too much of an asset in a market that has become soft. The asset is just sitting in that city—and you have to move it.

▶ Even more serious, the equipment may be broken, in which case it hits two reports: first the deadline report and now the slow-rent report, which kicks in at 90 days and highlights the deadlining. This makes certain that no one can hide a problem of this kind from us, at least not for very long.

And we want action. The computer spits out a slow-rent report for every location each month, showing:

1. The book value of the units that have gone over 90 days idle.

2. The dates on which they were last rented.

3. The action the manager is taking to get those slow rents off the book or back into service.

July	Aug.	Sept.	Oct.	Nov.	Dec.
2.4	1.8	2.0	1.7	1.6	2.0
1.5	1.5	1.6	1.1	1.4	1.3
1.3	1.2	1.4	1.1	1.0	1.1
1.2	1.1	1.1	1.1	1.1	1.2
1.0	1.1	1.1	1.0	0.9	1.1

Table 9.2. Slow rent/lost rent (by month, past 12 months).

Branch: ___9331___

						Month						
	Aug.	*Sept.*	*Oct.*	*Nov.*	*Dec.*	*Jan.*	*Feb.*	*Mar.*	*Apr.*	*May*	*June*	*July*
Slow rent investment ($1000)	166	87	107	39.7	25.6	28.9	112	65.2	36.2	44	42	93
Number of units	12	7	8	4	3	4	6	5	5	7	6	8
Lost rents ($1000)	2.3	0.7	1.0	—	—	0.5	0.7	0.5	1.0	0.7	0.8	1.2

We get back various comments or reports. The important point is to get an *acknowledgment of the situation and a response.*

Table 9.2 is a report for one of our branches showing the number of units on slow rent each month over 12 months, the investment cost represented, and the amount of money lost because no rent was coming in.

Table 9.3 is an action report from another branch showing the present status of the items that were last reported on slow rent and what the branch is doing about slow-rent situations still outstanding.

▶ The Deadline Report: Triggers Action When Equipment Is Broken

Deadline tells us that we have broken equipment and that we may need to hire more mechanics or send out the equipment for repair.

Table 9.3. Typical branch report: Equipment not rented in 90 days (over $5,000 investment).

I.C. Number	Description	Book Value	Date Last Rented	Action Taken
444-92-9006	Air tugger	$8,954	4/92	Quoting to sell
452-20-0046	2560E Hunter	$10,758	4/92	Currently on rent to Perdue Farms RA# 509856
776-96-8005	8-Pac Welder	$1,254	4/92	Currently on rent to McIntosh Mechanical RA# 509731

"Deadline" is defined as a unit that has been down for seven days or longer, again an arbitrary figure. If the unit has been waiting for repair less than seven days, perhaps all it needs is an oil filter, but the shop is busy and hasn't had time to change it. If the situation drags on for seven days, it can be assumed that the machine needs some serious remedial work.

Deadlining is an inherent part of any service business, and each type of industry has a different name for it. In the airline industry they call deadlined airplanes "hangar queens." No matter how tightly a business is run, equipment inevitably breaks down and requires repair.

Theoretically, we could drive deadlining down to zero if we were willing to put enough resources into repair work, but from a practical standpoint, the cost would be in excess of the benefit. A realistic goal is to get the deadline down to 1.5 percent of our overall fleet.

Table 9.4 shows our progress over nearly a decade in bringing the deadline problem under control, one single at a time. The slight upcurve in 1991 reflects the pressure on our maintenance and repair facilities because of the aging of the fleet.

Our deadline reports tell us where we are having problems and help us to ask the right questions to find solutions. Each of the branches prepares a monthly deadline report. It is the same kind of report we require for slow rent, and like slow rent, it *contains an action element*. It tells us why the unit has been deadlined and gives the estimated time it is going to take for repairs. If they are having trouble getting a piece of equipment back into action we want to know why:

▶ Does the shop have the expertise to repair that piece of equipment?
▶ Is the branch overfleeted and simply not bothering to repair the broken equipment because it has functioning units to put out on rent?

Table 9.4. Deadline as a percentage of inventory, 1984–1991.

Year	Percentage
1984	4.8
1985	3.2
1986	2.6
1987	2.0
1988	1.5
1989	1.1
1990	0.9
1991	1.4

▶ Or it is a matter of getting a part? If the branch has difficulty locating it, the purchasing department may need to help by going to the manufacturer for that part.

Putting off repairs is costly because you are eating depreciation and interest every day until you get it repaired. Our rule is that if a unit has to be repaired and you don't repair it, then you have to scrap it.

▶ Monitoring Overtime: A Problem in Every Service Business

Overtime is a critical factor not only in our business but in every service business. All service businesses run overtime, and overtime is expensive because it usually involves a time-and-a-half pay rate. A service business is not like a factory, where under ordinary circumstances you can pretty much plan your scheduling and minimize overtime. In the service industry, scheduling tends to be erratic and operating on overtime is the normal condition. We build this expectation into our planning, and we staff our branches on the assumption that overtime will run at a rate of 10 percent of payroll. The basic reason for this is that customer needs arise and you have to satisfy them or make a customer unhappy and lose the business. For example:

▶ You find there is no way to avoid making a delivery of equipment after hours or in the early morning hours.

▶ Equipment breaks down on the job and your crews have to work overtime so that the equipment can "make the rent," as the saying goes.

▶ Your people have to work on weekends—don't forget that we are on 24-hour call.

Overtime fits into the category of on-again-off-again problems. Over a period of years, overtime has become a concern about a half dozen times. When it gets higher than 10 percent on a national basis, we know we have a problem and go after it on a peer basis.

There are dramatic differences in overtime from branch to branch, as shown in Table 9.5, and when the problem starts to get out of hand, managers have to be alerted by seeing where they stand along this spectrum.

Table 9.5. Hertz Equipment Rental Corp. overtime ranking, worst to best.

Branch Number	Branch Location	October 1992
9730	Sacramento, CA	34.0
9638	Carson, CA	25.8
9631	Phoenix, AZ	24.6
9720	Reno, NV	24.2
9471	Denver, CO	23.8
9725	Salt Lake City, UT	23.0
9633	N. Hollywood, CA	22.9
9641	Palm Springs, CA	22.8
⋮	⋮	⋮
9412	S. Houston, TX	10.1
9414	N. Houston, TX	10.1
9136	Allentown, PA	8.2
9723	Seattle, WA	8.0
9164	Cleveland, OH	7.8
9318	Greensboro, NC	5.4
9323	Winston-Salem, NC	1.6

A number of problems can cause excessive overtime, some understandable and others remediable:

▶ *A sudden surge in business or unusual repair requirements may have occurred*—breakage that wasn't expected. If either of these is the case, we accept the situation for what it is.

▶ *Staffing was inadequate.* The branch may not have enough drivers or mechanics to handle the normal workload, let alone a surge in activity. If we determine that the overtime is due to inadequate staffing, the regional office can authorize the branch manager to increase the size of the work force.

▶ *There is a pattern of abuse.* The fact of life is that people get used to overtime as it gets built into their standard of living. A truck driver who has been running 5 to 10 hours overtime on a regular basis won't let that go easily when you try to take it away; the driver will find ways to court that overtime.

We have a lot of younger managers because of our policy of training our own managerial cadre, and many of them find that the hardest thing they have to learn is managing overtime. They are dealing with people who are senior to them, and they are confronted with basic standard-of-living issues, often involving heavy family or similar responsibilities. We

Table 9.6. Branch preventive maintenance status report.

	7/91	8/91	9/91	10/91	11/91
				Preventive Maintenance—over	
Number of units in fleet	213	206	203	202	200
Number of units not serviced in 90 days	22	32	54	60	56
Percentage not serviced in 90 days	10	15	26	29	28

have to work with our managers constantly to manage overtime, which in any case has a natural tendency to drift upward. Periodically we have to police overtime when it moves into double digits.

▶ *Preventive Maintenance: Making Sure It Actually Takes Place*

This report flags when a piece of equipment is due to go into shop for regular maintenance. In the equipment rental business, the old saying "Pay me now or pay me later" typically means, "Do the oil change now or buy the engine later." At HERC, we believe in protecting both the customer's interest and ours by paying now for an effective system of preventive maintenance (PM).

Our rule is that each piece of equipment will receive maintenance every 250 hours of use (the usual period recommended by manufacturers), or every 90 days. It is also our goal that at any given time 80 percent of our fleet is "PM'd," that is, has been serviced within the established time frames.

Here's how we assure this actually takes place:

▶ When maintenance or repair work is performed on HERC equipment, a repair order is written up just as is done in an automobile dealership.

▶ The data from that job are fed into our rental revenue analysis system.

▶ As a fail-safe measure, we feed the dates of the preventive maintenance orders for each item into the computer to make sure that all our equipment is being maintained within the 90-day period. This way, we can tell which of our branches is adequately performing its

$5,000 Investment, by Month							
Month							Current
12/91	1/92	2/92	3/92	4/92	5/92	6/92	Month
201	201	201	194	184	190	188	201
56	65	56	25	22	28	33	30
27	32	27	12	11	14	17	14

preventive maintenance, and we flag exceptions. Table 9.6 shows a typical branch preventive maintenance status report.

▶ When exceptions show up, we look for the underlying cause in the same way we do with deadlining, and we correct the problem (by increased staffing if necessary). If the exceptions begin to drift upward throughout the company, we raise the consciousness level through peer ranking. Table 9.7 shows extracts from a regional peer measurement.

First, we define what we want to accomplish, then we make sure we do it by feeding those shop orders into revenue rent analysis. This is a sophisticated process, and we are aided by a mainframe computer. If you have a small fleet, however, you can do it manually; it is the methodology that counts.

Table 9.7. Preventive maintenance peer ranking—regional basis.

Branch	Total over $5,000 Invest.	Over 90 Adj. Due	Adj. % of Fleet	Over 120 Total Due	% of Fleet
Richmond	195	15	7	1	0
Baltimore	143	21	14	8	5
Virginia Beach	218	59	27	26	16
Allentown	154	24	15	14	19
Pittsburgh	200	24	12	13	6
Boston	185	64	34	46	24
Cleveland	122	21	17	15	12
Pennsauken	199	43	21	21	10
Newark	187	54	28	36	19
Washington	141	34	24	20	14
N.E. Region	1,744	359	20	200	11

▶ *Delivery Cost: Try Not to Give It Away*

Delivering the equipment when and where the customers want it is a challenge.
This is a major service that customers demand and the competition offers.
Despite a delivery charge, it is a major area of cost that many people don't
recognize. The three revenue components in the rental business are:

1. The rental itself.
2. Insurance (loss and damage waiver).
3. The delivery charge.

The problem is that to secure the rental, you sometimes find yourself giving delivery away, with the result that the transaction nets out at a
loss because of the capital and running expenses entailed.

Each of our locations has two to five delivery trucks. These are big
rigs that can deliver anything from monstrous hydraulic excavators down
to bulldozers and pumps. They comprise a tractor with a so-called low-
boy—a long flatbed trailer with a hydraulic liftgate to load and unload
equipment. The tractor costs $75,000, and the lowboy, $20,000; so you are
looking at $95,000 for each delivery truck. The running costs also mount
up: You have to maintain the rig to keep it on the road, and you have to
pay for fuel, tolls, permits, a license, and the driver's salary.

For years, we didn't know what kind of a loss we were sustaining because we didn't have a detailed analysis and weren't calculating all the
costs. We tried to improve performance by peer-ranking delivery as a percentage of revenue. But it was a crude measurement that showed the ranking of the result, but not the ranking according to the actual losses
sustained. Now we have a peer-ranking report listing every location in the
country based on the actual expense run up by each truck and the resulting profit or loss. And we rank that from worst to best to create an awareness of these costs.

Table 9.8 shows the enormous range in delivery expense from location to location. The worst showing for September 1992 was in Palm
Springs, California, where we were losing $275 a day; the best was in Den-
ver, Colorado, where we had a profit of $8.50 a day. Because we need a
great deal of improvement in this revenue component, we are putting a
heavy emphasis on it, and we are seeing some results. We give our managers a target: We want them to charge at least $2 a loaded mile.

Managing delivery is an art. You have to be careful how much you
pressure your branches to charge the rate because disadvantageous

Table 9.8. Delivery revenue peer ranking, ranked worst to best, September 1992.

Rank	Branch No.	Branch Location	Delivery Revenue Per Truck Per Day	Delivery Expense Per Truck Per Day	Profit (Loss) Per Truck Per Day	September Number of Trucks	Total Profit (Loss) Per Day
1	9641	Palm Springs, CA	$106.19	$381.99	($275.80)	2	($ 551.60)
2	9730	Sacramento, CA	138.41	397.76	(259.35)	3	(778.05)
3	9643	Bakersfield, CA	39.79	291.56	(251.77)	5	(1,258.85)
4	9136	Allentown, PA	65.32	309.96	(244.64)	3	(733.92)
5	9637	San Diego, CA	44.76	286.63	(241.87)	2	(483.74)
6	9729	Fremont, CA	104.05	343.78	(239.73)	4	(958.92)
7	9645	Lancaster, CA	63.93	296.25	(232.32)	2	(464.64)
8	9417	Port Arthur, TX	76.19	304.60	(228.41)	2	(456.82)
9	9639	Ventura, CA	119.52	344.89	(225.37)	2	(450.74)
10	9631	Phoenix, AZ	57.38	277.05	(219.67)	2	(439.34)
⋮	⋮	⋮	⋮	⋮	⋮	⋮	⋮
68	9416	San Antonio, TX	219.52	276.40	(56.88)	2	(113.76)
69	9530	Chicago, IL	345.36	380.42	(35.06)	2	(70.12)
70	9412	S. Houston, TX	174.44	205.40	(30.96)	3	(92.88)
71	9725	Salt Lake City, UT	234.67	260.59	(25.92)	2	(51.84)
72	9414	N. Houston, TX	192.78	210.31	(17.53)	3	(52.59)
73	9661	Las Vegas, NV	206.63	218.58	(11.95)	3	(35.85)
74	9727	Richmond, CA	252.38	263.46	(11.08)	1	(11.08)
75	9323	Winston-Salem, NC	180.19	190.81	(10.62)	2	(21.24)
76	9203	Miami, FL	290.66	297.61	(6.95)	5	(34.75)
77	9120	Virginia Beach, VA	272.86	268.59	4.27	2	8.54
78	9471	Denver, CO	232.79	228.39	4.40	2	8.80
		Division	$130.18	$263.33	($133.15)	208	($27,695.20)

tradeoffs may ensue. Say the branch is delivering a backhoe that is being rented for $1,800 a month, and we're pushing for a delivery charge of $50 or better each way. If we put on too much pressure to get that delivery charge up, maybe the delivery rate will go to $150—but the rental rate may drop to $1,500. Here we are into the arcane art of pricing, a subject treated at length in Chapter 13.

▶ Active Accounts: A Search for the Right Criteria

When active accounts are growing, your business is healthy; if they are declining, it indicates a sick business. Active accounts are therefore a key index not only for HERC but for thousands of other businesses in our industry and many other industries and trades.

Table 9.9 shows monthly net changes in active accounts for the stores in one of our regions from October 1991 to October 1992, indicating the moderate growth we were able to achieve in customer base during a recession. This index took a great deal of effort and experimentation to get right. Its history illustrates vividly my adage that the important thing in learning how to measure any activity is to start somewhere, even if you begin by measuring the wrong thing. What we started to measure was *new* accounts, and it took us several years to discover that what we ought to be measuring was *active* accounts, a subtle difference that made all the difference.

In the early 1980s, measuring new account activity became imperative because of our need to expand our customer base. The larger the base, the more insulated you are from a downturn in business or from recession. If you have a small customer base and you lose one or two significant customers, you are in trouble, which is what happened to us when the Sun Belt oil economy collapsed in the early 1980s.

Up until then, construction rental activity in the Sun Belt was booming, and nowhere more so than in Houston, which became our most successful city. We enjoyed all the fruits of success; the phone rang constantly and we had stores posting ever-greater revenues in those good times. What we didn't fully appreciate was that several large contractors were giving us all our business. So when those jobs were completed and no

Table 9.9. Active customer base preceding 13 months.

Region	Branch	Average	10/91	11/91	12/91	01/92	02/92
SE	9318	99	95	97	94	93	91
	9321	160	151	143	140	144	121
	9322	144	160	128	134	137	143
	9323	116	108	112	107	108	97
	9325	258	250	252	249	253	255
	9326	148	142	155	150	132	144
	9330	106	84	95	89	91	95
	9331	169	170	166	165	167	172
	9332	153	140	148	144	143	146
	9333	123	126	123	120	123	125
	9336	176	173	171	172	165	150
	9337	151	154	131	135	140	138
	9338	224	199	197	201	214	201
	9339	176	144	155	156	158	177
Total		2,203	2,096	2,073	2,056	2,068	2,055

other activity showed up because there wasn't any, Houston became our worst-performing city. This painful but valuable lesson forced me to look carefully at the accounts throughout our whole national network of stores, and what I saw was that we had become complacent.

Our customer list numbered many thousands, but these weren't necessarily active accounts because of our dependence on the construction industry, which has many transients that move into a city, as in the case of Houston during its boom days, and then move on. We were beginning to make a major effort to diversify our customer list into the more stable industrial field and to develop national accounts. Above all, we needed to enlarge our overall customer base of active accounts. We needed a great many of them, and we had to focus the efforts of the salespeople by creating incentives to bring in new customers.

We set a goal for each salesperson of opening up seven new accounts a month, and we began measuring the branch's new-account performance and weighting the salespeople's performance review by how many accounts they opened. We ran up charts showing the number of accounts they had opened in the preceding 12 months. The average location had three salespeople, and if one of these three-person teams opened up 30 new accounts in a month, I would personally commend the management for its good performance; I used peer ranking to stimulate the whole process. We used the new account measurement for about four years because it was the best tool I had. Table 9.10 shows a typical new-account report for a branch in the form we used at that time.

03/92	04/92	05/92	06/92	07/92	08/92	09/92	10/92
96	98	96	101	105	110	107	109
155	158	152	156	165	164	206	221
134	146	146	148	144	147	149	152
114	124	117	120	128	129	122	127
244	262	249	270	268	276	264	261
138	156	155	151	151	144	150	162
108	100	111	109	117	117	129	129
172	168	164	165	167	169	171	175
156	160	158	158	149	156	164	170
119	121	119	117	122	130	131	129
165	171	168	180	186	195	195	194
134	141	147	149	155	157	176	201
215	233	246	240	244	245	237	245
184	184	186	184	187	189	190	191
2,134	2,222	2,214	2,248	2,288	2,328	2,391	2,466

Table 9.10. Typical branch report: monthly increases in new accounts over twelve months.

	Month											
	Aug.	Sept.	Oct.	Nov.	Dec.	Jan.	Feb.	Mar.	Apr.	May	June	July
Number of new accounts	28	17	42	32	33	34	29	31	27	34	41	44
Rental dollars generated ($1,000)	21.8	8.1	20.4	23.6	18.3	17.6	20.1	22.0	19.1	21.3	21.6	20.4

After a while, however, I began to notice that locations were opening 200 to 300 new accounts a year, yet the revenue growth did not reflect that large number of new accounts. I began to suspect that perhaps these accounts never really did business with HERC—and indeed that was what was happening. The salespeople were opening new accounts simply to show them on their reports. The application processing and credit check to enroll each new customer cost us $75, and on top of that, we were rewarding the salespeople for opening accounts that in many cases never did business with HERC.

I knew then that new customers were the wrong measure and that we needed to come up with a measure of active accounts that were actually producing revenues. I also realized the following things:

▶ How we defined an active account was not the critical issue, but rather that *we used the same measurement month after month on a consistent basis.*

▶ The actual number of active accounts was not the real criterion, but instead *the direction* in which the numbers were going. What we really needed to measure was our progress (or lack of it) in building our customer base.

▶ Nor was the time span we employed to define an active customer a crucial factor. Whether we defined an active account as someone who did business with us once in the preceding month, once in the past six months, or once last year was irrelevant just so long as we found a definition that would hold and consistently provide a yardstick by which all locations could be measured.

When the search was framed this way, the answer turned out to be *our current accounts receivable run,* which in effect was the continuously updated log of current accounts. I therefore went to the receivables department and asked for a report each month of the companies on the accounts receivables run. The flaw in this was that any account that paid up promptly could disappear from our active account list, whereas a delinquent account might show up. But these aberrances would wash out with consistent measurements over a period of time.

We now had a customer base for which I could hold local management responsible. We could not hold the managers accountable if a major strip center developer was gone, but we could make them answerable for the overall number of accounts the branches were doing business with. What we looked for was a net change in active accounts 12 months later.

We were now able to define what was an acceptable number of accounts per branch and salesperson and what was not acceptable. If we had a branch with less than 100 accounts, we admittedly had a problem: We knew from experience that this is an inadequate customer base for our kind of rental business. Under normal economic conditions, we would therefore require growth on the order of 100 to 125 more accounts a year. So, finally, *we had* a measurement tool that worked: *active accounts, which measure changes in rental revenue.* New accounts were just a step to get there.

The question is how you can introduce this into a system that doesn't have an accounts receivable department. When we opened up in France, this was the case; it was like starting a new company. So we had to resort to a simple methodology. Not having the ability to define a new account the way we did here, we defined it instead as anybody we did business with in the past three months. We then peer-ranked them by the salesperson's name and the names of the accounts. Table 9.11 is the active accounts listing for our location in Collegien, outside Paris. It is a way of posting each salesperson's accounts. This is a simple procedure that anyone can utilize—you don't have to have a sophisticated system. You can just post people's names and rank them.

▶ *Safety: A Preliminary Report on Another Common Problem*

Safety is a problem that has to be flagged in all businesses. Beyond the painful human cost of any injury to our employees, additional costs are incurred to cover the following resultant expenses:

▶ Workers' compensation.

▶ Medical costs.

Table 9.11. Active accounts per salesperson, Hertz Equipement France, September 1991.

Branch	Salesperson	New Account	Name
Collegien	Aury	6	ARC Air
			C.E.M. Constructions
			C.T.M.
			Maisons Favorites
			Mayer
			S.N.V.
	LeMoigne	8	Blairon
			Curado
			Pinson
			Polygest
			Polystock
			Sodenor
			S.E.M.
			Tere
	Poulain	4	Avirons de Joinville
			C.N.I.
			M.E.Q.
			S.G.T.P.
	Laks	12	Blockleys Brick
			Cogei
			Ex Excavation
			Gabo
			Gautier
			Leadview Const.
			Lehrer Govern
			Manu Ventilation
			Novaire
			Parador
			T.I.S.
			Vonie
Total Branch 01		30	

▶ Absenteeism of trained people who are recuperating from accidents.

▶ Overtime from the resultant understaffing.

▶ Insurance premiums.

Safety became part of our performance measurement in 1992. As recounted in Chapter 6, we were having many accidents and people weren't learning from them. Our customers wanted to deal with a safe company and we wanted to create a safe environment, so we went to work on this in our typical pragmatic fashion:

▶ We had people list their accidents, the dates of the accidents, the causes of the accidents, and how many they had experienced over the years. I wanted them to acknowledge the accidents and to focus on them.

▶ In addition to having the managers send in accident reports for each accident, we then structured these reports into our semi-annual branch business review meeting. Each manager now provides a chart showing:

1. The number of accidents that have occurred in that location.

2. A description of each accident.

3. A statement about actions taken to prevent future accidents.

Tables 9.12 and 9.13, and Figure 9.1 offer examples of all three kinds of reporting from branches. Table 9.12 focuses on the branch as to the number of accidents occurring over the past five years and as to the nature of the accidents over the past year. Table 9.13 deals with a branch safety plan to prevent accidents.

Figure 9.1 describes the company accident rate on a yearly basis versus industry standard and HERC's past year's experience. We are still in the early stages of developing these into a measurement system up to our standards, and we will continue to work on it. What you see in these reports is a listing of problems and the actions taken. We go beyond that and have them present a plan to do something about it. But we will have to

Table 9.12. Typical branch report of injuries.

Safety Records Branch __9332__

	Number of Employees	OSHA 200 Recordable Accidents	Injury Rate (Percentage)
1992 (YTD)	13	1	13.4
1991	15	4	26.1
1990	15	4	24.2
1989	13	6	38.7
1988	12	0	0

Accidents—Last 12 Running Months

Date	Name	Occupation	Description	Action
08/08/91	J. Smith	Mechanic	Rt. Ing. Hernia	Surgery
10/22/91	L. Larson	Administrator	Rt. Ing. Hernia	Surgery
01/30/92	K. Jackson	Shop Foreman	Laceration Rt. Hand	Sutures

Table 9.13. Typical branch report of actions taken.

BRANCH ____9332____

This Month's
Action Toward Safety

8/20   Safety Meeting—Topics
- Safety as a Way of Thinking
- Safe Lifting Procedures
- Motor Vehicle Safety
- Safety Equipment Available

Next Month's
Action Toward Safety

9/17   Safety Meeting—Topics
- Safe Tool Operations
- Eye Protection
- Safety Awareness, Self-Evaluations

move even beyond that and integrate the reporting into a more sophisticated model. Safety will eventually go to a peer measurement system, but we don't know enough about that yet. I can tell you, though, that in 1995 we are going to have a better reporting system than we have today. Our goal is that eventually the problem will disappear because we will have fixed it.

One thing we have learned is that *you need to look at safety on a consolidated basis.* You can't look at safety in one location only; you may overreact. You need to summarize on a national scale to see if you have a problem, and you need to bring it down to the local level to correct it. *Summarize to identify it; localize to act on it.*

You try to improve in small increments. If you can do a better measurement, you put that in. You make people aware of it and possibly reward them for it. Do that, and I guarantee you will gradually see results. The trouble is that everybody wants instant measurement—and instant improvement.

WRAP-UP
Pay Heed to the Uncertainty Principle

The uncertainty principle in quantum mechanics posits that under certain circumstances the act of measuring particles will in effect alter the conditions you are trying to measure.

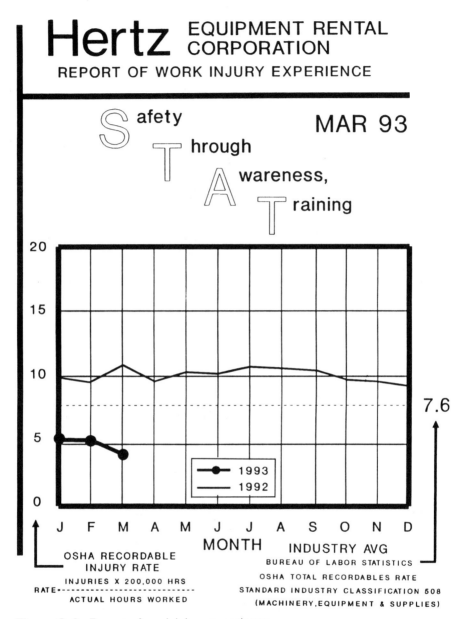

Figure 9.1. Report of work injury experience.

This contains a valid warning for anyone attempting to measure performance in the service industries. Carefully consider what you measure and how you measure it: You may end up inadvertently interfering with people's behavior in a way that defeats your own purposes.

HERC devised a way of measuring the new accounts opened by the salespeople and rewarded them on the basis of the new customers they secured. The intent was to increase revenue, but the result was actually just a long list of new customers—with no new business.

What was happening? The salespeople were simply opening new accounts for the sake of opening new accounts. HERC's solution was finally to adopt a way of measuring new accounts indirectly by using the number of active accounts as the unit of measurement.

HERC has also found that trying to control costs too zealously can have a compensatory effect that may nullify any gain you create. Two examples:

▶ Pressuring people to push customers into paying for delivery costs can led to counterbargaining by the customer to shave the rental price. Thus, what you gain by getting the delivery rate up where it belongs may result in reduced rental revenue.

▶ Much the same effect can also result when you lean too hard on your delivery people to cut back their overtime; they will find ways to court the overtime they feel is their due.

10

Keeping Track of Utilization

In this chapter we will look at our "on-yard" report, which tracks changes in utilization by showing every item in our inventory on a daily basis. This kind of information is indispensable in managing a quality service business. These are the statistics that keep us in continuous touch with the pulse of our business.

The history of the on-yard report offers a dramatic illustration of how difficult it is in any industry, especially the service industry, to obtain precise, timely, and consistent data when you attempt to put numbers on things hitherto unmeasured. In recounting the trials and errors we went through in developing this particular set of statistics, I hope to make a point that can help others up against similar challenges. The moral of this chapter: *Define tightly; hold people to it.*

▶ *Why Method 1 Failed: Unreliable Reporting*

When I first came to HERC, we developed a couple of simple methodologies to track our revenues. One of these was the monthly base described in Chapter 3, which told us something about our future revenue while the daily average was telling us about our daily business. If a branch had a $100,000 monthly base and a daily average of $2,000, we knew that over a 28-day period it was going to do $144,000 overall revenue. This gave us an understanding of the basic soundness of our business, but it still did not provide a sensitive reading of what was really going on.

We supplemented this with the current estimates of business that the field management filed every month for the next 30- and 60-day periods. In addition, at the beginning of each month they submitted their actual revenues for the month just ended. But we only obtained this information once a month; for the rest of the month we were in the dark from an analytical point of view about where the business was going and what was really happening out there. What we were looking for was some kind of continuous *check* on the utilization rate of our equipment. (Chapter 8 explores the importance of this factor.) To understand this, we had to know two things at any given time:

1. How many pieces of equipment are out on rental?
2. How many units are on-yard, *not* earning revenue?

Knowing just one of these did not add up to utilization; we had to know both. Accurate answers to these questions at any point in the cycle would provide signals enabling us to make instantaneous adjustments in policy.

We therefore made regular calls to the field managers to find out what was on their yard and to hear what they were doing in revenues. And each manager would give us an estimate, some accurate, some not accurate. We learned to discount the information when I realized that some managers were fully aware where they stood but didn't want to tell us because they were afraid we would take actions to control costs, while other managers, even some vice presidents, habitually estimated low and always did better when the figures came in. Every manager had certain idiosyncrasies when it came to measuring numbers, and I had to learn those personality factors to know whether the estimates were credible.

▶ *Method 2: Personal Site Inspection—A Sound Approach but Unworkable*

As a reality check, I did a lot of spot checking around the locations and evolved a kind of rough methodology for estimating utilization and revenue flow. I would do the following:

- ▶ Walk around the yard and count each piece and estimate its value.
- ▶ Go to the books to find the value of the equipment in inventory, say, $5 million.

▶ Subtract from that amount the $1.2 million worth of equipment I had found in the yard, which meant that the branch had $3.8 million on rent.

▶ Look at the rental agreements and then come up with some kind of utilization factor to arrive at the rental revenue.

If the pricing was worth 5 percent of the value of the equipment and there was $3.8 million worth of equipment out on rental, the branch would be doing $190,000 in revenue that month.

This methodology, though crude, yielded the information we needed to run an efficient business, but at that point there was no way to apply it to the system. All that I had was a snapshot of that one location for a single day. I could do a few locations firsthand a month, but for global figures, we had to go on relying on our informal polling of the field managers. For four years, therefore, it was a process of calling around each month and hoping that people's estimates would stick.

▶ *Reason for the Failure of Method 3: Managers Hid the Facts*

The first breakthrough came from a manager who was running one of our European operations. He had worked out an innovative listing, in broad categories, of all the equipment on the yard and on rent, coming up with a total for all the equipment. He did this on a weekly basis. He sent me the form he used, and I had it on my desk for some weeks without realizing there was a great deal of validity in his method. When I realized that he had hold of a less subjective way of doing an estimate, I sent the form to all the regional vice presidents and said we should start using it in the United States. At first everyone was doing something a little different, but we put more categories into the form and finally got everyone on a uniform reporting basis.

As soon as we began using the new system, we found that we had surprisingly high utilization rate, about 85 percent, which made us feel pretty good. We were further encouraged by the improvements we seemed to be getting in our fleet logistics. Here is the way the system worked:

▶ The regional office would collect the information by telephoning the branches every Friday and asking each manager how many backhoes were in the yard and so forth.

▶ The manager would look out the window and report the equipment visible in the lot.

▶ The regional vice president would collate the information and mail out the consolidated report to each of the branches each week, so that the local managers would at least have some fairly up-to-date information about where equipment was available.

▶ If a customer needed a backhoe and the branch didn't have one, the manager could now tell from the report where one was available rather than having to call branch after branch to locate one.

▶ If a location had an excess of backhoes, it would transfer one of them to the other location—or so we were led to believe.

But what was really happening was another story.

If the manager had only two or three backhoes in his yard, he would report during the weekly roundup that nothing was available, because backhoes are usually in pretty good demand and if he gave one up he might lose revenue. *Managers were not being truthful with each other* in order to protect their own equipment availability. This became apparent to me when I visited locations and discovered that I couldn't verify the figures. We also began to realize that the whole system was too crude—the categories, for instance, were too broad—and that it was not truly a management information system. We used it only about a year before we concluded that this informal way of doing business simply was not doing the job and that we had to find still a better way.

▶ *Success with Method 4: A Computerized System*

By then, HERC was into computerization, so we went to the computer people and told them we had to have a system that tabulates by machine what is on rent and what is not on rent. The computer people designed a system for us that seemed foolproof. When a rental agreement was printed on the computer, that sent the signal that the equipment was going out on rent. And when that piece of equipment was billed to the customer, it showed the machine coming off rent. This greatly improved the system, which at that point became known formally as the on-yard report.

And it was also at this point that a very interesting thing happened. The day we put the report on-line, our utilization dropped 10 percent across the whole system, shattering that rosy picture that we had been living with.

When that happened, I knew we had to radically revise our standards. People were always telling us that they needed more equipment, that they were so efficient they couldn't do any better with what they had. And as long as I thought we had 85 percent utilization, I believed them and worked to give them more equipment, thinking that the whole inventory was too tight. But the inventory was not so tight after all; the system of measuring had simply been inadequate.

In light of our new reporting, one of the big reasons for the inflation of the utilization figure became immediately apparent. The problem, in a word, was "commitments." By this, we mean the branch's reservations of specific pieces of equipment for customers at a specified time a few days or a week hence. The accepted way of reporting this went something like this: A branch manager had an inventory of 10 backhoes, 5 of which were out on rent and the other 5 were on yard and available for rental. The branch report therefore showed a 50 percent utilization on that category of equipment. A call came in on December 12 from a customer who ordered 3 backhoes to be delivered December 18. The branch manager now reported those "on rent" as of December 12, which raised the utilization rate from 50 percent to 80 percent, even though no new revenue from that order was coming in and wouldn't be coming in for another six days. The branch manager regarded such reporting as quite legitimate because of the commitment to produce those machines when the customer wanted them. It was contractual. They were reserved, but since there was no way to indicate that in the on-yard report, the transaction appeared as "on rent."

▶ A Firm Understanding about Making Precise Entries

The classic case was Las Vegas, where we have long had a contract to supply warehouse forklifts for the convention business. Conventions are big business in Las Vegas, and our branch keeps 75 of these forklifts in inventory to handle rushes of business. Even though the business was intermittent, the manager always showed the 75 forklifts as being utilized 100 percent of the time.

I said to him, "You are showing utilization very, very high, but you have all these machines in the yard."

He said, "We only use these for this one customer, and we have a contract, so I consider those things utilized 100 percent of the time."

I replied, "Yes, we do have a contract, but never the less, the customer is using the equipment only 50 percent of the time—and that is the way it has to be reported."

We finally got that straightened out. Now, when you look at the on-yard report, you will see maybe 41 machines—but not zero—duly reported "on yard." That tells us the system is working the way we want it to.

The rule is invariable: *Define tightly; hold people to it.* Otherwise you have no measuring system at all.

As long as the reporting is right so everyone knows exactly what is happening, there can be an allowance for contingency in any workable system. "Reservations" is one such area in our system. It presents an arena for bargaining, based on trust between peers, within the framework of the system. The on-yard report shows each manager daily just what is on yard in every location throughout the HERC network (see Figure 10.1). Nobody can hide anything; every manager sees what is available, and where, and has to take it from there.

Let's say a manager needs to fill an order for 3 backhoes and sees that the Denver branch has 10 available. He calls the manager in Denver, who explains that he has reservations for 6 of those machines and has to have a spare or two the way business is going, but he can loan out a couple. The inquirer must accept this answer, and this in fact is the way the system works. Generally, equipment is available when asked for, but in this hypothetical though typical case, the other manager then has to rustle up another machine somewhere else. Always be sure that your control system has breathing spaces of this kind built into it.

▶ A Basic Rule in Building Any System: Simplify, Simplify

Another rule I always follow in building any methodology for measurement purposes is simplify, simplify: *Build into it only what you need to accomplish the purpose you have in mind.*

For example, when we designed rental revenue analysis, we were after some complex and inclusive measurements and comparisons, so we threw into it every piece of equipment that HERC rents, from pneumatic drills to giant earthmovers. This was appropriate for what we needed to accomplish.

In contrast, when we built the on-yard report, we were seeking better daily control over the business through better utilization and estimation, and as a result we only needed to look at the big-ticket items, which in our business is where the action is. It wasn't necessary for us, and would only have been confusing, to look at every item in our inventory.

So we declared an arbitrary cutoff point of $5,000 in book value, and all the items under that we threw out of the on-yard report. That shrank the universe we were following from about 30,000 units to 15,000 units, which simplified our job and gave us more commensurable units to deal with.

If we were a small mom-and-pop rental company renting rototillers and snowblowers, $5,000 wouldn't be an appropriate cutoff, but for a rental equipment company dealing mainly in heavy equipment it makes good sense. We cast our on-yard report in units, and it works out that there is actually a close approximation between units and value.

▶ *The Mysterious Drop-off at the End of Each Month*

When we finally got the on-yard report on line in the spring of 1991, I had more computer-generated information than I ever had before. Thanks to this, I was finally able to solve the mystery of an odd revenue pattern that had been puzzling me from the time I arrived at HERC: Why did revenue track light during the early part of the month and always come in heavy at the end of the month?

This was no small matter. If we had 10,000 pieces of equipment out on rental, the number would drop to 9,500 in the 72 hours or so just before midnight on the last day of the month. Thus the figures were showing a drop of as much as 5 percent in utilization for no apparent reason. It had been this way through the two decades or more of the company's history, and nobody could ever figure it out. HERC did its accounting close at the end of the month. Were all our customers doing an accounting close at the end of every month? It hardly seemed likely that all construction sites were so budgeted that the superintendents had to turn in their rented equipment at the end of each month. Yet that is what seemed to have been

FICHE INDEX - AREA-9100 NORTHEAST

	9111 0526	9112 0527	9120 0527	9136 0527	9161 0527	9162 0527	9164 0526	9165 0527	9167 0527	9169 0527	REG ONYRD	REG ONRNT	REG DEADL	FLEET TOTAL	PRCNT ONRNT
100-160 COMPRESSOR	0	0	1	0	0	0	0	1	1	0	2	3	0	5	60%
185-190 COMPRESSOR	4	1	0	5	3	16	0	3	4	1	37	97	0	134	72%
250-450 COMPRESSOR	1	1	0	3	3	1	0	1	0	1	7	20	0	27	74%
750-825 COMPRESSOR	3	0	6	1	1	0	0	1	0	0	13	10	0	23	43%
1300-1600 COMPRESSOR	1	6	13	0	4	3	0	3	0	0	28	22	1	51	43%
PNEUMATIC ROLLER-RIDE ON	0	0	0	0	0	0	0	0	0	0	0	0	0	0	0%
WALK BEHIND ROLLER	3	2	1	2	2	1	0	1	2	3	17	5	0	22	23%
SMOOTH DRUM ROLLER-RIDE	1	0	1	1	4	2	0	2	0	0	9	10	0	19	53%
PAD FOOT ROLLER-RIDE ON	0	0	0	1	0	1	0	0	0	0	1	0	0	1	0%
DOZER	1	1	0	1	1	1	1	1	1	1	3	13	0	16	81%
CRAWLER LOADER	1	0	0	1	2	1	0	1	0	1	7	11	1	19	58%
FARM TRACTOR	0	0	0	0	0	0	0	0	0	0	0	0	0	0	0%
BACKHOE	3	2	3	7	4	7	6	5			42	157	1	200	79%
LANDSCAPE LOADER	0	0	1	0	1	0	0	1	0	0	1	4	0	5	80%
ROAD GRADER	0	0	0	1	0	0	0	0	0	0	2	1	0	3	33%
TRENCHER	2	1	1	0	2	2	0	2	0	2	7	5	0	12	42%
MINI EXCAVATOR	0	0	0	0	0	0	0	0	0	0	0	0	0	0	0%
EXCAVATOR	0	0	1	1	3	1	0	3	1	0	6	25	0	31	81%
SKIDSTEER LOADER	2	1	1	3	7	2	3	5			26	64	1	91	70%
WHEEL LOADER 2 CY & UNDE	0	2	0	0	0	0	0	0	0	0	2	3	0	5	60%
WHEEL LOADER ABOVE 2 CY	0	0	1	2	1	2	0	1	2	0	7	28	0	35	80%
CARRY DECK CRANE	1	0	0	0	2	0	0	0	0	0	3	0	0	3	0%
8-10 TON CRANE	0	0	1	1	1	1	0	1	1	1	7	9	0	16	56%
11-12 TON CRANE	2	1	1	1	0	1	0	1	0	1	7	22	1	30	73%
WAREHOUSE FORKLIFT	0	2	7	5	4	2	7	8	1	1	36	110	1	147	75%
UP TO 6K CONST F/L	4	1	1	1	0	2	1	2	1	1	11	37	0	48	77%

146

Figure 10.1. On-yard report.

	1	2	3	4	5	6	7	8	9	10					%
OVER 6K CONST F/L	0	0	0	0	0	0	0	0	0	0		0	0	0	0%
5-6K HI REACH FORKLIFT	0	1	1	1	1	1	1	0	1	0		7	51	58	88%
8-10K HI REACH FORKLIFT	0	1	2	2	2	0	1	1	1	1		6	27	33	82%
16'-25' SCISSOR LIFT	5	2	0	5	5	9	6	4	4	2		35	170	207	82%
26'-46' SCISSOR LIFT	0	0	0	1	1	4	3	1	1	0		12	11	23	48%
UP & OVER BOOM LIFT	5	1	1	1	1	0	0	2	1	1		10	37	47	79%
UNDER 41' BOOM LIFT	3	1	2	1	1	2	3	0	0	0		12	32	46	70%
42' TO 61' BOOM LIFT	4	2	4	1	1	1	1	4	4	0		19	59	82	72%
30' BOOM LIFT	1	0	1	1	2	2	1	5	5	0		5	12	17	71%
BUCKET TRUCK	0	1	1	0	0	0	0	1	1	1		6	1	7	14%
LIGHT TOWER	1	0	0	1	1	4	2	1	0	0		10	32	42	76%
10KW+ GENERATOR	1	1	1	0	0	3	4	2	2	0		11	19	30	63%
6+ INCH WATER PUMP	0	0	2	0	0	2	0	0	1	1		2	1	4	25%
FLATBED DUMP TRUCK	1	1	0	1	1	2	2	0	2	2		9	18	29	62%
BOX DUMP TRUCK	0	1	0	0	0	2	2	1	1	0		8	79	87	91%
PICKUP TRUCK/BRONCO	2	2	2	2	2	0	0	13	1	0		22	83	106	78%
12' STAKE TRUCK	0	0	2	0	0	0	0	0	0	0		0	6	6	100%
1800 GALLON WATER TRUCK	0	0	0	0	0	0	1	1	0	0		2	13	15	87%
3700-4000 GAL WATER TRUC	0	1	1	0	0	0	0	0	0	0		0	0	0	0%
HYD HAMMER/TAMPER	0	0	2	3	3	2	3	3	3	2		14	9	23	39%
ARROW HAMMER	0	0	0	0	0	0	0	0	0	0		0	0	0	0%
SWEEPER - RIDE ON	0	0	0	0	0	0	0	0	0	0		0	0	0	0%
UP TO 250 AMP WELDER	0	0	0	0	0	0	0	3	3	0		3	3	6	50%
300 AMP + WELDER	20	12	12	1	1	0	0	1	1	1		39	33	73	45%
MILLER 8 PAC	3	0	0	0	0	0	0	0	0	0		4	2	6	33%
TOTAL ON RENT	134	113	126	168	151	205	76	111	146	124		517	1354	1890	
TOTAL ON YARD	77	26	69	39	38	72	41	78	49	28			19		
FLEET TOTAL	211	140	201	207	192	277	122	190	196	154					
PERCENT ON RENT	64%	81%	63%	81%	79%	74%	62%	58%	74%	81%					
INVESTMENT UTILIZATION	69%	76%	64%	78%	79%	76%	67%	55%	74%	83%					

72% INVESTMENT UTILIZATION

147

happening every month over many years. After visiting every location 10 times, I was still getting the same answer: "Don't worry, Dan, the revenue will start tracking heavy at the end of the month."

In fine-tuning the on-yard report, we finally picked up a lag between the time that customers phoned in to take equipment off rental and the time it was actually picked up and logged in at the branch. The result was a float of 500 or so machines in a kind of limbo: neither off rental nor on yard. They just sat idly, earning nothing, at the customer's job site while simultaneously inflating our utilization figure.

The reason these units were sitting there, we discovered, was that they had been called off rent during the latter part of the month and were waiting to be picked up by our drivers. Rental business has a tendency to move upward in the latter part of any month, so our branches would get busy delivering more rentals, and they just didn't have time to pick up the returning equipment. These off-rent machines might have been sitting there since the twentieth or twenty-third of the month, but nothing much happened until the final days of the month when the branches realized their revenue estimates were short—and the only way to get the revenue was to log it into the daily report of business (DRB).

So at last they would rush their trucks out to pick up all this equipment that had come off rent earlier in the month. Even if the piece went off rent on the twentieth, the branch didn't log it in until the driver picked it up 10 days later. The branch wasn't trying to pad the figures, merely trying to get revenue the only way they could get it—by "DRBing it," as we say.

▶ The Heavy Cost of a Few Days' Lag in Reporting

Just about everything was wrong with this irregular performance that could possibly be wrong, and from just about everybody's standpoint. To leave our equipment around cluttering up the customer's site:

▶ Certainly looked slipshod on our part and undermined the image we were trying to create of quality service.

▶ Subjected our assets needlessly to theft or to damage by vandalism or other causes.

▶ Opened us to potential liability suits in the case of injury or accident.

▶ Built up overtime in drivers' pay thanks to that last-minute rush to sweep up equipment before the monthly closing.

▶ Kept several hundred pieces of equipment off the available list while branches had to scramble to fill customers' orders, making our system less efficient and responsive.

It was, in short, an excellent example of the small inadequacies that plague the whole service business—subtle, pervasive, difficult to isolate.

We went back to the computer people and said, "Look, this doesn't make sense. Isn't there a way, when the equipment is called off rent, even if not picked up, to key it in the computer so that it is off rent and hits the on-yard report?" They responded by setting up a simple keying operation; all that the branch had to do was punch in when the equipment came off rental, which would then hit the utilization report. We first installed our sophisticated computer reporting in April 1991, and in May 1992, we installed the key-in function. And just one day later, we lost another 3 percent of utilization by eliminating the lag between equipment coming off rent and being logged in.

▶ *Eliminating a Possibility of Human Failure*

The system was now tighter than ever, but there was still more work to do. Despite explicit instructions about keying in when the equipment came off rental, not everyone was doing it. I saw an on-yard report from Ventura, California, showing that the pieces of equipment on rent dropped from 150 one day to 120 the next day, so I called the manager and said, "What happened to the business?" The manager said, "Well, I had several days of pickups, and I didn't key them in." I said, "Look, this is wrong. You've got to key in." It took a while to get everybody on the same reporting basis, and eventually we had to call the regions and stores and demand that they do it.

By mid-1992, our system in my view finally became dead accurate. The few inaccuracies due to human error or failure still in the system had a negligable effect on its usefulness. These inaccuracies have now been entirely eliminated thanks to the advanced computerization we installed throughout our system.

Despite an occasional glitch or two, what we now possess is the fast reporting of daily trends that I had been hunting for from the time I came to HERC. At the close of each business day, the branches download their DRB into the Hertz computer in Oklahoma City; it is consolidated overnight; and the report is on my desk at 1:30 P.M. the next day. I am now getting detailed information only a few hours old from every store in the country showing just what is on rent and what is on yard.

In the old days, when I was trying to do estimations, I never knew where I was until the month closed and the reports came in. They told me that rentals always tracked strong at the end of the month; then the month would close and we would get in the numbers. Lo and behold, there was revenue. But until the current estimate came in during the second week of the next month, I still didn't understand what had happened the month before.

Now, instead of waiting until the second week of the following month, I know where I am at any hour of the day in any given month. I don't have to wait 40 days to know something. With our new system, the current estimate is just confirmation of what I already know. So I am ahead of the power curve instead of the power curve being ahead of me. I now control my destiny instead of it controlling me. I knew exactly what was going to happen to the monthly base in December 1992 because the on-yard report told me. I didn't have to sweat it out for 30 or 40 days, because in 30 or 40 days the world changes.

WRAP-UP
Warnings about Building an Early Warning System

A basic problem in any business is estimating your revenue in order to plan and control your business and expenses and to know what your profits are going to be. In the equipment rental business, we need at all times to know:

▶ Whether or not we are profitable.

▶ Whether the business is off, so that we can begin eliminating expenses, including the disposal of equipment.

▶ Whether the business is strong, so that we can bring in more equipment.

We badly need an early warning system to forecast our prospects so that we can make plans. The important thing to remember in setting up such a warning system is: *It will only be as accurate as the reporting that goes into it.*

Several factors can derail any system that you set up for retrieving information. The following factors can compromise the integrity of the information system you are trying to establish:

1. *People are confused about the meaning of a procedure.* This is not always easy to detect and takes patience during the formative stages of any project. But getting the wording down without ambiguities is the basic requirement for a system that works.

2. *People are too busy to file the information you need.* This is an ever-present possibility. It is difficult to create totally fail-safe systems, so this kind of neglect may take constant policing.

3. *The subjective factor may affect it.* If the information you need requires estimates, you will have to learn to discount the personal spin each person puts into his or her answers.

4. *People may not make the effort to take a truly accurate count.* HERC's managers often simply eyeballed the lot instead of going out and carefully tallying the equipment.

5. *People may protect themselves by hiding the true facts.* This is perhaps the most insidious factor of all because it goes to the trust level within an organization.

None of the preceding cautions will surprise anyone who has tried to build an information system. They are, however, a useful reminder of the practical difficulties that you will always face when you attempt this.

A final thought: There are no final answers to any of these problems, but searching for them will give you an education in organization and human nature.

Part Three

How to Price for Quality and Profit

11

The Precise
Art of Pricing

I take the empirical view that pricing is an art, not a science. It is something that you work out over time by coming at it from several different approaches, leaving yourself the flexibility to maneuver according to the inevitable pressures put on by the marketplace and the bottom line. Pricing could be best described as a precise art.

▶ Three Ways to Price

There are broadly three approaches to pricing in the service industry or in any industry, and I believe in working all three of them. None of the following stands alone; each has to be worked in tandem with the other two:

1. Pricing by what the market will bear.
2. Pricing by the cost of doing business.
3. Pricing by cash flow.

Pricing by What the Market Will Bear

First of all, you can price by asking what the market will bear. It is the oldest of all approaches—what will the traffic bear?—and is a perfectly valid place to start. The only difficulty with it is that, for most businesses,

155

it is not a very good place to wind up unless you don't mind being a pawn of fate and of the competition.

It takes sophistication to work this approach adequately, and over the years we have become more adept at employing it. We supplement our own in-company information by having analysts create a matrix of what the competitors are doing in a given market. This yields various kinds of helpful intelligence, answers to such questions as:

- What are the current prices in that market?
- At what point will the competitors start discounting?
- Do they discount for a favorite company?
- Will they discount for quantity or for periods of longer duration?
- Do they price basically by asking, "What is the market?"

All these data are vital when using the what-the-market-will-bear approach to pricing.

A lot of companies price on the what-the-market-will-bear basis, and it can work. The obvious flaw in this pricing method is that *it may or may not be profitable.* So you have to look at your cost of doing business and crank that into the equation somehow.

Pricing by the Cost of Doing Business

In the rental business, you have to figure costs for every unit in your fleet, and these are both fixed and variable costs. You must take into account such items as:

- The cost of your facility.
- Your parts expense.
- The cost of your personnel.
- The cost of your revenue-earning equipment, which triggers depreciation and interest cost.

With this information, you can start at the other end of the axis and work out accurately the price that will enable you to make a profit and flourish. The obvious flaw in this approach is that *the marketplace may not let you get the price you need.*

Pricing by Cash Flow

The last way of pricing is through cash flow because without an adequate cash flow you will soon be out of business. So cash flow has to figure somewhere in the pricing arsenal, too, and can legitimately influence short-term pricing decisions in slack seasons when demand drops off sharply. But if you price for cash flow solely and don't consider profitability, you will be out of business in the longer term—and you can cause havoc in the industry while you are doing that. That happens often in our industry.

People use unrealistic depreciation schedules and peg the life of a machine at, say, 10 years when it is actually 5 years. If you are on the 5-year schedule, then the competitor has a seemingly lower cost of doing business. In the end, however, when that competitor (1) disposes of the unit and replaces it with a new one or (2) pays off the loan on the old piece of equipment, which has a value on the balance sheet, the actual money may not be there. The seller takes a loss and may eventually go out of business—while prices in the marketplace are sliding downward.

▶ *Which Market Are You Aiming At?*

Whether we lean more heavily on one or the other of these approaches depends on the market we are aiming at, and this is where the strategy of pricing becomes complex indeed. It is a combination of knowing your costs and the marketplace and of balancing one against the other in often subtle ways.

Our pricing most nearly resembles a scientific process when we are bidding on some big account, a major chunk of new business. That's incremental business, and we want to make sure it is profitable. We therefore use fixed and variable cost analysis to set prices in a way that the textbooks on pricing would approve. We also use fixed and variable cost analysis when we buy from a supplier, because we don't want to buy a piece of equipment when the market won't support the cost of the purchase. Sometimes we will not buy an attractive piece of new equipment because we cannot get a return that will cover us.

At the other end of the spectrum is our core business, which provides our bread and butter. *Core business has to be priced to meet the market,* so we are immediately thrust into the whole intricate world of tradeoffs.

Pricing is an art filled with perennial, unsolved questions, and I can only tell you how we try to tackle these everlasting riddles.

▶ Making Sense of Pricing

We are just another company trying to maximize its returns. Like everyone else, we have some specific number in mind of the return on investment we want to achieve. Putting that figure into a formula with the costs provides us with the pricing we want to have on a given unit. Sometimes that pricing is not achievable, so we have to carry the item as a kind of loss-leader and make it up on some other piece of equipment. For example, backhoes are very competitive—everybody has backhoes—and they are a price-comparison item. Hydraulic excavators are another story: Since they cost $125,000, about three times the acquisition cost of a backhoe, not too many of our competitors carry them. Thus it may be possible to get a better return on the hydraulic excavators and make up for the low rental on the backhoe, so that the average return on investment meets our standard.

▶ Fixed Costs versus Variable Costs

Sometimes, you can cover your variable costs but not your fixed costs; if your business grows large enough, however, your fixed costs eventually come down. That's why some of the mass discounters are successful; their profit is minimal, but they have quantity. Your fixed costs remain the same whether you do any business. The question is: Did you price for the fixed costs and variable costs or just the variable costs?

Let us say you own an appliance store and you are going to sell a TV set with a variable cost of $400, the price you pay the wholesaler. Your fixed costs for your appliance store are $5,000, including rent, salaries, utilities, and so forth. If you sell 50 sets, your total cost is $500 per set, $400 variable and $100 fixed. If you sell 100 sets, the fixed costs are $50 apiece, and if you sell 1,000 sets, the fixed costs are $5. So with increased quantity, your fixed costs come down and your whole cost comes down.

In our case, if we can start putting more equipment out, that fixed cost gets amortized over a bigger base and in fact our total cost becomes less. So when you bid big jobs, you really must figure out how much fixed costs you are going to put in there. If you don't pay your fixed costs, you are going to be out of business.

▶ *The Results of Being a Price Leader*

When you price, you have to hope that your competition follows. You can't be out there all by yourself. Everybody wants price. Our problem is that we know we have the finest quality and we plan to be the price leader, with the result that everybody prices off us. Nobody prices over us, needless to say, nor do they price at us; they wait for us to price and then drop below us. They do not offer our quality of service, nor do they have the fleet we maintain. So, getting the pricing we need is often a real battle, not so much when the economy is good but markedly so when it is slack. Or to put it another way, when business is booming, any irregularities in pricing are obliterated by the flood of revenue that pours in. As we have now learned, that is a dangerous illusion. If a service business like ours is to remain truly profitable, pricing must be treated as a precise art at all times.

In the following two chapters of Part Three, we take a look at the ways in which we set pricing strategies and attempt to implement them.

WRAP-UP
The Strategy of Pricing

There are basically three ways to price; exclusive reliance on any one of them is usually unwise.

1. *Pricing by what the market will bear* is a good place to start the development of your own pricing—but, accepting the market price as your sole guide will make you a pawn of the market and your competitors.

2. *Pricing by the cost of doing business* is fine, provided the market allows you to cover your costs plus make a profit. This type of approach can lead to problems if the market will not let you get the price you need.

3. *Pricing by cash flow* is useful at slack seasons of the year, but long-term reliance on it without considering profitability can put you out of business.

If you are successful in business, it is probably because you have learned how to employ a flexible combination of all three methods, taking into account:

- ▶ Seasonal demand.
- ▶ The state of your inventories.
- ▶ Your knowledge of what your competition is charging.
- ▶ Your ability to cut expenses.
- ▶ Your relationships with key customers.
- ▶ Your natural skills as a bargainer.

Finally, to achieve success, you must not only take care of the preceding factors but also persuade your people to follow the established pricing guidelines; this is the subject of the next two chapters.

12

Why Centralized Control Is Necessary

When I came to HERC in 1982, every branch set its own prices. On my tours, I found that the rental prices for the 20 or so categories of equipment carried at one location were entirely different from the prices for the same pieces of equipment at the location I had visited just before it. In fact, the pieces of equipment offered were frequently quite different. When I asked for price lists, the manager often handed me nothing more than a piece of paper, sometimes not even typewritten. There was no consistency, no overall policy, no pretense about central pricing.

I respected the tradition of individual entrepreneurship that prevailed in the company at that time, and I was also aware that we had to pay attention to local and regional differences in competition and pricing. However, this nonsystem of pricing, though appropriate to the traditional equipment rental business, was too informal and relaxed for the era I needed to bring about at HERC. Here's why:

▶ We were moving toward industrial business and national accounts, and with such a chaotic situation, we would be unable to guarantee firm prices to our accounts from one city to another. We could not manage our pricing across the country with every location on a different basis.

▶ With such a medley of constantly changing prices, there was no way to predict how much revenue would result from any given increase or decrease in utilization. This hindered rational planning and decision making.

▸ The rapid advance in computerization was opening the possibility of vast control systems with great flexibility built into them.

This chapter describes how these and other economic and competitive forces moved us inevitably over the next decade toward an increasing centralization of the pricing function.

▸ Introducing Centralized Control

On October 1, 1983, I brought all our regional vice presidents together in one room at the Hertz headquarters in New Jersey, and we held a kind of curb exchange starting early in the morning and going on all day. We looked at every item of equipment in our inventory one by one, and I went around the room asking each manager two questions about each item:

▸ What do you charge?

▸ What can you charge?

I wanted them to agree on one price they thought they could realistically get. We spent 12 hours at this hectic business, and at the end of the day we had no less than 12 regional pricing structures covering 55 locations. But at least we had put on paper the prices for all categories of equipment on a daily, weekly, and monthly basis. Then we ran out the next morning and had a quick printer produce a price book; it couldn't have been simpler—just a set of pages stapled together. We air expressed copies to all our managers and salespeople.

That was step number one in the process, which was similar to the procedure we used in establishing our standard industrial code (SIC) descriptions. Within a day, step number two started with frantic phone calls from managers all around the country: "I can't live with this price," one manager would say; and another would insist, "I can't live with that one, I've got to charge more." We received all kinds of feedback. Within two weeks we had to print a revision, and within eight weeks we went through five revisions. As this process went on, we created special prices in, say, Raleigh, North Carolina, because what went for Greensboro didn't go for Raleigh a few miles away in the same state. Thus, we were able to become more sophisticated and adjust the pricing to different areas.

Achieving this fine tuning required a lot of effort and patience. But now we had a *basic control method* and could tell a national account what our rates were in specific areas (see Figures 12.1 and 12.2).

RENTAL RATE SCHEDULE

SOUTH TEXAS ZONE

EFFECTIVE OCTOBER 1, 1983

Austin, TX	(512) 444-8514
Beaumont, TX	(409) 722-3476
So. Houston, TX	(713) 641-2391
W. Houston, TX	(713) 578-8810
No. Houston, TX	(713) 692-5911
San Antonio, TX	(512) 661-4281

All rates F.O.B. Hertz Yards
Prices Subject to Change without Notice

Figure 12.1. Rental rate schedule.

EARTHMOVING AND EXCAVATING

	DAY	WEEK	4 WEEK
TRACTOR CRAWLER DSL, DOZER, LOADER			
450 Case (1 yd. 57 H.P.)	250	750	2200
550 Deere (1¼ yd. 72 H.P.)	300	900	2600
850 Case (1¾ yd. 83 H.P.)	300	900	2600
1150 Case (1¾ yd. 105 H.P.)	425	1275	3750
TRACTOR, LOADER, FARM, DSL, 3 PTH			
2600 - 3 PTH Diesel	85	250	750
420/445 Ford, 302A Deere (50 H.P.)	140	420	1260
TRACTOR, RT, DSL, LOADER & BACKHOE			
580 Case (14' - 1 yd.)	190	570	1710
310 J.D. (14' - ¾ yd.)	190	570	1710
410 J.D. (15' - 1 yd.)	200	600	1800
MAINTAINER - GRADER, DSL			
70 H.P. Fiat Alli 65B	300	900	2500
80 H.P. Deere 570B	335	1000	3000
TRENCHERS - RIDING			
Small 2200 - 2300 DIW,			
25 + 4, 30 + 4 Case	175	500	1500
Medium 3210 DIW, R-40 DIW	200	600	1800
Large 6510, Rock Saw	430	1290	3840
FRONT END LOADERS, 4WD, DSL			
¼ yd. 1835 Case (30 H.P.)	125	375	1125
½ yd. 1845 Case (50 H.P.)	175	500	1450
FRONT END LOADERS, 4WD, DSL, ARTICULATED			
1½ yd. W-14 Case, 444C Deere	270	800	2400
2 yd. W-20 Case, 544B Deere	325	960	2875
2½ yd. W-20 Case, 644B Deere	350	1050	3150

Figure 12.2. Price list.

This was a crude process, subjective in nature and representing only a rudimentary start in relating our rates to true costs. But at least we now had a complete set of "book" rates that we could quote to customers—if only for the purpose of immediately cutting them to meet the competition. That was a lot farther ahead than we had been before. We had a base, however fragile, on which to build a more secure pricing structure.

▶ *How to Lose Control of Your Pricing*

During the latter part of the 1980s, we worked out an accommodation with the field people that gave headquarters a loose rein on the play of prices. We established daily, weekly, and monthly rates, and we authorized our people to offer discounts according to the following schedule:

- ▶ Ten percent for coordinators and salespeople.
- ▶ Twenty percent for branch managers.
- ▶ Thirty percent for regional vice presidents.

But we did not enforce this schedule. We were making all kinds of money, and we let people violate the pricing guidelines pretty freely. Utilization was the game, and we permitted bargain discounts where needed to get the equipment out on rent. To get a job, we would sometimes discount it like a loss leader in a supermarket, and we wound up making still more money. Everything we did made money.

Those were the halcyon years for our industry: The Tax Reform Act of 1986 had just been passed, and the country was really rocking. The real estate developers were speculating with office buildings, warehouses, and housing, and we were reaping the benefits in the Sun Belt and everywhere else. Construction people needed our equipment to get their jobs done in time, and utilization continued to rise. In 1989, we had the best and most profitable year in our history.

The Deterioration of the Rates

Then the recession closed in on us. The developers went away, and the whole rate structure began deteriorating as all our competitors began fighting for business. In mid-1992, one of our most capable managers in the Northeast, whose facility is among the best managed throughout our system, described the situation to a visitor this way:

> There is a surplus of lift equipment in my market just as there is throughout the region. Market prices in that category have gone down dramatically in order for people to stay in business. We are now having to compete piece by piece with the competitors. Even with old customers, it comes down to shading the price by $100 or losing the business. I used to rent a 60-foot-man-hoist back in 1988 for $3,500 a month. Now I can't get more than $2,600. They cost the same to buy, and maintenance and other costs are the same; but there

aren't that many customers for aerial equipment. I guess companies weaker than ours are simply going out of business.

In this case, we were looking at a rate deterioration of somewhere between 15 and 25 percent, but many items in many locations experienced an even deeper pervasive erosion. Overall, the rate deterioration on individual items ranged from 20 to 40 percent. We had been the price leader and were in the habit of commanding a premium of 5 to 10 percent over our rivals during the good years. But we had a price book out there that was basically out of line; it was too high, and our people were discounting according to what they thought the market would bear. They cut prices down to the competitors' level in order to hold market share or just to get the equipment off the yards. And they were successful in keeping utilization high—a little too successful, as it turned out. We had in effect slipped over into the *cash flow model* of pricing.

A New Platform for a Return

By 1992, we had refined our utilization figures to such a degree that I could now see at all times just what was happening on every yard in the country as well as what was happening in the aggregate throughout the entire system. There was no question that time utilization was excellent; our people had indeed been successful in moving the equipment out of the yards. In fact, time utilization was at a record high, even better than it had been in that magic year of 1989. But it takes two things to make money; utilization *and price*. The result was that even with this wonderful utilization, we were making only a fraction of the profits we had made in 1989. To be sure, we were in the black, which was an achievement in itself during the recession years, when most of the rental industry was reportedly in the red. What we were getting was an education in the sensitive relationship between utilization and price, and in the futility of having one without the other.

This was reinforced by our discovery (thanks to the utilization analysis we now possessed) that if we had achieved the same level of utilization back in 1989 that we managed in 1992, we would have topped our 1989 record profits by yet another 15%. With this kind of efficiency, given the right kind of pricing, it seemed to me that we could get to the moon. Yet, we were scraping the bottom of a deep valley with no way to get out unless we somehow dug our way out by our own efforts. Certainly our competitors weren't going to do it for us. We were historically the price leaders, and it was our task to lead the way out of the valley. We could hardly look to the mom-and-pops or even to the larger regional companies, because as already noted, the competition bases their prices on ours.

I knew that price was the answer to many of our problems. Lack of revenue was damaging us in various ways:

▶ We had an aging fleet because we couldn't buy new equipment.

▶ We didn't have the capital to expand our facilities.

▶ We had reduced our training programs, kept our staffing down, confined our salary increases.

All this had happened because of lower profits.

The only alternative I could see was to risk *taking pricing actions that would lift revenue.*

▶ How to Take Back Control of Pricing

We announced to our management that it was now our policy to firm up the rates and that we wanted everyone to take a tougher line on quoting prices to the customers. But telling people to do this achieved absolutely nothing. Our 85 locations had some 200 sales coordinators and 200 salespeople setting prices, and what they wanted to do was get the equipment off the yards. With that number of people in the act, the situation was unmanageable. They simply did not do what we wanted and gave us all kinds of reasons why they couldn't: They were "just meeting the competition," a customer "negotiated me down," and so forth.

Nerving People to Try

I felt we could push the prices up if we really tried; people simply lacked the nerve. I could not prove this, however, and the weight of the available evidence on every side was against my gut reaction, which was all I had to go on.

I could not discount entirely the risk involved whenever you decide to tamper with your pricing, especially when you are in chaotic markets. That year, American Airlines had tried to rationalize and simplify its entire rate structure about the same time we were beginning our experiment with firming up prices. On the face of it, the airline's action seemed a sensible one that might have had some appeal to travelers, who were caught in a chaos of crazy pricing. But it brought down on the airline an even worse avalanche of rate cutting by the competition, forcing American Airlines to rescind its action at great cost.

One thing that gave me confidence that we could pull it off was the *quick turnaround* the daily utilization reports made possible. Thanks to these finely honed reports, we knew the utilization for every single store in the country, and for every single item in that store, down to a tenth of a percent. Furthermore, we could monitor changes in those figures daily. So if we had a problem, we would know immediately and could alter our course within 24 hours if necessary. We weren't in the position of an airline with a vast and complex pricing structure involving a maze of flights and services; to turn something of that kind around is like turning a battleship around in a bathtub.

Cautious Experimentation with Pricing

There still was some risk, however, and I knew I needed solid evidence that it would work if we were going to bring people along. To make sure of our ground, we therefore did some rather elaborate sampling, starting with two samples of 10 stores each. One group of stores was told not to discount the daily rate under any circumstance; the other was told not to discount the weekly rate. We decided to run the test for two months, during which time we would monitor it closely.

I traveled around these stores reinforcing the message we were sending out, which was, *Don't break the price.*

"If the customer comes to you and says that if you don't lower the rate you will lose the business, then lose the business," I kept telling them. "Don't give the discount; lose the business."

They came back and said, "What do you mean, we're going to lose the business?"

I said again, "Lose the business. I am telling you that we are going to take the risk to get the prices fixed. Lose the business."

As the test went along and we moved around the stores asking people what they thought, we got two strikingly different answers: The coordinators said they didn't really see any difference at all. But the managers said, "We're going to lose everything."

Our rejoinder to the managers was, "Stay with it." We told them to tabulate what their results were and come back to us if they had a problem. And what we found out was that for every 25 rental agreements closed successfully, we were losing only 2 for reasons of price. After just two weeks, we realized our gamble was paying off, but I still wanted to play it cautiously.

We now expanded the sampling from 10 to 20 locations: 20 with no discount on the daily rate, 20 with no discount on the weekly rate. When we saw that worked, we then doubled the size of the sample and went to 40-plus-40 locations, and that appeared to work, too. In all, we ran our tests for two months, and at the end of that period, we went back to the regions and told them we had a new firm pricing policy:

▶ There were to be no discounts at all on the daily rate and a maximum of 10 percent discount on the weekly rate.

▶ We also put a restraint on the monthly rate by holding discounting to 20 percent, beyond which division approval was required.

We realized that there would be hardship cases, so we asked the regions to identify what branches were so hotly competitive that they would lose market share if they had to conform. We were given a list of 20 such stores, and we exempted these from the price controls covering all the other stores in the system.

The Real Test: Price Increases

Our success with holding the price line emboldened me to take a step beyond and experiment with selective price *increases*. My feeling was that we were giving customers the best quality of service and the best new equipment, and therefore we ought to do better than merely match prices with competitors offering six-year-old equipment. I wanted to get back that premium we had when we were the industry price leader. We therefore selected certain items of equipment that were showing strong utilization and we prescribed increases on these items of at least 2 to 10 percent in the daily, weekly, and monthly rates depending on their rate of utilization. We mandated these selected increases in the book rates for the entire system, and once again it worked, giving us back a little of our edge.

Utilization was now as high as it had ever been, our new pricing was sticking, and our profits were increasing. In July 1992, the month we completed our tests, we picked up no less than a quarter of a million dollars in added revenue—where the pessimists had thought we would lose money. I never understood how people could keep saying this. There was no way we could miss getting more revenue if the pricing policy was being administered tightly and utilization was at least holding. Even if utilization had gotten a little worse, we would still have been better off. But as it turned out, utilization improved, so we had made a good start on the long road to recovering an adequate revenue that would yield a suitable return on our investment. It might take a year and a half or perhaps two years before we had pricing fixed. After all, we were confronting a serious, prolonged, industrywide erosion of rates that had occurred over several years. But at least we had made a good beginning. It was once more a case of making steady, continuous improvement by hitting 1,000 singles.

We came out of this experience with a new understanding of the relationship of price to utilization that could be stated as a ratio: *An increase of 1 percent in pricing is worth more than an increase of 1 percent in utilization.* It is a worthwhile formula to remember in shaping future pricing strategy.

▶ *Time to Take a Tough Stance*

Our success in raising the price level did not come without a tough struggle, not so much with our competitors as with a mind-set among our own employees. It was a formidable challenge to get all those two hundred people out there who were responsible for setting the rates to support the new pricing policy.

We were dealing with the general tendency among people in service businesses to cut prices in the belief that it is the right way to keep customers. Because they assume they cannot get the higher rate, they rationalize that they can support the company's interests by going for utilization at the expense of price. It is also easier to do that than to face down a customer across the counter or on the phone by sticking firmly to a quoted price. People in sales want to please others, so when they are under pressure from both sides they try to keep the customer happy by cutting the price and then mollify the boss by calling it "negotiating."

When we did our sampling, we wanted to be sure that our firm no-discount policies were being observed, so we set up auditing procedures in the branches. We soon found out that, despite all our best efforts at persuasion, there was considerable disregard of the pricing guidelines. Midway in the sampling period, I felt compelled to put out a memo saying bluntly that anyone who broke the policy intentionally would be disciplined up to termination of employment. Admittedly, it was a terse, tough, message, and it created much resentment. I received a number of phone calls from executives and managers who complained that it wouldn't work. They also told me that I had ruined employee morale.

Despite this tough stance, it was apparent that some price breaking was still going on. So as I traveled the circuit on my store visits during the summer and fall of 1992, I carried on the same kind of missionary work that I had done in the field when we introduced other innovative measures such as the national account program and the safety program. I had to convince people that the concept would work—and that we were unequivocally serious about it.

Dialogue with a Coordinator

Every branch in HERC keeps its current file of rental contracts in the "tub," a big hanging-file drawer under the coordinator's desk out in the front sales area. When I visit a branch, I make a ritual of going through the tub to check each sales contract to get a sense of what is going on in that business. Each contract contains, for example, the rates that the coordinator quoted to the customer while negotiating the deal.

I had the following dialogue with a coordinator as I was going through the tub in one of our southern branches. My mixture of mentoring, Dutch uncling, chivying, and cheerleading reads something like the earlier dialogue in this chapter. It was reenforced, however, by my additional experience and my firm conviction that this was the way to go, and the only way.

> **KAPLAN:** Tell me about this rental agreement. You held the weekly rate, you held the daily, but you cracked the monthly.
>
> **COORDINATOR:** Competition.
>
> **KAPLAN:** The region doesn't have the authority to approve this level of discount. They only have the authority to go to 25 percent. This contract is beyond that. Now tell me about this one. Here you lifted the daily, you lifted the weekly, but you lowered the monthly.
>
> **COORDINATOR:** We wouldn't be able to get $1,500.
>
> **KAPLAN:** What did you quote them, then? Looks like $1,300. Why wouldn't you try to get the $1,500?
>
> **COORDINATOR:** I didn't think they would pay that.
>
> **KAPLAN:** All they can do is say no, then you can always back off. The problem here is that if you believe that you are not going to get it, and in fact quote them a low rate, then you are never going to get it. It's that simple: If you aren't going to ask for it, you are not going to get it. If the customer's problem is $1,500, try

$1,400. But if you say that, that's what you're going to get. We've got to overcome this tendency to underquote by our co-ordinators.

What is your utilization rate in this branch on backhoes— 70 or 80 percent? So what are you losing if the customer hangs up? You can rent the same backhoe to someone else. There is always risk in trying to get a price increase, but the answer is that it is worth the risk. And we are going to lose rentals. What I want is for all of you to take the risk and maybe get it.

Here's another one. Do they have a contract?

COORDINATOR: Yes. They have a service contract.

KAPLAN: Let me tell you the problem here, because this is a real problem. You lifted the daily. You broke the weekly—you simply can't do that. And you lowered the monthly.

You cannot discount the weekly rate—I'm telling you so you don't do it again. This isn't permitted. For doing this, you could be terminated without a blink of the eye. I don't want to hurt somebody. The last thing we want in the world is to hurt our people. We don't want that.

The other problem is that lowered monthly rate. The question is, Why do that? Why not try to get it all? You just have to go after it.

The proof of the pudding is that at the end last month, thanks to the new pricing, we picked up a quarter of a million dollars in the division. That should give everyone some courage. So what I'm saying is, take the risk, try it. I'm not saying you are going to get them all. You may lose some. What I'm saying is when you have a resistance problem with a customer, try it.

A Message for Managers

Although lest it may seem that I was being unduly harsh, I wasn't singling out this coordinator; I was carrying this same message everywhere I went. The next day I was in another branch a few miles away, and I delivered the following monologue to the branch manager and the staff as a group.

KAPLAN: The problem of the branch is rate. Your utilization ranges from 76 percent up to 90 percent. You realistically can't get more utilization. You're taking the easy way out and are discounting yourself to death. You are close to your business plan, but you are losing money. I don't want to feel that I would have to take away your ability to negotiate on the monthlies.

Why do you feel you have to discount? You can take the initiative—it's summertime and our utilization is at its highest point. Remember, I'm willing to give away a point of utilization for a point of rate.

I think the coordinator here is not legitimately defending the pricing. He is the one who is making or breaking the pricing. We have to work to give him the courage to do better. He has to have the backbone to stand up to the pressure.

The only one who can dig you out is you. I know you can do it at the branch level. My whole point is: Get the rates improved. Only you can make the difference. Think how hard a guy in the shop works to save money on a drive motor. He is killing himself back there to save $25, and here you are pouring it out the front door with rates. You can see the inconsistency.

It is very easy to tell you to price, and I know it is tough actually to do it. It takes judgment—good judgment—and it takes guts. You've got to reinforce how important it is. If you willfully violate the pricing rules, we will terminate.

I was talking as much to the manager of that branch as I was to the coordinator behind the counter or the salespeople who go out into the field to negotiate face to face with the customers. I have in mind a remark made by that manager in our Northeast region whom I quoted earlier in this chapter:

> Talking up the rates depends more on me—that is where the reinforcement has to come from. You can tell the salespeople to toughen up the rates, but they are not going to be doing anything about it. They keep coming back to me, and I am the one who has to say no.

Compensation Creates Believers

Did I really hurt morale with my tough order? I felt the charge keenly and spent a good deal of effort trying to find out if this had truly happened.

Yes, morale was affected in the beginning, but within a few weeks this passed when people began to see positive results from the lifting of prices. Everybody grumbled during July about the new pricing, but when we rolled up the revenue for that month, people were surprised to see their branches were getting $15,000 and $20,000 more revenue than they thought. (I made a point of this in my dialogue with the coordinator.) They were becoming believers.

In some degree, everyone involved in improving pricing is affected by our compensation system, which is keyed to the branch's success in meeting its business plan. Under the prior relaxed pricing system, as revenue dropped during the recession, they were always complaining that they had to work harder to make a living. As they now began to experience gains in revenue, people became somewhat reconciled to the new system because they felt it in their pocketbooks.

▶ The Shift from an Entrepreneurial Model to a Systems-Driven Model

I say "somewhat" reconciled for a good reason. From the beginning, part of the resentment against the new controlled pricing stemmed from a realization that it inevitably would take pricing authority away from the branches. That was something brand new, and the managers in particular didn't like that. We were changing the methodology from an entrepreneurial operation to a systems-driven operation, because we now had an information system telling us how to do it. We were no longer letting them make those decisions.

This major transition was necessary because we were determined to run a big company and keep it viable in this era. You can't have two hundred people making pricing decisions. To maximize profit, pricing decisions have to be made in a *consistent* and *orderly* way, and the new computerized communications systems make this possible. Centralized pricing under these circumstances becomes inevitable.

A Pricing System for All Seasons

My thinking about our entrepreneurially based pricing system changed markedly over the years when our industry seesawed from a boom into a recession and then moved slowly toward recovery. I observed:

▶ Our original nonsystem in pricing worked well when customers were clamoring for our services. When things are good, an entrepreneurial mode of pricing gives managers a lot of room to move around and make deals that more or less satisfy everyone and keep the customers happy. My role in that process was a satisfactory one.

I wandered around motivating everyone in my capacity as a cheer-leader. I wanted to believe in what I was doing, and the proof that it was working seemed apparent in the profits we were rolling up.

▶ When business turned down, I saw that our nonsystem didn't work so well any more; and as our control systems became more sophisticated and sensitive, I began to see the flaws in the entrepreneurial mode. Although managerial initiative in pricing seems to work well on the *upside,* it does not work effectively on the *downside.* The managers start disbelieving all they know as the competition begins to cut prices. They start behaving like mom-and-pop entrepreneurs rather than corporate entrepreneurs and take cover by price cutting instead of looking a little farther into the future. Like our coordinators down on the firing line, they feel they are doing the right things to make the company better, but they are actually hurting the company.

An Improved Overview and Better Performance

Our managers did not like losing their pricing autonomy one little bit, and I don't blame them for that. I am sorry we had to take it away, because we lost some of the contributions that able entrepreneurs can make to the company. The other side of this is that there are not all that many highly capable managers in any enterprise. By going over to a systems-driven system, we improved the company's overall level of performance in pricing.

A computerized information system provides a far more detailed and far-reaching overview of what is happening in the marketplace and in the company than any manager can possibly have from the perspective of a single location. Nor will he or she understand the implications of a given set of pricing actions at the local level with the precision of the machine. Through it, we can grasp the effects these actions have on complicated intertwined factors such as utilization, return on investment, and fleet renewal—all those things that ultimately affect quality of service.

It is impossible for us to keep a tight control over pricing when we have large numbers of people making sensitive decisions on their own or under varying guidelines from their supervisors. They are frequently working under intense pressure, distracted by constant phone calls or other interruptions. Our coordinators, who handle this job, are our management trainees, with no more than two years of experience at the most, and often with only a few weeks or months. Delegating too much latitude in pricing to relatively inexperienced people is not in the best interests of the company. It demands too much of them. Now that we have highly sophisticated information systems, we don't need to risk that.

Also, it is easier to manage a pricing system with controls than to manage the old entrepreneurial nonsystem. This is a system I can build on; I couldn't do that with the old one. The managers find it easier to handle, too. They were always complaining that they were inundated with paperwork as a result of our efforts to track pricing. Now, with all our controls, the job is simpler for everyone. Nor are we getting the surprises and problems we used to have, and my corporate bosses are happier because they feel more secure about us.

Now that I have control over pricing, I have no intention of relinquishing it.

WRAP-UP
Entrepreneurial versus Systems-Driven Pricing

If your organization has many locations and you permit local managers a lot of latitude in setting prices, you will find that:

1. Your pricing policy works quite well when the economy is rolling and the demand for your services or goods is strong.
2. The policy does not work well on the downside of the market, when managers lose faith in what they know about pricing and take cover by following the competitors in cutting prices.

Another problem is that the setting of individual prices often tends to be in the hands of many people at lower levels in the company. You cannot control prices when several hundred people, often relatively inexperienced, are involved.

There should always be some flexibility in the pricing system to allow for local competitive conditions. But this *flexibility should be limited to a narrow band of prices and to carefully specified cases.* Authority to reduce rates must be specifically delegated and the whole system rigorously enforced.

If you have a large system, you need a mainframe computer to control pricing; controlling it manually is possible but difficult. A computerized system provides a far more detailed and far-reaching picture of the marketplace than any one manager can have. It also makes possible almost instantaneous revisions in pricing strategy in response to sudden changes in the marketplace.

13

Selling a Menu of Services

The so-called service encounter is more aptly called "dialogue" because that term is more descriptive of what really goes on during the crucial contact between a salesperson and customer. In my business, the dialogue that either makes or breaks the transaction typically occurs during a telephone conversation between the customer and one of our sales coordinators. The sales coordinator is a key actor on our customer service team; he or she is in a position either to cinch the sale or lose it. This chapter tells what we expect of our coordinators in their role as salespeople—they play several crucially important roles—and how we train them to sell our menu of services.

▶ The Service Dialogue

Every time I dine in a restaurant, I smile when the waiter or waitress comes around to my table and starts selling me the appetizers. I always look forward to this—and it always happens. After taking the beverage order, he or she tries to sell the appetizers, then moves on to the specials of the day, the soup, then the salad, finally the dessert. But always the appetizers first, and the employee's whole personality goes into the act. I often say to a person, "How would you like to come to work for the Hertz Equipment Rental Corporation? If you can sell the appetizers like this, you can be a success with us." If any of our management are with me, I always turn to them and say, "Why can't our sales coordinators sell like that?"

I am serious about that. I notice that whenever the waiter puts effort into selling me appetizers, really throws his personality into it, I am going to get good service as well. The person who truly sells the appetizers is the one who takes care of me and attends to my wants and needs—hands me a napkin, tidies up my place, sees that my water glass is full, and so on. Such solicitude confirms my view that selling and service not only are completely compatible but in fact reinforce one another. At the root of both effective selling and good service is the willingness of the salesperson to get into a dialogue with the customer, to know how to move with the situation as it unfolds, to sense what the customer wants and is willing to pay for, and to play into that with adroit suggestions about the items on the menu. No matter what goods or services you are offering, *effective selling and service start with a dialogue.*

The script and the cast are different in each service business. Sometimes the crucial dialogue is carried on by a salesclerk, sometimes by a telemarketer, sometimes by a detail person, and so forth. Sometimes the service contact person is merely an order taker, as in the fast-food business, where little dialogue is required beyond "What beverage will you have?" and "Do you want an order of french fries with that?" Just about any teenager can master that. At the other extreme is, say, the investment banking business, where MBAs and lawyers spend untold hours selling a complex financial product to a corporate client. I guess you might put HERC somewhere between those two extremes in terms of the level of the dialogue and the expertise of people we hire to do the dialoguing.

A Mixed Mode of Telephone and Personal Calls

We don't utilize national media advertising in our business. We locate our stores in high-density locations and depend mainly on direct selling by our salespeople to bring in business through visits to potential national and local customers, as described in earlier chapters of this book. We actually employ a mixed mode of direct selling, because we supplement this by direct selling over the phone. Each of our stores covers a rather large geographical territory, and since the number of personal calls even the most energetic salesperson can make is limited, telemarketing is an important adjunct for us. It opens up new prospects for our small sales staffs and extends their range. As a result, our business usually involves some combination of personal sales visits and telephone calls.

Customers also come our way by thumbing through the yellow pages or simply because they have spotted our store along the highway. But no matter how the business originates or where it comes from, it is almost invariably closed by a telephone call. That's the call that comes in to our sales coordinator when the potential customer actually has a specific job lined up next week, needs a certain piece of equipment, and has to know about rental cost, availability, delivery, and so forth.

That's when the customer sits down at the table in our restaurant, so to speak, and is ready to order. It is then up to the sales coordinator to start selling the HERC menu of services.

Why We Hire Promotable People

Selling over the phone is more difficult for many people than selling face to face. It requires people who can respond to the unseen person at the other end of the line, who can convey a sense of welcoming the call, of being interested in the person's problem or need, of being ready to help as best they can. For this task, we need people who are educated and alert, and who can learn how to hold an intelligent dialogue.

Sales coordinator is the main entry-level job at HERC for people who want to move on into sales and management positions. We don't expect or want them to be sales coordinators for very long, but while they are in that position, we want them to put their personality into telephone conversations, in the same way a waiter or waitress puts personality into selling the appetizers. *We find that promotable people do this the most effectively for us* (see Chapter 17).

▶ *Developing the Dialogue*

In other equipment rental businesses, the job performed by our sales coordinators generally represents a final career move. More often than not, it is filled by someone who started out in the shop and who is now going to answer telephone calls as a lifetime position. When the phone rings in the office of Joe's Equipment Rental Company, the ensuing dialogue typically goes something like this:

> "Joe's Rental."
> "Do you have a backhoe?"
> "Yes, we do."
> "What's the weekly rent?"
> "Fifteen hundred."
> "OK, I'll call you back."

And that's the end of that.

First, Get the Facts

When a phone call comes in to one of our stores, we want the dialogue to begin like this:

> "Hello. This is Hertz Equipment Rental. My name is Sally. How can I help you?"
> "Do you have a backhoe?"
> "Yes, sir, we do. May I ask your name and what company you are with?"

The coordinator follows this up with a series of questions to elicit:

▶ The caller's phone number.

▶ What kind of job the equipment is needed for.

▶ When it is needed.

▶ Where it is needed.

▶ For how long.

Assume that the caller is asking for a piece of equipment we have in the yard, or that we can obtain from another HERC location, or that will shortly come off rental and be available in time. Answers to the coordinator's questions provide the information needed to determine exactly what the requirements of the job are and precisely what size of equipment and what model is appropriate. When all this has been agreed on, and not until then, do we want the coordinator to discuss price—but not quite yet.

Learn to Parry Questions about Price

When someone calls up and starts off with, "I want to rent a backhoe for four days, what's the rate?" the coordinator fends this off by interposing questions as smoothly as possible until he or she knows more. There is a tendency on the part of nearly everyone, sellers and buyers alike, to rush into discussing price. I wonder why there is this great anxiety to get this matter of price settled as soon as possible. Like good rug merchants in an Eastern bazaar, we at HERC want to stave off that issue until the person on our end of the line has a chance to engage the person on the other end of the line in a conversational give and take. We want to know something about our callers, *who they are, and what they need and want*.

Perhaps the equipment is only going to have TV cameras sitting on it all day at a football game, or stand idle holding up a platform for days at a golf tournament. On the other hand, it could be intended for demolition work. By obtaining such information, the coordinator can get some idea of the risk of abuse and possible damage, which can then be taken into consideration when discussing price.

Focus on Quality and Service

Before getting to price, our coordinators focus first on quality, service, and the other features that differentiate us from our competitors. Here is a possible gambit: "Did you know that we have a new John Deere 310 backhoe? And that the price is such and such?"

It is not that we charge any more for a brand-new piece of factory-fresh equipment; our rates are identical for a new unit and for one that is maybe two years old. The coordinator is simply trying to anticipate the customer's next remark, which may go something like this: "Well, Joe's Rental will rent me a machine for two hundred under your price."

"I believe you, sir," our coordinator replies. "But did they mention the age or condition of the machine they're renting you?"

The point is not lost on the person at the other end of the line, who knows as well as we do that our competitors typically carry six- or eight-year-old equipment. This gambit gives us an edge in the negotiation over rates that may follow, especially if we are talking monthly rates. Drawing attention to our quality equipment and service *helps justify* our holding on to that higher book rate we have worked so hard to establish.

How to Raise a Delicate Point

The coordinator's trials are not yet over; the delivery charge must still be negotiated, and the average customer doesn't want to hear about that. What he or she *wants* to hear is that the delivery cost is going to be included in the rental price. Or, to borrow my restaurant analogy, the customer wants to order the prix fixe dinner—and we are firmly promoting the à la carte menu and the appetizers. The caller is bound to be disappointed and may say so in no uncertain terms. So the coordinator, to keep the dialogue going, says something like this: "I don't know whether you realize it, sir, but your job site is 30 miles away from our store. And we have to maintain a $95,000 truck to deliver these heavy pieces to our customers, not to mention pay the driver's salary. It's costing us a lot of money to get this backhoe to you."

Comes this response from the other end of the line: "OK, champ, that's your problem. Joe's Rental won't charge me anything for delivery."

Try to Get *Something*

The coordinator is now in a sticky position. Trying to hang in there with our standard mileage rate for delivery may mean losing the customer and nixing the sale for good. Or in an effort to get the top rate, the coordinator may simply inspire the customer to renegotiate the rental price down as compensation, and we don't want either. As mentioned in an earlier chapter, we found that when we leaned on people too hard to get the full delivery price, what we gained there was simply lost in a tradeoff for a lower rental. So our standing order to our coordinators goes like this:

> Whenever there is a standoff on delivery price, at least try to get something. If need be, charge only $5. Once you establish $5, you can go back another time and get $10, then maybe $15, and so on. In other words, if you can't sell the $10 appetizer, try the $3 salad—*try to get something*. Why let the competition call the tune?

And Keep on Trying

When I go into a branch and ask why the delivery revenue is so low, and people tell me they can't get orders because the competition gives equipment away, I tell them they are defeated before they start: "You are never going to get customers with a negative attitude—never. Start dialoguing," I urge them. "Let the customer know what is involved in delivery. If you get into a full and reasonable dialogue and still the customer doesn't buy, well, I'll accept that. But nothing short of that, because I know what can happen when people try."

I have seen places that were doing a horrendously bad job of selling delivery turn around and do a great job, and I have seen the reverse happen. How can that be? The answer lies in *how well motivated* the sales coordinator is to get the business. During my branch visits, I listen carefully to the coordinators' phone conversations with customers, and I can always tell when they are handling them properly. When a coordinator says to me, "We're trying," I know we are going to come out all right.

▶ *What a Coordinator Does*

We expect a lot of the sales coordinator, who literally is in the middle of things. The coordinator sits right behind the desk just inside the door, surrounded by phones, a computer terminal, manuals, and logbooks. He or she is our customers' first HERC contact when they call us on the phone or walk through our front door.

Every business has some one person who holds this key position as the *chief contact* with the customer. Typically, however, the information and responsibilities that are needed to carry out the function properly are dispersed too widely among superiors or fellow workers. We have made a point not only of putting the coordinator in the nerve center, but also of providing the needed tools to work with, as well as full access to information and channels of communication. With all these threads in hand, the coordinator can deal with customers intelligently and knowledgeably.

Life at the Nerve Center

It is hardly the kind of job in which a person can deal quietly with one customer or task at a time before moving on the next. While the coordinator is handling a walk-in customer, a second customer is calling to complain about a service problem. Still another customer rings up on another phone to say, "I'll take that rental." Then, while the coordinator is notifying the back shop about the service problem, a delivery driver phones in to ask, "I'm over at Elmcrest and Pine, how do I find Joe Smith's place from here?" And while all this is going on, the coordinator is trying to write up the service contracts and log in the rentals on the computer, feeding in the data that go into the daily report of business and the utilization reports.

Meanwhile, coordinators also are expected to fulfill other tasks:

▶ *Enter all the phone inquiries in a telephone log as the conversation proceeds.* This is an absolute must. If for some reason we lose the prospect at the other end of the line, we can turn the information over to the outside salespeople as a potential sales lead.

▶ *Keep a running report of what we call "lost rents."* This shows us the revenue we lose because we do not stock some piece of equipment the caller needs. We review this information continuously to decide whether we should add the wanted item into our inventory. It could be something we do not ordinarily stock, such as wood chippers, but if we get enough calls for that item, we may want to put it in. This is an important way of keeping abreast of changing market demand.

▶ *Act as the connecting link between the other people in the local branch, as well as between that branch and other branches.* They are exactly that: coordinators. They let the salespeople know about potential customers; they schedule deliveries and pickups. In short, they handle just about everything that comes along in the course of the day's business, from routine actions to sudden emergencies.

The Menu of Services

The coordinator's sales job by itself is a demanding one. Besides selling the basic rental, our people have to sell the full menu of the things we are providing. We want to sell not only a delivery charge, but also a fueling charge and an insurance charge. In addition, there is the sale of used equipment, which is crucial to our overall operations. Through our quarterly publication *The Source,* we have an international market in used construction equipment, but the action takes place locally. These resale units are sold out of the yards at each of the branches, and it is up to the coordinator on location to describe this equipment to prospective buyers and to negotiate delivery (if the buyer requests it), as well as other details.

And There Is also Telemarketing

Among the routine chores we expect the coordinator to handle is telemarketing, which entails making targeted phone calls to prospects in our customer base to find out if they can use our service.

Admittedly, this is a hard thing to do. I know few people who are really comfortable with making *cold calls.* People don't like asking others to give them their business, especially over the phone with all its impersonality. Telemarketing is also tedious and discouraging because you have to make a lot of calls to achieve what we call our "hit ratio."

Let's say you make a hundred phone calls and find only 15 people interested, and then it turns out that only 2 or 3 of those 15 are really going to rent. From the company's standpoint, getting two or three pieces of equipment out on rent is worth a hundred phone calls, especially when business is slow and we have excess equipment in the yard. It may take two days to rent a backhoe, but a backhoe rents for $1,500 a month and the person on the phone is earning around $2,000 a month, so the effort is certainly worthwhile. But it can be difficult to get people to see that.

We try to encourage the branch managers to hold meetings with the coordinators and sales staffs to trade information, ideas, and contacts. They can talk over the new equipment they are getting in, like that John Deere 310 backhoe. The coordinator now has a pretext for making those phone calls; the backhoe is something to talk about—a way to get into the dialogue. But people still balk at telemarketing because we are asking them to spend their idle time making those hundred calls. Frankly, they hate it, and a lot of times they make phone calls that are pointless but easier to handle than the targeted calls. Some of our branch managers do not fully recognize our dedication to telemarketing and therefore do not infuse others with a sense of how vital it is to keep at this task.

▶ Teaching Basic Telephone Skills

The courteous and effective use of the phone is a basic skill that all our coordinators must master. We employ a full-time sales trainer, and we send our trainees to class basically to learn how to answer the phone. Other businesses don't seem to regard this as important, but we do. The voice at our end of the line may be the first contact the caller has ever had with our company, and we want that first impression to be a favorable one. But there is more to it than that.

Getting People to Come to the Point

Besides extending courtesy and respect in any phone conversation, our coordinators must also observe a kind of phone discipline. There is an art to handling a dialogue over the phone and steering it toward a productive conclusion. Curiously enough, the problem for most salespeople isn't curtness or rudeness, but rather the opposite. When it comes to the selling part of the dialogue, salespeople need to learn *how to come to the point and ask for the business.*

Salespeople who answer the telephone like to make people happy. If the rack rate on some unit is $100, they don't want to ask for $100, they want to give it to the caller for $95 or $90. They always want to discount, which reduces me to that frustration I have talked about in other chapters. I always ask, "Why on earth do you want to do that?" Even when people don't ask for it, the coordinators still want to lower the price. They hunt for the lowest rate and work to come up with the best deal they can maneuver. We try to make them aware that we are providing quality and need to be paid for all that. This means that we have to teach our coordinators, who are also our future managers, the *basic economics* of our business. It is essential that they understand what goes into revenue and how the rental prices maintain revenue.

Because of the complexity and diversity of our equipment, many people assume our sales personnel should come out of the shop and have a thorough technical grounding. Although that background has been more or less a tradition in our industry, we see no need for that level of expertise. We have found we can readily teach our sales recruits what they need to know about the technical side of the business with a short training course. We give them some on-the-job training in the back shop, where they check out the equipment and drive it around the yard. We also teach them how to find their way around in a specifications catalog, so they can quickly look up what they need to know when they are talking with customers. They learn enough about the equipment to handle intelligently the technical aspects of the job they will be doing for HERC, first as coordinators and then as salespeople in the field.

Selling a Set of Values

Our objective is not to make our salespeople into technicians, but to train them to *serve the customer's needs and sell quality of service.* What they are ultimately selling, whether they are taking a phone call or talking in a customer's office, is something both tangible (a rental product) and intangible (a set of values). Quality of service translates not only into newer and better equipment than anyone else in our business offers, but also into a whole array of services, from availability of the equipment the customer needs to radio-equipped service vehicles if anything goes wrong. Those intangibles *are* the quality.

HERC is not the same as Joe's Rental. We are not the low-cost producer, we are the high-cost producer with the premium product; and we don't give the product away for the lowest price. If you are serious about offering quality of service, as we are, you will eventually have to tackle the price issue head-on in some way. You will have to demonstrate how other vitally important services must be weighed against sheer price, and to make this convincing requires skill. Our way is to train able people to hold intelligent conversations, help them to function as a team, and then hope that everything we have taught about product, service, and company comes together by the end of the sales conversation. That about defines the art of selling quality service: *Bring all the ingredients of the meal together—and sell the appetizers.*

WRAP-UP

The Importance of Basic Telephone Skills

In many service industries, the sales dialogue that makes or breaks the transaction has the following characteristics:

▶ Wherever the business originates, it is most often closed over the phone.

▶ It is handled by a sales clerk or by some lower-level person within the organization. In the case of our rental business, the person on the spot is the sales coordinator, an entry-level position.

▶ It involves not only the sale of the main item but a menu of auxiliary services, which affect the total profitability of the transaction. In the rental business, that includes delivery of the equipment to the customer, insurance on the equipment, and fueling.

Selling over the phone is a difficult art. Effective coordinators can do the following:

▶ Enter into a dialogue with the customer.

▶ Put personality into the call.

▶ Ascertain the customer's identity and needs.

▶ Draw attention to quality before discussing price.

▶ Establish a price for the basic service.

▶ Sell the other items on the menu.

To handle these responsibilities successfully, the coordinator needs to:

▶ Have training in the basic telephone skills.

▶ Participate in meetings with the branch managers and salespeople to trade information and ideas.

Ultimately, the coordinator's purpose is to serve the customers' needs and sell quality of service. Experience shows that the candidates who are most likely to do this effectively are people who are promotable, who are on the success path into the cadre of managers and salespeople.

Part Four

Expanding into
International Markets

14

Thirteen Rules for
Companies Going Abroad

merican firms that go abroad tend to be a little too complacent about their own success and overconfident about their ability to take on any competition. My advice to firms considering a move abroad: Think carefully about what you are doing and why. Think about it again. Then think about it still one more time.

HERC was doing so well in business at home in the late 1980s that we were totally confident we could go to Europe and show the equipment rental industry there a level of sophistication never seen before. When we looked at what is called the "plant-hire" industry in Europe, it seemed to be a backward business. It was a big industry still competing in the way it was done 30 years ago. That opened up a wonderful opportunity for us, or so we thought. We had the systems, we had the technology, we had the image, and we had the Hertz name, which was outstanding in Europe. We also had the funding, and we were going to take Europe by storm.

Seven years later, we are still in Europe and are operating in two countries, Spain and France. We plan to stay in both and to expand to other countries as opportunities open up. While the many cautionary lessons we learned along the way have not brought our plans to a halt, they have greatly altered both the timing of our moves and the way in which we will go about making them. We have been tempered by our many sobering experiences. In this chapter, I have explained the lessons we learned and summarized them as 13 rules. They should be helpful to other companies that contemplate becoming international operations.

My very first piece of advice is contained in Rule 1: *Don't be misled by instant success.* When we first went to Europe, we were very successful, and I am here to tell you that just about the worst thing that can happen to you when you go abroad is too much success too fast.

▶ *Early Success in Britain Despite Resistance*

We decided to make our first move into Europe by buying an established company in the United Kingdom. We hired a company to represent us, and they found 10 prospects for us to look over in the plant-hire industry. I went there in 1986 and selected for purchase a small, entrepreneurially driven company, which was making a lot of money relative to its size, despite what we considered to be poor facilities. Their problem was that they did not have resources, and they spent more time trying to buy equipment and finance their business than expanding it. We started putting money into the business, and our investment increased annually from $5 million to $14 million to $26 million. We gave them new equipment and still more new equipment, and we gave them bigger and better facilities, and profits rose.

Things went so well that when equipment would come in from the manufacturer, we would have the trucking firm go right to the customer and drop it off. The managing directors who ran the company would keep asking me how much equipment I wanted to put into some depot and how large we should grow the fleet.

They would call me on the phone and say, "Dan, I'm looking out over the yard, and it's empty."

I would reply, "We'll buy more equipment until you can see it in the yard."

I told them that we had the resources to keep expanding the company, and they loved it. They were seeing a capitalized company for the first time; we were seeing a company with miserable facilities and with people working under almost hardship conditions, but still making all kinds of money. They were saying all the right kinds of things, and I respected them as people and for their expertise. I had come over to put the HERC system in, but they were doing better than we were at that time, so I let them have their head.

The Greater the Success, the Greater the Resistance

The British managers had been in business for a long time and had a lot of experience in the plant-hire industry, which actually was older historically than its counterpart in the United States. They were knowledgeable to the point of being arrogant. They thought they were smarter and worked harder than anyone else in the world, including the Americans. They were indeed knowledgeable, and they did work hard; I found no fault with this. The problem was to persuade them to accept U.S. systems. Being senior and strong-willed, they intimidated the young managers we sent over to run the company. They resisted virtually every change our people tried to make, although they were actually very loose in their operations. It was even a struggle to get them to file expense accounts; they didn't know much about such things and they resented them. Our British managers also insisted on having percs like those big automobiles that are so important to European executives.

We wanted the future; they wanted the past, and we gave it to them. In retrospect, I should have changed the *key management* instead of leaving the original team in place; we should have put *our imprint* firmly on the company from the beginning. We should also have changed the whole mix of business early on. In the end, we did replace the British top team with our own local people and impose our own policies, but this was well along in the game.

This episode points directly to one of the problems you are apt to have if, instead of starting a new operation, you buy an established European company. For anything you propose, you will find resistance that is proportional to the firm's success. This paradox is stated by Rule 2: *The more successful a European company is, and therefore the more attractive it is to purchase, the less likely it is that you will make a go of it.*

▶ Importing Ideas from Home: Which Ones Work, Which Don't

During our British tenure, we experimented with some American concepts of doing business, with what I am forced to admit was a mixed showing of success. These are worth looking at for insights into what general kinds of imported ideas will work in Europe and what kinds probably won't.

A Nuts-and-Bolts Policy That Succeeded

An idea that worked had to do with a nuts-and-bolts issue involving rental policy. European plant-hire companies generally offer two kinds of rentals:

▶ "Operated," which means that the supplier rents a major piece of equipment like a backhoe with an operator.

▶ "Nonoperated," which means renting it bare, as we customarily do in this country.

We came over to Britain thoroughly imbued with the American concept of renting equipment bare; we were sure that it was a better way to do business, and we decided to push it. We convinced a major manufacturer that it presented an opportunity for them to sell their equipment to a larger customer base, and they gave us incentives to put in their equipment on a nonoperated basis. The idea took hold and the plant-hire industry followed our lead in a flash. We were looked on as a pioneer, and this quick success gave me perhaps rather exalted ideas of what we could do.

An Ambitious Project That Did Not Work

A much more ambitious idea that did not work called for the construction of a prototype facility like the ones we were then building in the United States (see Chapter 5), only this one was to be even bigger and grander. We were frankly interested in building our image, so we decided to locate in the Docklands area of London. The Docklands (better known in the United States as Canary Wharf) was a hot development and its name conveyed a sense of excitement and movement to the business world that seemed to suit our purposes admirably. Actually, while image building was the magnet that pulled the whole rather grandiose project together, we had several motives in putting up such a building and locating it there:

1. It would upgrade the British perception of the plant-hire industry so that we could attract highly qualified, promotable people. In the United States, we were hiring almost no one without a college degree at that time, whereas in England not more than 5 percent of our entire staff had the equivalent of a college education. No one with a university degree would go into plant-hire. It was stigmatized in class terms as a "trade," and no one with any social pretensions wanted anything to do with it. We found it virtually impossible to hire college-level people and to build the quality we wanted into our English operations. The search for some way to make our company attractive to such people was the genesis of our prototype project.

2. The facility would greatly improve the working conditions of our shop employees, which candidly I thought were deplorable. On my first visit to the United Kingdom, I saw people working under what to me were intolerable conditions in dark, messy shops. They complained very little and did not seem really unhappy. My value system said to me, "What remarkable people. How can they work under such incredible conditions?" It seemed to me the epitome of dedication, and I valued that and their standard of work.

3. It was to be the first of three similar stores with which we hoped to blanket the London market. Our underlying concept was to serve the London market along the lines of our American logistical model, which calls for the spacing of stores about 50 miles apart. By contrast, the typical plant-hire depot in the United Kingdom is no bigger than the backyard of somebody's house, and the tendency is to locate them every few miles. This follows the general pattern of retailing in Europe. In London, a competitor might have 15 depots, whereas we wanted to run with three superstores. In addition, the Docklands site would put our operations right in the center of the construction going on there, as well as closer than any of competitors to the activity generally taking place in the heart of London.

European Indifference to Image-Building

Our glittering, state-of-the-art facility was to cost $1 million, and the costs mounted because of piling work that was necessary for any construction in the Docklands area. When that depot was completed, it covered an acre and a half, and was in startling contrast to the cramped, grimy, nondescript depots of our competitors. Because no one in the entire plant-hire business in Europe had ever seen anything like it before, the depot attracted a lot of publicity, which we took as a signal to build the second million-dollar store in London. But that was about all we got out of it: publicity.

Public acclaim notwithstanding, the project did nothing for us. Nobody we intended to reach really cared; it was as though the event hadn't happened at all for all that it did to accomplish our various objectives. From all of this, I derived Rule 3: *Image building in Europe doesn't pay the same dividends that it does in the United States.* Facilities built by companies in this country tend to be major corporate statements; they are meant to present an image and tend to be accepted as such. No so in Europe; our idea of image leaves the Europeans unimpressed. It certainly did little or nothing to attract those educated people we wanted. I also had to draw some rueful conclusions about two other premises:

1. In the United States, we operate on a grand scale. We gravitate toward the supermarket, the warehouse store, the large rental facility. We feel our way is more efficient, whereas the Europeans feel their way—small places with small overheads—is more efficient. I am now willing to concede that, for their conditions, their approach is better.

2. In looking at working conditions with American eyes, I was misled by our U.S. standard of living, which is still somewhat superior to the way people live in most other countries. I felt nothing but sympathy for these people who were working under such conditions and working so hard. My feeling now is to let that go when you move abroad. To our British mechanics (fitters) these were simply normal working conditions.

This leads me to Rule 4: *Upgrading the working environment beyond local expectations is apt to do little more than increase your costs.*

▶ Don't Lose Confidence in Your Own Expertise

Avoidable Errors

Because Britain was our first experience abroad, such errors as building superstores could be attributed mainly to our lack of understanding about local preferences and social conditions. This, however, was not true of errors that we permitted in the logistics of fleet management, an area in which we had accumulated a considerable body of expertise (see Chapter 6). It was this kind of oversight that caused me to formulate Rule 5: *Don't become so distracted that you lose confidence in the soundness of the basic methodologies that have worked successfully for you at home.* Following are three instances in which we backed off from this rule:

1. *We failed to balance the fleet in time.* The company had a lot of the small earthmovers the Europeans favor: miniexcavators, which are small backhoes on tracks; and so-called dumpers, small vehicles that substitute for a dump truck and can be maneuvered around a tight construction site. They already had quite a few of these, and somehow we let them put in even more, neglecting another of our sacred precepts: *Balance the fleet mix.* We eventually did diversify into light towers, generators, and pumps, but too late.

2. *We failed to diversify our customer base.* We didn't do the kind of SIC coding we had done in the United States; we stayed instead with the customer base they had. Because London is an old city and there are not

many empty spaces, demolition is a driver of the plant-hire business. Demolition companies and railroads made up our customer base; about four
customers accounted for 25 percent of our revenue. This, again, was a violation of all that we had learned from the moment I arrived at HERC.

3. *We concentrated our stores in the London area.* London was such a
strong market that we let ourselves be talked into building our distribution network there rather than dispersing it regionally, thus defying all
we had learned about logistics in the United States. We eventually did go
into Birmingham and Southampton with stores, but this was a timorous
move, once again made too late.

Taking Our Losses and Moving On

During the good years, none of these latent flaws surfaced. We began 1989
with what looked like another good year, so we tripled our investment
from 1987, and still our revenues rose along with our profits. That lulled
us into thinking that we must be doing some things right. As it happened,
we were making some progress in training people on our systems. At the
same time we were making money in the United States, and I felt there
was nothing to prevent me from going to the moon.

The European economies are more volatile than the U.S. economy; the
Europeans themselves refer to them as "stop or go." In 1989, the British
economy went abruptly from "go" to "stop"—and caught us with our woe-
fully lopsided customer base, our partially diversified fleet, and our heavy
dependence on London, which took the first hit as the economy went down.
All our successes started reversing on us, and as an added blow some of our
key people went into business against us. Just about everything went wrong,
and when 1990 turned out to be worse than 1989, we decided to close, and
did so in 1991.

We are used to dominating the market in this country. When we
closed in England, we were an insignificant factor in the market. There is
probably more equipment rental per gross domestic product in England
than in any other country in the world, and HERC was ranked somewhere
between 50 and 75 among these companies. Far from controlling the industry, we were forced to meet it. Hertz companies are market leaders and
work best when they are establishing the pricing and operating in their
own way.

The recession was deep, and the economic data I was getting said that
the next couple of years were going to be worse. Rental rates in England at
that time were running between 2 and 3 percent a month of the first cost of

the equipment. If an item cost $10,000, it was bringing in $200 to $300 a month in rent, not enough to pay for depreciation and interest and variable costs, let alone fixed costs. Somehow we had managed to maneuver ourselves into the position of a mom-and-pop rental business, which is not where a Hertz company likes to come from. The only people who were going to survive were the ones with deep investment and who had no chance to get out.

Fortunately for us, we were in a position to take our losses and move on. In fact, while things were still looking good in Britain, we had already begun to expand our European foothold into Spain and France, so that by the time we closed down the British operations, we were well into these ventures.

▶ *A Fast Start in Spain with Our Own Operation*

Several powerful economic magnets drew us to Spain:

- ▶ The road system was in horrible condition and would take 15 or 20 years to rebuild.

- ▶ The electrical power system was inadequate and there was a big need for electrical generators, much more so than in the United States.

- ▶ The telephone system was wretched, and it took up to six months to get a phone line installed.

For an equipment rental company, Spain was thus a land of opportunity; the entire infrastructure needed development. This was confirmed by data showing that manufacturers' equipment sales were increasing. These hopeful signs were corroborated by the growth of Spain's gross national product, which from year to year was climbing more rapidly than any other economy in Europe. The projections of future growth were highly optimistic.

In addition to these long-term prospects, there were two impending short-term projects of great magnitude: Expo '92 in Seville and the Olympics in Barcelona. These were two of the world's three major construction projects at that time, the third being Euro-Disney in France. This time, with so much activity going on, we decided to go into a country completely on our own and not get caught up in all the old baggage that an acquired company can bring with it. The Spanish government was doing everything it could to promote Spain and the major cities, and from the moment we opened up in Madrid in September 1989, we began experiencing wonderful revenues. Driving on the fast track, we were in Barcelona and Seville the following year, and in 1991 we were in Valencia. Since Spain had no national equipment rental company, overnight we became the largest equipment rental company in the country.

What We Did Right in Spain

Our early experience in Spain was refreshingly different from that in Britain. From the beginning we had

▶ A diversified fleet.

▶ A diversified customer base.

▶ A proficient country manager who did not resist U.S. systems, but respected them.

We were in a totally explosive situation, and we took off. In Madrid, we were operating out of trailers hooked together on unimproved land with gravel. In Seville, we were doing hundreds of thousands of dollars a month, and we couldn't even get a line telephone; we operated with one cellular phone. Thanks to the high rental rates typical of a boom market, we were extremely profitable. We were growing and growing, and every time I visited Spain they called for more equipment. We poured equipment into the hot spots, but as it turned out, the pace was too fast for our inadequate systems, especially our accounting controls. We simply outgrew our systems, and it was in our receivables controls where trouble first showed up.

Build Your Accounting System First

I had not paid sufficient heed to the warning I had been given that Spanish firms are slow payers. Whereas payment terms in this country are net 10 to net 30 days, in Spain they are commonly net 90 or even 120 days. (In 1993, they were net 150 and sometimes even 180 in Spain.) They had a bad reputation for delinquency, but I figured that if the receivables were aged, this would be offset by the high rental rates we were getting; in other words, the customers would be paying for it and we could therefore tolerate the slow pay. But the load got too heavy for us to handle, and the invoices were going out two weeks late in the billing cycle. All the signals were there that we weren't collecting the money. Somehow, our able country manager ignored the signals and went on renting to everybody without making thorough credit checks. So a lot of the business we wrote subsequently went bad, and we had to write it off the books.

Things got so badly out of hand in our receivables department that we did not even know from what account money had been received. We eventually had to rebuild a whole receivables collection group and go back and reconstruct a year and half of invoices. It took hours and hours to trace all those invoices back to the customers.

It was from this experience that I derived Rule 6: *Put in an accounting and receivables system first and don't operate that system until your controls are in place and your crew is thoroughly trained.* In fact, even before you do that, hire a good controller to develop the procedures and systems. Above all, get your systems in first, then thoroughly train your new staff to use these systems before opening your shop for business. Based on what we learned in Spain, the preparatory phase should last six months at a minimum, during which time you can be setting up your first facility, a staff, and doing all those other things you have to do to start an enterprise.

You are betting your systems, and you had better get them right before you take in a franc, a pound, a mark, or a peseta.

All this is costly, but remember that you are building for tomorrow. Be willing to lose some money rather than losing more money later. To recall that saying in our business: *Pay me now, or pay me later.*

▶ *The Effects of Recession: A Costly, Difficult Closing*

Our accounting mess was worsened by the turndown in the Spanish economy in the early 1990s. For us, it began with the opening of Expo '92, when the construction work stopped in Seville; this was repeated in Barcelona when the Olympics opened. The Olympics did provide some continuing business because they needed generators, forklifts, and other equipment during the games. The construction that had been stimulated by those events had been enormous: hotels, roads, sewer plants, stores, you name it. But the anticipated work on the decrepit Spanish infrastructure that had brought us to Spain never materialized.

The government had used Expo '92 and the Olympics to showcase the country as a beautiful land of opportunity, and it had poured money into preparing for these events, which superheated the economy. It was counting on this stimulus to attract foreign capital, which was to flow into all kinds of private development. But the whole promotional scheme toppled when the government ran out of money and was unable to pay its debts, let alone finance more infrastructure. Thereupon the Spanish economy, which is essentially driven by public works, came to a sudden stop and went into a steep recession.

The Agony of Shutting Down a Branch

When we finally decided that we had to reduce the fleet, cut back expenses, and lay people off, no one could accept this. At this point, we realized that one of the things you must expect abroad is that you have *less mobility* in your movements than you have at home. In the United States, when an automobile plant does a turnaround for two weeks, people are laid off for two weeks. This kind of thing simply is not a part of the mentality in Spain and some other European countries; they do not close plants or trim the work force. The attitude we encountered was, "What do you mean you are going to lay people off?" I was trying to send an extremely urgent message that we had to cut costs. But our people never seemed to get it, and they stonewalled.

Many employees in Spain have work agreements, so if you are going to lay someone off in January and the agreement ends in June, you still have that person on the payroll until June. The worker is even more protected in Spain than in other European countries. If you want to sever anyone, you owe 45 days of severance pay for each year of service, and you must go to the courts for permission. If you have senior employees, it can become extremely expensive. A major corporation that wants to shut down must accept these heavy social responsibilities. Employment is viewed as a right, not something you can back away from. It is a rare company that shuts down.

Closing out the Seville operation was very costly in terms of the severance and penalties we had to pay; the amount was staggering. It also cost us a lot of ill will from our former employees, the unions, and customers. I was told point-blank by a left-wing union official, "You betrayed us. You came in here and told us that you were here to stay; and now you are backing out. You pay up or we'll make it tough for you." From the standpoint of the American way of doing business, we had no choice except to close down Seville because of the losses and the bleakness of the picture. The decision was painful for us, but in the end, it may be the action that will save our Spanish operations from having to close down entirely as happened in Britain. When we talked about austerity measures, we sent up a strong signal that we had better be taken seriously.

▶ Getting in Position to Remain in Spain

We now have a sophisticated receivables system in Spain, and we know better how to operate our business there: how to staff it, diversify it, and build the customer base more intelligently. What we cannot do is fix that stop-and-go, public-works-driven economy, and as of mid-1993, the economy was still stalled. We believe it will reverse itself at some point; although we don't know when that will happen, we are nevertheless planning to stay in Spain.

As of 1993, Spain was still absorbing a good deal of my travel time. I felt relatively comfortable with the direction the Madrid operation was taking, but I was still seriously concerned with what was going on in Barcelona. To save the operation there, we issued the country manager a firm order to take the following steps to protect the business plan or risk shutting down Barcelona during the next quarter of the year:

- ▶ Use the sales coordinators in a telemarketing effort to revive dormant accounts, stimulate active accounts, and target customers through lists and directories.
- ▶ Set a timetable for reducing all aged receivables, with no write-offs after a certain date.
- ▶ Eliminate 10 jobs throughout the system that I listed by title.
- ▶ Provide a list of proposed fleet reductions, and close the Barcelona substation immediately.

"You are the country manager," I wrote. "You must be positive with your staff and take action to minimize the losses in Spain. You should not wait for me to direct you. You must manage!"

▶ A Fast-Track Start in France with a Deceptive Beginning

We looked at a couple of French companies and negotiated with them, but they had a lot of problems, so we decided once again to start afresh. In 1988, we bought land near the Euro-Disney site, we hired a French national who had worked for a U.S. company and was fluent in English. We brought him to the United States for training, and he was articulate. We had already done a whole study on HERC entering France, and we built a basic strategic plan, incorporating some of the lessons we were learning in the United Kingdom. Our first year was not a good one, but we were successful the second year—deceptively so, as it turned out once again.

We went into France the same way we went into Spain. In each case, the economy was hot, and we moved in quickly. A fast-track, bare-bones entry into a market works fine in the United States, where you have an established logistical network and plenty of backup if you get into trouble. But it is not advisable to do that in Europe, with its stop-and-go economies. One minute your fragile system may be swamped by a surge in the economy, and the next minute the tide may be out, leaving you with insufficient revenue to cover even your fixed costs. This leads to Rule 7: *Be wary of the fast track; go into Europe with your eyes fixed on the long, steady haul.*

Adding to the Overhead Burden

Our first site was in Collègien, near Euro-Disney, which was one of the magnets that had brought us to France in the first place. We bought a piece of property, fenced it in, threw down some gravel, and worked out of a trailer to get the operation going as quickly as possible. We followed this up with a million-dollar-plus HERC prototype building; it is so elaborate that today Collègien is the largest HERC facility either here or abroad. After that, we opened up branches at Coignières and Gennevillières in Paris and another branch in Lyons, all of them premier facilities. The trouble was that we had not learned our British lesson about the folly of building beyond the expectations of people.

Our image building had the unfortunate effect of loading a high overhead onto the French operation. Here we were breaking the rule we follow in the United States of starting modestly with facilities that are in scale with the market. If the market grows, we can turn that facility into a substation for a new larger facility nearby. The rule of thumb in our industry is to spend no more than 5 percent of revenue on one facility, and we are spending more than that in France. We are what you might call facility-poor in France.

This has compounded the inevitable problem associated with starting up an operation in a new country, namely, your *excessive overhead* until you can spread it over a wider base of operations.

The Inherently Higher Costs Abroad

When you launch an operation abroad, it is incorporated as its own company, which means it has to have its own balance sheet, income statement, policies, and procedures. You are small and at first cannot afford all the managerial and supervising functions you have in the headquarters at home. The general manager of the country performs many of these tasks at the outset. He has to have considerable assistance from the home office in such areas as marketing literature (in translation), the development of personnel policies and procedures, and all the rest.

Obviously, there is no need for a full headquarters staff to be in place on day one, but you do have to have more than just a one- or two-person office, and that becomes costly. You need good accounting controls, as we learned in Spain, and you need a general management system. You need people who are bilingual and have breadth of experience, and such people have to be well compensated. This is recognized by Rule 8: *Your fixed headquarters costs abroad will always be inherently higher than they are in your U.S. headquarters.* That puts pressure on to dilute the costs as rapidly as possible; if operating results are poor and expansion is delayed, you have a problem.

The kind of thing you can do in this country—start up a new operation and be in the black the first year—is highly unlikely to happen abroad. Even in this country, such a feat is difficult; to bring it off you need the network of logistical and sales support described in earlier chapters of this book. *It can take years for a company to grow large enough to absorb the high headquarters cost you encounter in the beginning.* In the United States, each regional staff supervises 12 to 15 stores, and we currently have 85 stores nationally. We gain tremendous efficiency through size. In both France and Spain, we have about 10 headquarters people supervising five or so stores apiece. Thus, we still have top-heavy staffs that are too expensive for small operations.

These factors make realistic planning an imperative in going abroad. Not only must you defray the costs of top-heavy staffs but you must also crank in the start-up costs caused by the long training and preparation exemplified in our Spanish experience. This is covered by Rule 9: *Adopt a realistic plan and stay with it.* This will give you a buffer against the vagaries of these stop-or-go economies, and if indeed you do need to postpone the venture or fold it, you will not suffer insupportable financial losses. (What you define as "insupportable" depends on the realism of your contingency planning.)

▶ *The Importance of Knowing When to Bear Down*

As was true in England, we have had great difficulty in France hiring promotable people. For the most part, our French sales coordinators are pleasant people with nice voices who would make fine receptionists and fit in nicely in other service businesses that are less demanding than ours. On the whole, they simply are not the people who can fuel the expansion of our branches. Once again, we fell into the mores of the country and did not follow our own sound judgment based on our wealth of experience at home.

This failing is reflected in Rule 10: *When hiring people abroad, do not be deflected by the local job stereotyping.* Hire the people you need to run the business according to *your* style—and be willing to pay the price to get them. Even overpay them if necessary, because they are your future management if you are serious about staying in that country.

We have another problem in France that also cuts across our American experience. Whereas in the United States, our core business is monthly business, our stores in France do primarily a daily business. The French construction industry likes to take equipment out on a very short-term basis, preferably a day at a time. As we saw in Chapter 3, daily business is a more expensive business to handle, requiring more trucking, more washing, more phone calls, more invoicing. While Euro-Disney was driving our business, we didn't seem to have a problem; the overheated market also overheated the daily rates. But I knew that eventually Euro-Disney would cool down, and I kept urging our country manager to switch over to monthly rates. He was convinced, however, that this was the wrong policy, and he was so knowledgeable and knew the terrain so thoroughly, that I was afraid to risk it and backed off. In the end, when our pricing eroded disastrously, we had to tackle the daily–monthly rate issue anyway.

Rule 11: *If you know you are right from your own experience, listen patiently to the evidence on the other side, then go ahead with your plan.* Make it happen. This is what we should have done in England and France.

▶ *The Dangers in Relying on Superevents*

In 1992, the ceiling fell on us. Euro-Disney opened in the second quarter of 1992, and the next phase of construction was to commence in the third quarter. Disney opened the gates to the public, and as anticipated, our equipment came back while we awaited phase two. But the tourists didn't flock to Disney, the expansion was postponed, and we found ourselves overfleeted.

Rule 12: *Do not, unless you want to live like a gypsy, depend on superevents.* Don't build for a carnival; build for every day. If windfalls occur, enjoy them, but don't depend on them for your livelihood. And don't be seduced by grandiose commitments made by corporations and governments; they can easily disappear when things go sour, as with our operation in Spain. The irony here is that we violated our own basic rule about centering our attention on the core business and treating everything else as incremental.

As we entered our fifth year in France, we were still not enjoying sustained profitability, and we decided that a change in strategic direction was imperative. I therefore sent the country manager a firm memo about hiring and pricing policies.

> ▸ I told him, first of all, to hire only college-educated people into sales and management jobs and to start replacing every coordinator with a college-trained person.

> ▸ Next, I said, "Our pricing strategy is cumbersome, and is one of the prime causes of lower-than-anticipated revenue." I told him to go over to a simplified schedule of rates similar to our U.S. pricing system. And I prescribed the same cold-turkey cure we had taken in the United States during 1992: a drastic limitation on price discounting (see Chapter 12).

Following my premise that the art of taking systems abroad is knowing when to bear down, when to compromise, and when to back off, this was a case where it was essential to bear down. We fought through the battle of the discounted rates on our own turf and know a good deal about the dynamics at work in this situation. I may be proved wrong, but I think we are going to be able to innovate successfully by bringing American practices into this situation, just as we succeeded in gaining acceptance of "nonoperated" rentals in England.

▸ Our Prudent New Policy for Europe: Switch to the Local Track

We are planning to expand in Europe by cashing in on all the experience we gained from our British, French, and Spanish ventures. Just where we intend to expand is proprietary information, but we have had a skeleton staff in training for some months. We have learned from our hard-earned experience:

> ▸ We made sure that at least a month of their training was devoted just to receivables.

▶ We had a controller on board from the beginning, a top-flight person with solid corporate experience in Europe.

▶ We were computerized from the beginning.

These preparations cost us hundreds of thousands of dollars without a dollar dropping into the till; nor do we expect for this to happen soon. We have given up the idea of a fast takeoff in order to guarantee long-term stability.

When we originally went into Europe, we had an overall strategic plan for growth, but it did not take realistic account of the financial consequences. We had a plan based on success, and we were not prepared for anything else. We had no contingency plans, so we couldn't handle surprises—and surprises were what we got from about day two on. We feel that we have now brought our sights down to a realistic level. We're willing to go slower so that we can avoid surprises. We are far behind where we intended to be according to our European timetable, but we are more comfortable on the local track.

Here is some other cautionary wisdom that we learned in Europe and would like to share with others: Beware of "the great American tourist,"— that executive you send over to assist your European operation.

Europe is filled with great restaurants, antiquities, museums, concert halls, markets, castles, battlegrounds, and all imaginable kinds of cultural, historic, and scenic attractions. And every European subsidiary is filled with cordial people who are eager to show you the sights. Europeans are naturally hospitable and social people; they love dining, wining, and entertaining guests. They will spend all the time you want showing you around. My impression is that they are masters at distracting you with the glories of Europe, which helps keep you off their backs and sends you back home happy—and not too much wiser about the branch. You can send good operating managers over there who get so caught up with experiencing Europe that they are not operating managers any more. The same applies to the accounting and operations people you send over for short assignments. They can all become the great American tourist.

That can create a relationship that weakens the respect your European management might have for the home office. Your local managers will get the wrong signal; that you are not serious and not interested in your business. It is even more important to be firm about the corporate culture you want in Europe than at home, because you are a foreign company and everything you do is exaggerated. So the conduct of your people, wherever they go or whatever they do in the presence of their European colleagues, will be noted and have its effect.

My final piece of advice is stated in Rule 13: *Expect to spend a lot of your time with your branches abroad, especially in the beginning—particularly if you are a hands-on manager.*

WRAP-UP
Can You Keep the American Edge Abroad?

A recent McKinsey & Company study indicates that the United States has a 15 to 25 percent lead over other advanced industrial countries in *service* productivity.[1] This edge undoubtedly reflects not only the scale of our market and of our service industries but also the ingenuity we have put into designing efficient systems.

When a service company goes abroad, the question is, Can it effectively translate its systems into an alien environment and have them still yield much the same efficiencies they achieve at home?

The answer is, Yes, if you play from strength and avoid wasting your time, energy, and resources trying to alter conditions that you can't change. The point is to concentrate on the ones that you can do something about.

1. *Be aware of the statutory restrictions that will inevitably limit your actions.* These apply across the board to other industries, too. As an example, the people who work for you will be nationals, and there are protective laws in most countries that prevent sudden actions on people. Laying off people or closing an operation is hard to do in Europe, with the result that you have less mobility in moving around your resources.

2. *Don't invest in programs to change cultural and social attitudes that affect your business.* People in Britain, for instance, look on the "plant-hire" (equipment rental) business as only a cut above sanitation work. Expensive public relations programs are unlikely to change such perceptions. Europeans are indifferent to American image building.

3. *You will have to work around differences in scale and dissimilarities in trade practices.* In this country, we build the logistics of equipment rental around superstores 45 miles apart. The cramped European pattern is to locate small facilities only a few miles apart. Their rental period tends to be shorter; the customers abuse the equipment more; fleet mix tends to be different; they run smaller equipment, again, because of space constrictions.

---

[1] Thomas A. Stewart, U.S. Productivity: "First But Fading," *Fortune*, Oct. 19, 1992, p. 54.

Differences of scale are mostly created by the geography, but some trade practices probably can be modified. The length of the rental period, for instance, is partly a function of the rate, which allows for some experimentation with valid American expertise in fine tuning. As a result of all these differences, your European cost structure will be inherently higher than it is at home.

4. *The real possibilities lie in applying the statistics-based control systems that underlie American efficiency.* This is working from strength. A particularly apt illustration is the elaborate control system that HERC has worked out for fleet renewal, which is balanced against return on investment.

No system runs itself. Your success will rest primarily on:

▶ The *ability* of the people you hire, and their willingness to cope with an alien system and adapt it to the work,
▶ The *tenacity* with which you supervise the operation directly and keep people up to standards that you know from experience are necessary for excellence.

So in the end, it is *people* on whom you have to concentrate.

Part Five

Creating a New
Corporate Environment

15

The First Turnaround Task: Reassuring People

Rebuilding the management team at HERC began on my first day with the company and has occupied me ever since. Doing it the way I did it, by patching and fixing, is much more difficult than coming in and making a clean sweep as so many corporate turnaround leaders do.

I do not believe in those clean sweeps. Sure, they make it easier for the person taking over, who can get rid of any latent dissidents and surrounds him- or herself with people who are beholden to that new leader. The stockholders and financial analysts applaud this kind of dramatic gesture as a welcome sign of vigorous and decisive action. But it doesn't play well with me; I know firsthand what damage it can cause. It fails to utilize valuable human resources and experience available within the company, while eroding the base on which a healthy corporate culture must be built.

▶ The Kata Tataki Problem: A Spreading Anxiety

Likewise, this kind of wholesale action causes an excessive amount of human pain. *Any severings or displacements cause pain,* and no true leader can ever duck this issue or should ever try to. Even the amount of displacement and reorganization that I had to effect can and did cause a good deal of pain in many people—hardly comfortable knowledge to live with if you are the one doing it. The person in command must shoulder and carry this

213

weight to be a true leader. Accepting the responsibility to guard the
health and well-being of the whole enterprise requires taking individual
actions that are often painful, and all you can do is to ameliorate this as
best you can.

In any company, news of separations or the shifting around of people
and jobs travels rapidly through the grapevine. Even Japanese firms have
become aware of this today as they restructure their operations to meet
the ever-toughening conditions that international competition is impos-
ing on all industries. For decades, Japanese companies have been bastions
of internal stability, offering cradle-to-grave security for employees. Now,
however, they are shifting and closing operations, downgrading people
into inferior jobs, laying workers off, and even severing managers and executives from the payroll, actions all formerly unheard of. The Japanese
have begun talking fearfully of *kata tataki,* meaning a tap on the shoulder.

I am witness to the speed with which news of *kata tataki* spreads
around a company, of the devastating effect this can have on morale, and
also of the great difficulty of countering this effectively.

My problem back then was to do what I could to assure people that
we were not contemplating widespread dismissals and demotions and
that people who were performing their work adequately were not in dan-
ger of losing their jobs or being transferred. But that in itself is a rather
threatening message. It is like saying to people that Big Brother is watching them and they had better measure up or else. How do you handle such
a delicate and sensitive situation? I frankly admit I have no grand answer
to this problem, which seems to have global implications in our era, affecting industries much the same way whether they are in the East, the
West, the Third World, or wherever. There aren't any simplistic solutions
for such crises, because each situation is unique to that particular company, in that particular national and corporate culture, and at that particular moment.

In responding to our own situation, I had nothing more to go on
than my intuition, having never faced that kind of problem before. My approach was straightforward and honest:

▶ I talked publicly to our people in broad terms about the changes
   we were having to make to bring HERC up to speed as a company.
▶ I followed this up as best I could on a selective basis by reassuring
   various groups of people privately about their own jobs.

Older managers were particularly subject to *kata tataki* insecurity
during our difficult transition period as they saw younger people being

hired and promoted. There was no doubt that we were becoming, by design and intent, a younger company. This naturally had to create anxiety in our older people in senior positions. As a result, we might have begun losing some of our most valuable players at a moment when we could ill afford to lose them. So I did what I could in my travels to reassure this group of highly vulnerable people whose talents and experience we so badly needed.

▶ *Making Use of the Grapevine to Send Signals*

Not long ago, I was having dinner with a veteran manager, who is still with the company and today runs one of our most successful branches in the South. We had a guest dining with us that evening, and the branch manager took the occasion to express his continuing gratitude to me for having given that reassurance to him and other senior colleagues back in those days of upheaval and transition. I told him how much I valued that. Later, the guest expressed curiosity about the meaning of this conversation, and I explained that it was more than merely an exchange of pleasantries. I had recognized at the time his feelings about the trend toward youth in the company. It had been important for me to take the time to tell him that this actually increased his value as a highly competent senior manager in acting as a role model for his younger peers. I had wanted that man to know how much he was giving the company besides just pretax profits. He had a particular talent for developing management and people that was equal to, or greater in value than the profits from his branch.

I was doing more than reassuring just this one highly valued person: I was also giving a signal that I knew would be passed around selectively and picked up by others who needed to hear it. Chapter 18 discusses the important role that giving signals plays in my approach to building a corporate culture; here I was employing it to boost morale and reassure people wherever I legitimately and plausibly could.

In doing my rounds to touch the iron, I made a special point of encouraging the competent and hardworking people I encountered, letting them know how much the company valued them. This kind of feedback gets around and tells people the kind of standards and work ethics you expect. While it is equally important to let people know directly when their performance isn't up to scratch, I much prefer to play the cheerleader than the taskmaster. Actually, both roles have a place in a repertoire of signals.

WRAP-UP

Every Transition Causes Pain

When you have to take drastic measures in a turnaround situation, it will inevitably hurt those who are severed or displaced and create fear in those around them.

There is no painless way to handle such a transition, but these brief guidelines to overall policy may be helpful:

▶ Be open, honest, and direct.

▶ Talk publicly in broad terms about the changes that must be made in the company.

▶ Follow this up selectively with reassurance to individuals about the security of their jobs.

▶ Let people know why they are valued. This will get around the company and give people signals about the kind of work ethic you expect in the company's new era.

16

Restructuring Management Jobs

From the beginning, I realized that I would have to make many changes in the staffing of the company. It took me just a little longer to realize that this would involve a great deal more than just shifting people around and perhaps bringing in a few new people here and there to fill certain jobs. Management at the headquarters and regional levels as then constituted was not functioning efficiently in serving the needs either of the field organization or the customers. In my view, management serves the people who serve the customers; this is the key to success in the service industry. The rule is: *Keep your management structure lean and keep its attention focused sharply on the needs of the customer and the field staff that directly serves the customer.* This chapter describes how I went about implementing this precept.

▶ *The Barriers to Promoting from Within*

My original intent was to bring new people into key positions by promoting from within. I believed then, and I believe even more firmly now, that this is the best personnel policy. *Wherever possible, promote from within.* Go outside your company to fill a position only when the needed skills simply are not available within the organization.

My premise is that you are better off dealing with a known quantity than with an unknown one. The inside candidate for a job may give you some cause for hesitation, but you still know a great deal more about that person than you do about someone from the outside. Even if the odds on the inside candidate succeeding in the job are only 50/50, you are still better off promoting from within. You simply do not know what is going to happen to the outsider in this new situation.

Promoting from within also gives strong signals about the kind of corporate culture you want to build. It shows that you greatly value your people and respect their personal hopes and aspirations. It also helps to build a work ethic into the corporate environment by demonstrating that effort and hard work will be repaid by promotion to more responsible positions in the company. This kind of environment also makes your company more attractive to the kind of recruits you want to draw to your company in building a management cadre for the future. People will feel that they can make a satisfying career in your company and find reward for their effort and diligence.

For these reasons, I would have much preferred from the beginning to locate within the company the talent and experience needed to shore up management. But I immediately ran into two difficulties that made me realize how much work we had to do before we could make this policy work:

1. The company lacked any organized management development system at that time, which meant there was no pool of trained managerial talent on which to draw. The whole idea of using the sales coordinators as the basis for management training was still in the future. We had to create a training program as we went along, a process that is described in Chapter 17.

2. We needed to develop job descriptions for the functions the new people would be expected to fulfill. This was at the root of the managerial inadequacy throughout the company. HERC did not need to (1) overhaul its management structures, (2) eliminate levels of management, or (3) create new jobs. What we needed were job descriptions to define the functions required of managers in an efficiently run service business. This is the task that I describe in this chapter.

In addition to all this, poor morale afflicted the organization from bottom to top. The continual losses, failed promises, mismanagement, and lack of purpose and direction affected, in one way or another, the performance of everyone in the company. I was faced with having to revitalize the corporate culture so that a new team could function and flourish.

▸ *Step 1: Improving the Headquarters Staff*

As an enterprise, we were a loser, and we had to do some serious soul searching in that situation. I saw that I would have to make major personnel changes in the headquarters staff. I knew I had to have people around me who could provide sound advice and expertise as we went about the enormous task of shaking up a whole enterprise. Getting the headquarters staff fixed and in place was therefore my top personnel priority, and I set about attending to this in the first weeks after my arrival.

At that point in our history, HERC still suffered from problems inherent in the parochial character of the equipment rental industry. We lacked the depth and sophistication of expertise to build the kind of company I had in mind. I needed true experts, people of caliber who were leaders in their respective fields. I therefore had to resort to a mixed mode of staffing, drawing on inside talent where that was possible and also going outside when that had to be.

The head of sales and the head of operations had to come from within because we needed people who were intimate with our own ways of selling and operating. Fortunately, a former head of operations, who had left the company before 1982 because of dissatisfaction with the company management, let us know that he wanted to come back under the new regime, and we snapped him up. We were equally fortunate in having a functioning sales department, with good people in operating locations to draw on.

When we came to some of the other areas, the story was different. We just did not have a real marketing organization—no depth to it—and we had to go outside. I wanted a person who was experienced in direct mail marketing, and HERC had no one like that. Nor was there any use trying to recruit such an expert anywhere else in the equipment rental industry; direct mail had never been used as a sales tool in our industry. So I hunted around for industries with marketing people whose experience in direct mail could be applied to the rental industry.

I sometimes had to try out two or even three people in a position before I found the right person. I kept at this until we had new department heads in the following areas:

▸ Finance.

▸ Personnel.

▸ Operations.

▶ Sales.

▶ Marketing.

Meanwhile, we were also *redefining these positions,* establishing new criteria for them and new goals and objectives for their departments. The reorientation of the marketing function toward direct mail was an example of this. At the end of two months, we had a new top team with redefined responsibilities, and we were now ready to tackle the other management problems down the line.

▶ Do the Regional Offices Perform a Valid Function?

Feeling confident that I had people around me who knew what they were doing and could be trusted, my next step was to put some of them on a plane with me and start moving in on the field organization. That was when we were doing those horrendous 100-hour weeks described in the early chapters of this book. We had to get out there and find out what was going on, and for two years we were out on the road. The vice president of operations, the heads of personnel and sales, and many others traveled with me around the country, meeting people down the line and trying to measure the quality of the management. Sometimes we did 20 cities a week.

As we made these moves, we became increasingly aware that the regional offices were not functioning well; all managerial functions were breaking down and the entire regional management team had to be strengthened. There was even a time during my early tenure when I questioned whether we should have regional staffs at all, whether we could simply eliminate them and thereby save money with no loss of control or efficiency. Further evaluation showed that the regional staffs could serve a valid operational function and make a genuine contribution—if their problems could be resolved.

The prescribed officer cadre for each region comprised the following:

1. Vice president.
2. Manager.
3. Sales director.
4. Controller.

We looked hard at this structure and concluded that it was necessary and costs justified if the people performed the functions we envisaged. But what we also began to see was that it wouldn't be enough just to say that the regional vice president is not functioning, so we will replace that person and fix the problem. This brought us finally to the key question: Exactly what are the appropriate functions of these top jobs? We needed to develop a carefully thought-out, step-by-step approach that might even have to stretch out over a year, since it would involve not only building a new team in each case but redefining functions as we went.

▶ *The Regional Vice Presidents: A Search for Activists*

We tackled the regional vice presidents first, determined either to bring all of them up to speed or to replace them if that didn't work. We hoped, one by one, to put highly capable and dependable persons in place and then use their skills to work out the functions of their staffs, thus involving them in the development of their own teams. It didn't turn out as neatly as that, and there were some weak spots before we found the right combination in each case.

It was difficult getting across to some of the regional vice presidents the new activist mode of managing that we expected of them. In the southern region, some of the branches were never visited; one branch manager told me that he hadn't seen the regional vice president in three or four years and that he had never seen the president of the company. He emphasized the importance of these visits to his people—how it propped up their morale to know that people at the top cared about them enough to pay a visit. This reinforced for me the wisdom of our new hit-the-road policy.

I recall driving with one of our regional vice presidents on an interstate highway in the South trying to convince him that we were serious about our vice presidents visiting branches to touch the iron and get to know the people. He told me that he was an inspirational leader and that he could motivate people from where he sat in his regional office. That made me angry. Here I was spending my life on the road—at that very moment indeed, I was driving him around his own territory—and here he was sitting in my car and telling me that his inspirational style made it unnecessary for him to do what I was doing. I ripped that wheel over and came to a screeching halt, and I said, "If you're not going to be a traveling vice president and go to the branches, you can get out of the car now. You're through with this company."

I don't like making a display of my temper, but sometimes it is the only way to get something important across. I knew that if I did not respond firmly to that provocation there wouldn't be too much chance that the new policy would ever get off the ground. This was not unlike the forceful action I took recently in threatening to separate people if they didn't follow the new pricing guidelines. There are different ways to send signals that are appropriate to the occasion.

I was trying to get across to that regional vice president the message that there was no room for a bureaucracy or for bureaucratic attitudes in the new HERC that was coming into being. We don't need executives who sit in their offices cheering on the people on the firing line. They would simply become a needless layer of command that slows down response time to real situations in the field. We need a lean organization in which supervisors' energies are fully engaged with the only thing that matters: giving direct assistance to the employees who serve the customers.

Footnote: That regional vice president who made me so irate stayed in the car and did become a traveling vice president; he made sure, however, that he never stayed away from home more than two or three days at a time. This annoyed me, but his performance was good, and I accepted it. You can force things only so far.

▶ Giving the Regional Sales Directors a Supportive Role

We proceeded in an orderly and methodical way through the regional cadres, fixing one position at a time before we moved on to the next one. We began with the sales directors.

As we saw it, the job of sales director was to hire and train salespeople who would act as functional support to the branch managers in improving the quality of their sales staffs. But the sales directors weren't into this mode at all. They were not hiring and training people; they were simply doing whatever the regional vice presidents wanted them to do. Some of them just seemed to hang around until the end of the month, when they would come to life, call a bunch of prospects, and sell them some used equipment to make a profit for the region. Others seemed to feel that their job was mainly to travel with the regional vice presidents and carry their bags. I couldn't see the benefit from their work, and what was worse, the people in the branches couldn't see any benefit, either. They just saw people who were being paid well and were not contributing anything, which hurt morale and damaged the image we were trying to create of a tight, lean operation without waste.

We had to redefine formally the sales director's job so that it stressed a basic training function. In this scheme, the job responsibilities included:

▶ Hiring, training, and mentoring the sales force.

▶ Visiting the branches in a supportive sales role.

▶ Making sales calls with the local salespeople.

▶ Counseling the salespeople on how to improve their performance.

We knew we couldn't just decree that kind of radical change in thinking without first doing some missionary work with their bosses, the regional vice presidents. Without their support, the program we were setting up would have a dim chance of survival. We therefore had our vice president of sales at headquarters begin working with the regional vice presidents to make sure they understood the new functional requirements of the job. The vice president of sales and the regional vice president *together* selected the candidate for the position of sales director. In that way, we made certain that the person picked for the job not only had the backing of the immediate supervisor, but likewise was oriented toward our new emphasis on training and development. Fortunately, this was a case where we could promote from within because we had an ample pool of good people in our sales force who were qualified for the job as we had redefined it.

Even with all this, we still encountered resistance. Several of the regional vice presidents had developed close ties with their sales directors over the years, and they defended their subordinates—insisted that they were doing well and lobbied us to leave them alone. They weren't doing well at all, but I had no wish to get rid of them arbitrarily and hurt morale.

We therefore tried to get the bosses to see for themselves why these people were inadequate and how this was lowering the performance of the whole sales staff. I had to do a lot of coaxing and educating before they could grasp our new expectations. It took me about five months to get one particular vice president to concede that his sales director really wasn't up to the demands of the job. It was tiring, dogged work, but I never let up because I knew *we could not allow a superior to protect a subordinate whose work was inferior;* if that began happening again, HERC would be headed right back to being the loser it had been.

▶ *Getting the Regional Managers to Stay Close to the Branches*

Next on our list were the regional managers.

The regional manager:

▶ Keeps a close watch on the mix of the fleet in the region and makes sure that it is generating the appropriate revenue.

▶ Works with the branches to transfer equipment where it can get the highest utilization.

▶ Determines what brands of equipment are favored and should be ordered.

▶ Keeps an eye on what equipment is operational and what is not.

▶ Works with the branch manager on maintenance and repair problems so that equipment gets fixed and goes back on rental.

In short, the regional manager is general supervisor of logistics in that region, charged specifically with maintaining a close liaison with the branches.

This is the way the job of the regional manager is now structured, but in those days it was so ill-defined that little work was getting done. The regional managers did indeed travel around the circuit, but exactly what they were really doing when they got to a location I never could quite figure out. The visiting regional manager would go into an office, close the door, and presumably get on the phone and work on fleet matters. These managers seemed to be doing deals and swaps, but exactly what was accomplished, no one ever knew.

We worked jointly with the regional vice presidents and our headquarters staff in defining exactly what we wanted these people to do. We then repeated the process that we had used in developing the new breed of sales managers. When we had finished training the regional managers and put them into the field, it was with the understanding that a good proportion of their time would go into developing close working relationships with the branch managers. The branch managers had been told that we wanted them to run an efficient operation, realize a good pretax profit, and produce good sales, but they hadn't been told how to get there. So we assigned the regional managers the task of educating the branch managers in these skills.

And that is how we got our regional managers into the front lines with the rest of the troops.

▶ *Bringing the Controllers into the Picture*

We left the regional controllers until last because they at least were doing the job they were supposed to be doing, even though not in the way we wanted it done.

Our accounting is highly technical, involving a great number of coded accounts, and we do an accounting close at the end of the month. Something always seemed to go wrong during the close, and often the controllers had to spend two or three days with the branch managers to get the numbers straightened out. The problem was that the controllers had never taught the branch managers the basic accounting that was necessary in the equipment rental business. When we did a close, so many errors cropped up that it took hours and hours just to reconcile the accounts from one store. It was a kind of comedy of errors in which the branch managers didn't know how or what to enter and the controllers were totally frustrated because they felt no one was willing to help them.

We eventually had to turn over the entire cadre of controllers. In some cases, we brought new talent in from outside the company; in others, we promoted from within our accounting and internal audit departments. In this way, we pieced together a new group of controllers and secured the expertise we needed to run our accounts properly. Our closings greatly improved. But as it turned out, it was not enough just to bring these new people into the management team. We also had to take care of a basic communications problem.

We are an equipment rental company, not an accounting firm, and the accountants felt isolated when we sent them into regional offices or branches, where everyone talked a different language. They were into accounting and everyone else was into the service business. Our controllers felt that they were not being recognized for their contribution. So we put on a whole program to emphasize their direct relationship with what was going on around them and made them feel part of the management team—not just specialists working in their own detached compartments.

With that piece in place, we finally had functioning management teams in the regional offices. Not only were the branches closing the monthly accounts about three hours after quitting time, but we felt confident that in general the regions were giving the branches generally the broad support in sales and logistics they needed to function properly.

WRAP-UP
How to Get Consensus When You Redefine a Job

Here is a methodology that may help anyone struggling to set up systems that have a chance of working.

Human beings make systems work. This is nowhere more true than in the service industry where the systems often *are* people, not automated machines or production lines. It takes finesse to establish viable human systems. The process may start modestly, perhaps with finding a replacement for a specific job. That effort often ends with redefining the job, as happened in a number of cases when HERC decided that it needed to look at the functions being performed by its management. When you redefine a job, you are actually creating a new human system by altering relationships among people and also the relationships with other departments and units.

Whenever a job opens up, you get the opportunity to see if something more can be done to make that job more effective in terms of the whole organization. Beyond that, you should consider what someone new can bring to the old job. So before you make the move to hire someone, first go over the ground thoroughly in the way HERC did:

▶ Decide the overall organizational goal you want to achieve.

▶ Redefine the job, if necessary, in the light of that.

▶ Make sure the supervisor fully understands the expectations about the new job and is comfortable with the new concept.

▶ Bring the supervisor closely into the whole process by working closely with him or her in selecting the candidates for the job and helping to develop the training program.

Only then is it wise to move on to the final stage of the process, the actual training of the new recruit. This is a way of getting consensus about the new human system before we put it in place.

17

Attracting
Promotable People

Fixing our staff management proved to be much easier and quicker than altering our line management. Because our customer base had always been construction, our branch managers were people who fitted comfortably into that environment. Perhaps one out of four branch managers had a college degree; most of them had started out in the back shop. They knew all about the equipment, but their horizon of service was confined pretty much to the needs of the local construction people they had grown up with. Now that we were cultivating national and industrial accounts and adding new layers of service, we needed a more knowledgeable and sophisticated person who could be comfortable with varied customers and with answering a variety of needs.

This chapter describes how we rose to this challenge and its far-reaching effects on hiring and promotion policies, for both the white-collar and the blue-collar streams of people within the company.

▶ When It Becomes Time to Stop and Begin Over

Whenever we needed to replace a branch manager in those days, the regional vice president would always come up with someone whose background had almost invariably been in the shop. I found this frustrating and would object on the grounds that the candidate basically didn't have the breadth of experience, education, or skills needed to run a quality service business. The regional vice president would then counter by saying something of this sort, "This guy's a carpenter [mechanic, electrician] and knows the construction industry"; when I still demurred, he would say, "Well, Dan, can you suggest someone better?"

The plain fact was that I couldn't. After scratching around in what few lists of names I had, I had to concede that I knew no better solution. Nor was there any other place to which I could turn. There was no pool of qualified people to tap within the company and there was no point in looking outside inasmuch as our competitors had the same problem. Inevitably, I had to agree to put that shop person into the job because it was the best we could do. But it never turned out to be more than a short-term fix, because in the end that person was not up to selling the appetizers and delivering quality service to our customers.

Don't Play from Weakness

We used to do much the same thing when we rode around the country asking local chambers of commerce where to locate and accepting their ready and plausible answers. Once again, we were playing from weakness. We weren't holding to standards, we were just filling holes, which was no way to build a company with a future. As we went along, we were learning how to fix all those other problems we faced: the location problem, the equipment problem, the national sales problem, the environmental problem, the technical and logistical problems. But here we were with a serious *people* problem and we had no answer for it—and people are the heart of the service business.

I came out of a corporate background where you could get help in fixing any people problem you might encounter. You called in the personnel department, and they supplied qualified candidates to fill any holes or weak spots. But nothing like that was possible now. When I went to sleep at night, I knew that—unlike the little cobbler in the fairy tale, who comes in during the night and has all the shoes repaired and lined up nicely by the next morning—no one was going to come in and save me. This was yet another problem that we would have to solve somehow from within, but not in the same way we had been able to tackle the people problem at the staff and regional levels. This one was going to take longer to solve because we were going to have to develop the people ourselves.

Be Willing to Pay the Short-Term Cost

I finally worked up the intestinal fortitude to stop hiring branch managers the way we had been doing it. When a vacancy occurred, we simply blocked the job and refused to approve a successor until we found a qualified person to fill it. I knew that might take some time, and indeed at one point we had as many as five branches without managers while we searched for the right people to fill them. I also knew that the short-term costs we would have to pay for this would be more than offset by the long-term gains we would get from effective leadership at the branch level throughout our whole system. Whatever the cost, we simply had to stop doing what we were then doing and start over again, and I needed to send up a dramatic signal that this was now going to happen. I did it, however, with the thought that I had an ace in the hole that could eventually begin to turn the situation around.

▶ *How the Success Path for Managers Evolved*

From my earliest days at HERC, I had encouraged the hiring of young people right out of college into the job of sales coordinator. It wasn't a formal training program, but I saw how key the sales coordinator was in the scheme of things and realized that by putting bright young people into these jobs they would eventually get a rounded education in our business that would qualify for them for other jobs up the ladder. Until then we had been in the Joe's Rental Equipment mode and had been bringing people out of the shop to get behind the phones at the front desk and act as coordinators. Our gambit worked, and it wasn't long before we had begun to develop some pretty terrific sales coordinators from among this crop of college graduates. I especially recall a group in Tampa who were so outstanding that we put one of them into the branch manager's job after he had been with the company for about a year.

Beware of Pushing People Ahead Too Soon

It was deceptive at the outset. When these bright young people first moved into the front office, everything would seem to go smoothly, and in fact, the operation would often start showing phenomenal results. Why? Because people rally around when someone is promoted from the floor. Everyone works harder: mechanics, salespeople, the young boss's old colleagues behind the sales coordinator's desk. Generally, people know their jobs and do what they have to do without having to be told. During the honeymoon period, the people around the new young boss feel empowerered and go about their jobs, and they do so with spirit. Then comes the time for tough decisions.

▶ Is it all right for this person to work overtime?

▶ Should a salary increase be given or withheld?

At that point, the line is drawn: The new boss is no longer people's old buddy; that co-worker is now management.

Problems like these always arise, and the young boss doesn't have the experience or the training to solve them. There is a fight between two guys in the shop, and the manager doesn't know how to resolve it. Or the sales force isn't functioning adequately, but without experience as a salesperson, how can the manager give the guidance that will increase revenue? We would see these gaps appearing, so I would go to the manager and say, "Look, Joe, I know you are having trouble because we didn't give you the right kind of training, and there are a lot of things like managing a sales force you missed out on." Then I would promise, "We'll do everything we can to back you up and work with you so that you can master these things and move ahead." But it would not help, and in the end the person would fail anyway. No amount of training or counseling at that stage could have helped. The manager simply did not have the maturity of judgment that comes only with time through direct hands-on experience.

When you try to jump people from Class A baseball into the major leagues, guess what happens? They fail because they are not ready. If we had been willing to leave these people as sales coordinators for a time and then had seasoned them further by moving them to outside sales for a while, maybe in three or four years they could have become great branch managers. But we pushed them too fast. Sometimes in the early days, we were taking people with six months' experience—people who looked like stars—and we moved them up to branch manager. Naturally, they were willing to do it because they became part of management, improved their salary, and got a bonus and a car. From that time on, no one has ever made it directly from sales coordinator to branch manager. We were, in effect, taking people with great futures and snuffing out their careers.

Creating a Two-Entry Program

We had been too hasty. We realized that shortcuts of this kind never work; the only thing that does work is in-depth management training. It was at this point that we started the associates program.

We hired people out of college and put them through a year's training by giving them a carefully planned experience in other jobs within the branch and region in order to qualify them for the job of branch manager. We started out with one associate doing his or her internship in each of our six regions; today we have two associates per region. We have also integrated this program with our program for hiring and training the sales coordinators.

Today, there are two ways of entry into the HERC management cadre. You can come in as a sales coordinator or as an associate; in either case, the basic requirement is a college degree. Actually, we prefer to use our coordinators as the basic pool from which we draw our associate recruits. At some point, he or she is going to be put through the coordinator's experience in any case. The basic difference between the two is that the associate program puts someone on a faster career track. The main point is that, in either case, whether the person comes in through one program or the other, *everybody we hire is promotable.* When you come down to it, that is the bedrock requirement for entry into the management pool from which we now draw virtually every one of our managers and executives, whether they are staff or line. Promotable people are people who have incentives built into them, the kind we want in our company and the kind we hope our company attracts because of its policy of promotion from within.

The Success Sequence

We anticipate that usually within 15 or 20 months in the coordinator's hot seat, a person is ready to go into the sales force and represent the company out in the field. At the very outside, they stay two years in the coordinator's slot, so that we keep constantly supplying a source of new management. *When a sales coordinator moves on, that beings the cycle which makes us our future management: from coordinator (and/or associate) to outside sales person to branch manager to regional manager or sales director, finally to regional vice president.* All our present regional vice presidents went through this sequence; these are people who know their business because they themselves have done every key job.

During the heady years of our fast growth in the latter part of the 1980s, when we finally had our promote-from-within policy working, some coordinators made it up to regional vice president in five years. By the early 1990s, that had become pretty hard to do. Our system of promotion works best when the company opens up new branches. That is one of the reasons why the economic stagnation that occurred in the late eighties and early nineties was so painful for us. Our whole management development system was designed deliberately with growth in mind. Some strains in our system appeared when expansion leveled off.

Appealing to Highly Motivated People

Our system has a fairly high attrition rate built into it. When you hire young people directly out of school, you have to realize that your job may be just their first port of call as they find out what they really want to do in life. They are trying things out. Our coordinator slot can require a 10-hour day, maybe even a 12-hour day. Young people just coming out of college tend to think they have been trained to be president of the company. They now face the reality that what they are going to be doing at Hertz Equipment Rental is answering the phone and making outgoing calls—they're not going to be president of the company. A fair number drop out and look for something else or some other company that suits them better.

When I visit colleges, I am aware of a certain naivete in the business students I meet. They are filled to the brim with marketing, accounting, personnel, psychology, and economics, but seem unaware they will seldom use these skills on their first job. I tell them candidly that we expect hard work from our management cadre. I tell them we are looking for highly motivated people who are comfortable with the fairly rough-and-tumble environment of a service business that caters to the operators of heavy-duty equipment. I don't think our business is ever going to appeal very much to the Ivy League stereotype with unrealistic expectations. I warn students that I am looking for young graduates who fully expect and are willing to work hard for what they will get out of life.

The Satisfaction of Working for the Market Leader

We are just right for such people. They like our defined career path, and they are pleased to be working for a prestigious company that builds its management from within. We run with straightforward policies and procedures—there are no hidden agendas. Generally speaking, if you work hard you will get promoted and succeed. It isn't a business in which some uncle or cousin is going to come up and take the position you have earned.

For many people, there is a unique satisfaction in working for Hertz or some other number one market leader in any industry or business. The reputation and the quality image of the leader rubs off on you. If you're working for the number one company, you're a winner, too—everybody who works for that company is viewed as a winner. When a company wins a Malcolm Baldridge Award, every employee shares in the glow of that. Working for such a company means personal recognition from people in the industry and from peers and friends. When I talk with people today and mention whom I work for, they are impressed because the name conveys an image around the world.

Working for Hertz is something of a challenge when compared with working for Joe's Equipment Rental. You have a great deal laid upon you: One is protecting a name known around the world, which is a lot to live up to. Keeping up appearances is no joke with us; we expect our equipment and facilities to be in top condition at all times, and our people are constantly aware of this standard. The name carries with it that implication. Strict compliance with all regulations creates still another burden for us. Simply stated, customers—and management—expect more of me and the division than is expected of other companies in our business. But the point is that the thing we really have going for us at all times and in all places, along the highway as well as over the phone, is our name. In its field, it is the best name in the world, and it's our basic inheritance.

▶ *The Support System for the Work Force*

Working for HERC has other attractions as well. We have the resources to backup our employees' work and give them the satisfaction of getting their job done efficiently:

- ▶ We are better equipped to deal with customer complaints than our competitors.
- ▶ We have a whole fleet of radio-controlled service trucks.
- ▶ Our service people go out there and fix what's broken.
- ▶ Each of our shops can do major equipment repairs.
- ▶ We have system-wide service and the flexibility to adapt to many different kinds of situations.

We have the assets and the tools to do the job better than anyone else in our industry.

What Appeals to Blue-Collar People

As we upgraded our equipment and facilities during the development years, we did everything we could to provide the blue-collar group with the tools and equipment they needed to do their work, as well as up-to-date, safe surroundings in which to do it. This made their work easier, more agreeable, and more satisfactory in almost every way.

We were also aware of the kinds of incentives and psychological support that our blue-collar people wanted and needed.

In general, they were looking for somewhat different signals from those to which our sales force and our management team responded. The number one concern of our mechanics and drivers was job security. They fully understand vision and the importance of making tomorrow better than today, and they could see the same problems that everyone else saw: that we were under poor management and weren't getting sufficient revenue. They sensed what was happening, and they felt insecure about their jobs and about the company. What they wanted above all was assurance that the branch they were working for would be there tomorrow and the day after that. They needed to hear that we were planning to stay in that city and make that branch grow and prosper; in other words, that HERC was a viable company with a future that included them.

Motivation through Training Courses

As we were getting the company into the right condition, we found the mechanics had a special morale problem that was rather simple to fix. It can be summed up in one word: training. Most of them had never had any training from HERC, yet they had been able somehow to keep that tired, old, pre-1982 fleet running. That was dramatic evidence of the native skills our people possessed. If they could keep that worn-out equipment running, think what they could do with the new equipment we were bringing in. We knew that we did not have to go out and look for new mechanics, we only had to find a way to give recognition to the people already there. And this is precisely what they lacked: recognition. They had worn themselves out on that decrepit equipment without anyone much caring or noticing.

Motivating the Mechanics

We therefore went to the manufacturers of the equipment we bought and asked them to supply factory training, and they did. They provided this at their own expense, and what it cost us was mainly the airline fares to get our people there; in many cases, the manufacturers provided lodging and food as well as the actual training. The program clicked with the mechanics. It gave them a wonderful chance to hone their skills, as well as get a break from everyday routine, and the manufacturers treated them hospitably and made them feel like important people. Even more than that, they realized that HERC had been willing to invest in them, and this is what really turned them on. They came back feeling that their professional status as highly skilled and productive people had been recognized and honored.

The factory training program has become a standard feature at HERC. We try to send 60 percent of our mechanics to factory training every year to any one of a dozen schools, with the training program varying according to our changing mix of products. There is always something new for our people to learn as we bring in new models and new kinds of equipment. This makes it mutually beneficial to all parties involved.

Motivating the Truck Drivers

Meanwhile, we sent our truck drivers to defensive driving courses. But what mattered most to them was simply the arrival of new vehicles as we moved along with our fleet renewal program and replaced the beat-up equipment they had been wrestling with for so many years. You can always tell when a truck driver is happy: You will find him out there washing and polishing his truck as though he owned it himself. I recently talked for a long time with one of our truck drivers in the Salt Lake City branch, who told me that he regarded his line of work as a profession in itself. He wasn't looking to move on; this was his career. From talking to countless people on my touching-iron trips, I find this a typical attitude among many skilled workers.

A Sequence of Promotion for Blue-Collar People

Within the blue-collar ranks, we have developed a sequence of promotion similar to the one we developed for the management side of the business.

▶ The lowest ranking job is that of yardman, whose assignment is to clean, grease, and oil the equipment, move equipment around the yard, and so forth.

▶ The next step up is the B-level mechanic position, which is the entry level job for mechanics.

▶ From there, the path leads to A-level mechanic, to lead mechanic, to shop supervisor. Our larger locations have all those positions.

▶ At the apex of this pyramid is the regional maintenance manager.

We recently created the position of regional maintenance manager with the intent of professionalizing this whole cadre of workers. Like the regional sales manager, the maintenance manager is expected to recruit and train people, as well as to work on difficult problems and to supervise the safety program. There was no such job when I came to HERC; by establishing this position, we have helped to build esprit and make people aware of the *potentials on the blue-collar side* of the business. Part of this person's job is to encourage people to move on up the promotional ladder.

Today, we have two separate streams of employees within HERC: the coordinator-sales-management stream and the yardman-mechanic-driver stream. The split is about three-to-two in favor of the management-sales group. The reason for this imbalance is that *HERC is driven by direct sales,* so that the number of salespeople is proportionally greater for us than would be the case in a service company oriented toward the consumer market. Our salespeople, both national and local, together with our coordinators, total more than 400 employees, which means that between a quarter and a third of our total work force is engaged directly in the "service encounter" with the customers.

There is no longer much movement at HERC across the line from the blue-collar to the white-collar side, nor do I encourage this. We know from experience that mostly it doesn't work, as witness the long struggle we had to get college-educated people into the sales coordinator and branch manager slots rather than to fill these from the shop. (As noted earlier, about 9 out of 10 of our branch managers today have a college education.) I do encourage the crossover if the person is willing to go back to school and earn a degree. We have one branch manager today who did rise from yardman in this fashion; he went right up through the whole sequence— mechanic, truck driver, and so forth. He is in his late twenties; he is extremely ambitious and capable; he is an exception.

People Like Turnarounds

People in general like to work in turnaround situations; they like to be involved in something creative; that is human nature. If people see you are committed, they want to buy in and be a part of it. They will be willing to put in an effort that is beyond your imagining when they see something is happening. We all remember reading about the excitement at Chrysler a few years ago when it was being turned around. Well, I found that kind of excitement within my business during the 1980s when we were making our comeback and creating a stir in our industry. When that kind of thing happens, you find the world beating a path to your door even if you are only a small company.

One of my greatest personal satisfactions came from seeing people who had left the company prior to 1982 beating a path back to us. They had left because they didn't like the way the division was being run, but now they saw some hope and wanted to come back and work for us. There were not just a few of these people, there were dozens, and most of them were among our best employees, who have since risen to responsible managerial positions. This was the most eloquent testimony I had that we were on the right path as a company.

WRAP-UP
An Agenda for Overhauling the Organization

When an entire organization has to be fixed to make it work properly, the first question is what *type* of organization is needed to manage the company. If we assume that the general organization of the company appears adequate to do the job, what it needs is fixing, not a thorough overhaul. Since it is impossible to do everything at once, here is a suggested agenda:

▶ Starting with the top jobs in the company and working down through the management structure, look at the criteria for each position.

▶ Redefine each job in the light of the new goals you have for the company.

▶ Make clear to the person filling that position what is expected, and hold him or her to it.

▶ Decide then whether that person is capable of fulfilling the redefined criteria or needs to be replaced.

▶ When holes develop because you cannot find eligible people to fill that job, don't settle for just anyone. *Run with the job open until you find the right person.* Otherwise, you run the risk of perpetuating the weak management the company has had.

▶ Be careful about filling openings with young management trainees, however bright and capable they are, because you run the risk of promoting people before they are completely seasoned and ready.

▶ Remember: *It takes time to develop a pool of managerial talent.* A program for developing people within the company who will be capable of meeting the new exacting standards of the company should be high on your agenda as you go about all the other steps.

18

Sending the Right
Signals to Employees

We were doing a lot more in those early days than just filling managerial posts and restructuring jobs. We were making sure that the people out there understood that their top management was committed to the company, that we were listening. We also made ourselves highly visible as we traveled around the country. Here the grapevine worked to our advantage and spread the news of our arrivals and departures.

This is how we went about building a new working environment, or what was really a new corporate culture, from those first weeks on. I don't recall saying anything about a "corporate culture" in those days; I certainly didn't make any grand pronouncements about it. That is not my style—I am an activist. In this chapter, I focus on how I employed that style to bring our local managers along with us in building a new corporate culture. Their participation was essential to our success.

▶ *The Branch Manager Is the Key*
Person on the Spot

In a service business like ours, the branch or store manager is the one who is responsible for inspiring and motivating the work force. Individually, each of our managers is accountable for only 10 to 20 people, but collectively that adds up to almost all the people in our company. We don't have huge, automated, and impersonal production facilities employing hundreds or even

239

thousands of people. We are not even like big retail chains, which ordinarily have depots supplying their stores. Because of its nature, the equipment rental business tends not to cluster facilities, equipment, or people. This has been reinforced by our own lean way of operating. Our biggest aggregation of people is at our Oklahoma City accounting center, a relatively new operation that was set up when we took receivables out of the branches and consolidated the function. It employs 60 people.

You can't be much more dispersed than we are, and because of this, the Hertz Equipment Rental Corporation as such is not a tangible presence to most of our employees, merely an abstraction. It is something "they" run out of some obscure place in New Jersey. For our employees, the reality of HERC is that particular store where they work. That may be in Monroe, Louisiana, let us say. The manager of that facility in Monroe, along with fellow workers in the shop or behind the front desk, represents the world of HERC. People may drop in from the divisional or regional headquarters from time to time and shake things up a little, but those dozen or so people in Monroe are the ones with whom the individual has to get along on a daily basis. Each person looks to the group and its leader, the manager, for clues as to his or her own standing in the community and what the prospects are. Companies like to advertise that "we are people," which is true enough, but I think it would be more accurate for HERC to say that we are 85 small communities.

How to Avoid Turnover

No matter where we go, people are interested in one burning question: "Is my job secure?" If things seem to be getting out of hand in that branch—if, for example, some people are being treated unfairly while others are getting all kinds of petty privileges—that naturally has to make the mechanic in the shop or the salesperson out on the road uneasy and anxious. Inevitably, one or two of our people will begin seriously looking around for another job. When eventually one of them leaves, someone new will then have to be brought in and trained. That is costly and time consuming, and it cuts back on a branch's efficiency and profits until the new salesperson or mechanic gets up to speed. Meanwhile, the gap shifts burdens onto others, strains relationships, frays tempers, and contributes to a downward spiral in morale.

An important message we tried to bring to managers as we toured the circuit was that there was to be no favoritism. A worker who did a good job was to be recognized for it; if he or she did poorly, actions would occur. People were to be evaluated and promoted on merit alone. I have read a lot of different ideas about corporate culture, but in my own thinking, a sound culture is based on three simple concepts:

1. Fairness.
2. The work ethic.
3. High standards of conduct.

These are the rules I try to live by personally, and they are the ones I try to bring to others through my own conduct. There are other important values, but these three must be present if there is to be the mutual trust that is essential for a viable corporate culture.

The Power of Personal Example

The message for our branch managers was that it was their responsibility to set standards through their personal example.

▶ Is the manager coming in late and leaving early?
▶ Or is he or she coming in at seven and leaving at six?

Demanding, yes. But doing it one way or the other can make a big difference in employee morale, attitudes, and behavior. The branch manager is the company to the people at that location and sets an example not only that matters to us but in the end is vitally important to the success of that profit center manager. It will determine whether the mechanic is merely a parts changer or really gets down there under the machine and fixes the broken part, thus saving money. Or whether the salesperson makes an extra telephone call that rents a piece of equipment to help meet the business plan this month.

Those people are going to take their cue from that manager, who is selling the corporate culture to the people working there. It is vitally important that the person running the profit center understand his or her actions provide the standards for all the employees. The manager's conduct gives the signals that guarantee a stable environment.

▶ Listening to What Others Are Saying

What I mean by signals is the kind of thing we ourselves were doing during those 100-hour, 20-city weeks on the road. We were in effect saying to people:

We aren't asking you to do anything that we aren't willing to do. A great deal of work needs to be done to get this company into first-class shape. We are not sitting behind our desks telling you to do it; we're out here with you in the stores and lots working alongside you. We're paying the price, too, and working our butts off. We are trying to show you that we are truly committed to this company and to your welfare. We want to hear from you what is wrong with the company, and with your help we will try to fix it.

What We Did about Compensation

One of the things we were hearing was that our compensation plan was not motivating people and was not competitive. Yet the stories varied from branch to branch and were not consistent from one area to another. I didn't know whether we were underpaying or overpaying people. We therefore retained an outside consulting group to conduct a salary survey, which would tell us the average earnings of a branch manager in our industry, what kind of compensation was normal for a salesperson, and so on. But we couldn't apply that data precisely to our operations because there was no national company in the equipment rental industry aside from HERC. For the other local and regional companies, big differentials in rates between different areas didn't matter, whereas for us they did. Besides, other companies in our field didn't have the number of professional and educated people we had, which pushed our rates up.

In the end we had to piece together our own compensation plan by extrapolating from other national organizations that were similar to ours. The dealer organizations of manufacturing companies were one such source, truck rental companies were another. So at last we had a compensation plan that recognized experience and also took into account the differences in the cost of living in California compared with, say, Mississippi. Since this latter factor can amount to a considerable differential, we use cost-of-living data in determining our wage rates for all major cities.

From the beginning, I had also known there was something else wrong with our compensation policy that created a certain unfairness. The branch managers were on a bonus plan and the sales people were on commission, but the sales coordinators were on straight salary. I had to find some way to tie them into the whole operation. Every branch had a business plan, a revenue target, for each month of the year. What we said was that if the branch hit the monthly mark, we would give each coordinator incentive pay of a couple hundred dollars. In this way, I was able to create a more equitable incentive policy and bring people together in one sales team moving toward a common goal: revenue.

Giving Some Structure to the Work Life

Meanwhile, we were tackling all the technical, mechanical, and logistical problems that we looked at in the earlier chapters of this book, such as cleaning up our yards, getting rid of surplus and broken equipment, setting up accounting and control systems, and pinning down the exact identity of our customers. These tasks, which kept us occupied for many months, were indications of the haphazard, careless procedures and habits that had characterized the HERC environment.

Work hours provide an example of the kind of things we had to fix. We noticed in our travels that some places started at five o'clock in the morning, some at seven, some at eight. Closing hours were equally capricious, as were holiday schedules; every store seemed to have its own idea of which holidays it would observe. It was ridiculous, but it was only one instance of the inconsistent work and personnel policies that characterized our whole operation. So we began tightening up with pronouncements such as:

▶ These are the hours the stores are going to be open, and these are the hours the stores are going to be closed.

▶ These are the holidays that are going to be observed.

We were putting in place a framework for the company that would give structure to the employees' work lives—consistent and equitable policies that applied everywhere, from Monroe, Louisiana, to Park Ridge, New Jersey, our home base.

▶ *What Personal Involvement by the Leader Means*

A corporate culture invariably reflects the personal style of the leader, and mine is admittedly a demanding style requiring a great deal both of others and of myself. To be an activist, you must become involved with what is going on around you, no matter where you are and no matter what is happening. You have to be willing to be part of the scene, an actor in it. The one thing you can't afford to do is to be aloof, to turn away as though you haven't seen or heard; that completely blows your credibility. *You have to handle what has been put in front of you, and you have to handle it right there on the spot.* That means being willing to be connected with people in a way that creates mutual trust and understanding.

How to Reaffirm People

When I get into a city, the first thing I do is to sit down with the branch manager and tell him or her what is going on in the company. I try to fill the person in on the things I have been working on and the things the company is getting into. I do this as informally and openly as I can, sharing my frank views about moves we may have to make to take care of new trends, say, in the marketplace or the economy. We go on with this talk when we wind up the day with dinner together, when I take the opportunity to state my forthright opinions about how I think this particular branch operation is shaping up. Visitors present at these sessions are often a little startled by the openness with which I talk about the affairs of HERC and about person-alities, but I can assure you that this isn't idle gossip. I want to draw that manager into management and impart a sense of presence in the bigger pic-ture. By sharing information that is somewhat sensitive, I am signaling that I trust the person's discretion to sort out what can safely be passed on. I am taking the manager into my confidence.

What I am trying to do is to empower that person by showing my trust; I try to provide the reassurance that comes from knowing this. I want the staff to know that I believe in their manager, that I think he or she is an important person. I am saying, "I approve of your management," and this, in effect, is a reaffirmation. When I leave that site, I want that manager to feel better about him- or herself and the company because of having an improved image.

One of my major objectives when I am traveling is to build a one-on-one relationship with each manager. I think of it as a safety net. I want all my branch managers to know that if they are in a crisis of some kind they are free to pick up that phone and call me. Before they leave the company or do something equally drastic, I want them to call me with full assur-ance that this won't be considered some kind of breach of the chain of command. There is something of an art in creating this kind of open-line communication and handling it adroitly. But it can be done.

The Case of the Despairing Manager

In one big city in the Midwest, we were not doing well financially; we were trying to crack a tough market, and we were continuing to show very poor results. I was visiting there once when the manager was mak-ing a presentation to the regional people, and as I watched him strug-gling, I knew that something was wrong. He looked disheveled and out of it. I sensed that he was frustrated with the company, was question-ing his own ability to manage, and was trying to decide if he wanted to stay with HERC. So when I got back to the office the next day, I phoned him.

I said, "Ken, I just want to tell you I've never seen you look worse. What is going on with your life? I believe in you, and I'm telling you that you can do the job. You don't have to be afraid. You are the best guy to get revenue—you're my best revenue manager. You're doubting yourself. Go out there and make it happen."

He replied, "Thank you, Dan, thank you. I needed that. I can't tell you what that says. This phone call means everything to me."

I didn't try to probe any deeper into his emotional difficulties but sim-ply said, "You can do it, Ken. I've known you for a long time. If you look like you're beaten, nobody is going to follow you. You can do it—you can make it happen. I don't have to tell you more than that. All you have to do is stop doubting yourself."

This kind of interchange cannot be faked. You have to care, and you have to know the person you are talking to or you will not pick up the signals that something is wrong. If you communicate effectively, it will strengthen your relationship, and you will empower the person. But be-fore you get into this kind of conversation, you had better be sure you know the person well. Otherwise, you may misread the situation and end by causing pain and damaging the relationship. This takes a lot of patient work.

How to Make a Breakthrough

In my contacts with the managers, I always search for the "hot button"—the consuming interest, idea, or dream with a special meaning for that person. When I make contact with it, I feel an emotional warmth that helps me relate to him or her. Sometimes this is very hard to locate, but I always keep trying.

During a visit at a location in California, the manager and I went out to a nearby restaurant and had pizzas for lunch, and when we were fin-ished, he asked me if he could take the leftover slices back to the fellows in the shop. A lightbulb lit up in my mind, because I had never been able to break through to this man in two years. I called over to the waitress and said, "Three full pizzas to go." That man's face lit up. The $20 I spent for those three pizzas made a connection with him that is still valid. It was my way of breaking through. It made me feel good that he cared about those people, and we suddenly had a shared interest and we felt good about each other. Those pizzas made all the difference.

There are many ways to make that kind of difference, and you have to be on the watch for them. It is a sensitive business, and your effort has to be motivated by a genuine interest in others—I can't stress that enough. If it isn't genuine, people will see through it quickly.

Look for Opportunities to Help People

Whenever I am on the road, I scout out situations where I can involve myself in some way that will help people.

- ▶ If there is a piece of equipment that needs a part they can't find, I will call the head of purchasing right on the spot and have him get the manufacturer direct.
- ▶ If there is a personnel issue, I will call the head of personnel to resolve the problem.
- ▶ If there is a financial problem, I will call the comptroller.

In each case, I see that the matter is followed through. I always look for problems of this kind—and I always find them. In doing so, I am trying to get across a simple message: *I am here to help you.* I want people to know that I look on every problem, even if it involves only a few dollars, as important to me; by inference it should be important to them, too. What I am really saying is that details are always important and that everyone must take responsibility for getting them right; otherwise systems won't work. I want my activist style to rub off on others so that they learn how to make things happen, too.

Once I become a participant in any situation, I become totally involved and try to get it wrapped up before I leave that place and go on to something else. A willingness to be totally involved this way is to me what gives the activist leader credibility. I can't think of a better way to show that I care for you than to be concerned about your problem enough to work along with you in solving it. The activist leader doesn't listen politely and then delegate the problem to someone else to take care of. He or she gets down into the gritty details of a problem, masters them as rapidly as possible, and follows through until there is a resolution.

The basic rule in practicing the activist style of management is that you can never overlook or turn away from any situation, no matter how difficult or unpleasant, when it comes to your attention.

▶ *The Gray Areas of Conduct*

Strengthening the Ethical Corporate Culture

One day when I was reviewing the rental agreements at a branch, I found that there was a PGA golf tour going on in that city and that the people in the branch had bartered the use of our equipment for tickets. I was upset about that. Not only was the bartered equipment in high demand and should have been rented, but the whole transaction was in a gray area of conduct—a very gray area indeed, as it turned out. If they had wanted to support a local cause or charity, there was an established company procedure for that. They resorted to bartering so they could attend the event for their own pleasure. The salespeople were out there with their friends— not their customers, just friends.

I gave that branch a piece of my mind. And when I got back to my office, I investigated further, I found that these bartering deals were happening all around the country. So I issued a strict policy rule: *No bartering of anything without direct approval from headquarters.* I knew that occasionally there were reasons for bartering deals that could be justified on either business or eleemosynary grounds. I didn't want to shut it down so tightly that there was no recourse; I simply wanted to get it under firm control. It was a signal about the kind of ethical corporate culture we wanted to have.

Big Problems Start Small

There were occasions when our branches sold off old batteries and put the money into a slush fund for the employees' Christmas party. But we had a policy stating how to fund Christmas parties; a slush fund is nothing but a signal for tomorrow's problem. This is how problems start, with local people bypassing the policy. You cannot tolerate this kind of thing at the pettiest level, even so much as the filching of a spark plug by someone who wants to put it in his own vehicle. That spark plug costs maybe only $1.25, but you have to make a point of it. When somebody does something unethical, you have to react to it and prosecute it if necessary. *You have to maintain a single ethical standard, as painful and difficult as it is.* You have to let people know that they are working for Hertz and that you are not going to tolerate anything but the highest ethics.

This message starts at the top and reverberates throughout the system. Every one of our locations has a fuel pump, and I have driven into the yard countless times with my gas tank nearly empty. It would be very easy to drive over to that fuel pump and fill up, but the only liberty I have ever taken was to give a yardman some money to go out and refuel my car at a local gas station. If I dipped into the company supply, I would be sending out a message that said, "Well, if it's OK for the president of the company, I guess he can't complain if I fill up my tank once in a while." And so it goes.

When I am on the road and go out to dinner with HERC people, I don't order expensive dinners or have many drinks. We can't afford to be lavish, and I also want to teach moderation. In the early days, I always made sure we went to inexpensive restaurants, and for the first year I wouldn't even order a bottle of wine. I said that we couldn't afford it and didn't deserve it. I have relaxed this admittedly austere standard designed for a time when austerity was our ticket to survival. Nevertheless, I remain aware that whatever signal the leader gives out, the human tendency is to take that in and loosen it a little. If you have two drinks with people, they are going to see this as a signal to have three drinks or more; if you have three drinks, five or six drinks is OK. Whatever you do, they are going to accept that as the standard, except that they are going to go a little farther.

Eating with the people I work with is critically important to me, especially having dinner with them. I look on these meals essentially as business occasions taking place in a relaxed and pleasant atmosphere, where we can all get to know each other a little better. I expect people to conduct themselves with the realization that they are part of the management of a major corporation. The vice presidents of the corporation have to remember the significance of that role; when they are on their own representing the company, *they* are the corporation. There is a strict message being delivered here: This is not a party, it is a business occasion, and we have only one standard.

▶ *Paying a Personal Price as a Leader*

I said earlier in this book that being a leader means that you have to pay a high personal price. When you have a European operation or a location in some other time zone, you sometimes have to get out of bed at three or four o'clock in the morning to reach people by phone in their offices at normal business hours. It is unpleasant to do this, but it is a way of giving a signal, setting a standard, even though sometimes you don't feel up to it. There are times when you are going on a business trip to Europe and have to fly all night and then work all day. That is tough to do, and it isn't recommended for everybody. But if you have the stamina to do it, there is a powerful message in it. You don't talk about it; your actions simply define the way you work.

Sometimes you are ill, but you have to show up anyway, because for the other people, this conversation with the president may be the most important one they are going to hold this year. If you work late into the night, people still expect you to arrive bright and early in the morning and then work late again the next night. If you are hungry and feel like digging into a lobster, you may not be able to indulge your craving because you would be giving the wrong signal. Or if you have a drink and you think you would enjoy another one, you may not be able to order it because you don't want to give the wrong signal. Standards are a two-way street, and if you don't treat them that way, you can pretty much kiss them off.

The Message Is Moderation

Being a leader and setting a standard is a job that requires effort and consistency, 7 days a week, 24 hours a day, 365 days a year. You have to live it, breathe it, and sell it all the time. You have to be consistent. The messages I preach I also try to live by. I have a comfortable home life and perform many of the tasks around my home from cutting the grass to shoveling snow. I try not to mix business and pleasure, and I try to keep my business and personal lives separate. Still, I think that basically I am the same person working for Hertz as I am on my own.

My approach may seem old-fashioned, even a little straitlaced to some, but actually it is a timely and appropriate one for the new age of moderation into which we appear finally to be moving. You need only to look at what is happening to some of the great corporate giants of our time as they struggle to cut back, downscale, and get rid of layers of unnecessary expenditure to catch my meaning. The role of leadership that my company has been able to play in its sector of the economy has been in large measure due to the austerity of our own corporate lifestyle. President Clinton is sounding this note of moderation to the country as a whole, which may signal a significant change in our national lifestyle. I don't see how as a nation we are going to recapture our former role of world leadership without some kind of belt tightening.

Running a company in moderation means:

▶ Staying on top of your systems.
▶ Keeping your staff lean.

▶ Reinforcing the work ethic.

▶ Maintaining cost controls.

▶ Not getting caught up by corner-office mentality.

If you do these things, you will keep your company in synch with the economy. You are not going to find yourself upside down some day. Nor will you wake up some morning and wonder how you ever got out of line, moved away from the customer, or got into an inappropriate cost structure. If you are continuously diligent about the things we've been talking about, you're going to stay in fighting trim all the time. You won't land in the fix of many companies who have taken their eye off things.

Many times during the day or when I am on a plane or falling asleep, thoughts come into my mind about how to take action to improve HERC: pricing, how to make a better deal with a vendor, targeting an SIC code, getting a better penetration of business with a customer. But whatever the idea may be, basically it tells people I am an activist. I am not going to be satisfied with the status quo. I am always looking for a way to improve things by hitting a single at a time. Just by taking that approach, I encourage others to do it the same way. So I am continually trying, and some of my ideas are good and some aren't.

When Does a Leader Stop Doing All This?

When I go to the locations, I always go through all the rental agreements. I've done it so many times I don't need to do it any more. In the beginning, the manager stood anxiously over my shoulder. Now, my inspection is a point of pride; the staff want me to see how everything is in order. So I must do that. It takes me 20 minutes, but they are expecting me to do it. And from there, I go on out into the yard, touch the iron, inspect the shop, and shake hands exactly as described in Chapter 1. It is a kind of ritual that I have down to a dead routine. It is the same wherever I go. People come to me and say, "When will you stop? Why do you do this? When does this end?" The answer is that as long as I am healthy, it never ends.

It's not that I have to do it any more for the same reasons I once did it. Today, I have all the information coming into me that I need to stay on top of the business: all those exhaustive reports on inventory and so forth. I know what I'm going to find before I check rental agreements or go out on the lot. My information system is so much more sophisticated than it was 10 years ago that from a control standpoint, why go out of my office?

I know what the monthly base is. I know how much equipment is on the yard. I know what the national accounts are. I even know the quality of the people.

Why, then, do I still continue to go on touching the iron? I do it precisely because it is a kind of ritual and people expect it of me, but it accomplishes a lot of other things, too:

▶ It helps to build morale and provides a consistent linkage with the past.

▶ It gives me a chance to talk with old acquaintances, meet new people, and generally to keep in touch with the human side of the business.

▶ It enables me to pick up new ideas and sometimes an inkling of coming trouble.

▶ It provides me with the forum in which I can send up all those signals discussed in this chapter, the ones that shape the corporate culture.

You cannot do all this from a corner office.

WRAP-UP
Tasks of the Leader

In attempting to create a new corporate culture, the activist leader:

▶ Gives support and guidance to the local manager who, in the end, is responsible for inspiring and motivating the work force.

▶ Helps the local manager understand the power of personal example (e.g., the manager cannot expect the work force to keep regular hours at work if he or she does not).

▶ Listens carefully to what people are saying and responds to legitimate policy grievances as soon as possible.

▶ Participates fully in any action that is going on and handles immediately any problems that arise.

▶ Gives managers a sense of being part of the large corporate picture.

▶ Reaffirms managers publicly before their own staffs.

▶ Makes an effort to establish personal connections with each manager.

▶ Never avoids a head-on confrontation about unethical practices however small—big problems of this kind start as small ones.

▶ Is willing to pay a personal price as a leader, which often involves pushing beyond the personal limits of patience, endurance, or capabilities.

Above all, remember that whatever the leader does or says becomes a signal—the leader is always on show.

Postscript:
Build Your Own System

F ew people today seem to be willing to do the hard work that leads to success. Almost everybody is looking for shortcuts, instant answers, easy-to-apply solutions. Not long after an article about the way HERC measures peer performance appeared in a business magazine, a number of people called or wrote asking me to send them our system. From their remarks, I gathered that they thought it was something cut, dried, and packaged that they could simply apply to their enterprise and make it work just like that.

I remember especially a colonel in the Pentagon who was a supervisor of the huge post exchange there. He called me saying plaintively that his superior officer had read the article, and would I please send him as quickly as possible instructions on how to set up a similar system so he could get that superior off his back. I sent him a generous selection of HERC statistical reports. I politely suggested that he study these in order to build a peer performance measurement of his own and that perhaps one or two of our peer performance statistics might prove of value to him in doing this.

He did not get the point, nor did any of the other inquirers. They were thinking about solutions, and I was thinking about processes. They were thinking about systems, and I was thinking about methodologies that get you to systems. They were thinking about answers, and I was thinking about questions, and not necessarily about the "right" questions, either. As I have repeated throughout this book, you don't have to start with the right questions: Just get in there, dig around, get your hands dirty. Find out enough about what is going on so you can begin asking questions, any questions. If you are persistent, you will finally learn enough to begin asking the right questions, at which point you will be able to develop systems that really work for you.

But don't wait until then to start building your systems. *Systems don't have to be right at first;* in fact, I doubt there is such a thing as a "right" system. If you were to be so unfortunate as to find what you believe is the right system, you might forget that it was right only at that particular moment in time. And you might be tempted to stick with it long after it had been obsoleted by change. You always must be mindful that the one thing you can be sure of is that change is rapid.

The first part of this book is about an *evolutionary process* that keeps adjusting our systems of measurement and control to ever-new conditions. Evolution in this context is equivalent to hitting a single at a time, which keeps working you around the bases toward the better (not perfect) systems that we constantly strive for. You will find that there are no shortcuts in this process, which again is good because shortcuts lead only to future dead ends. This book thoroughly endorses the *kaizen* approach: Strive for constant improvement, and make tomorrow better than today.

The earlier part of this book is also about putting numbers to things, including performance and other activities that are elusive and hard to measure. *Quantification is an absolute must* to achieve quality of service and at the same time maintain profitability. I cannot design a system for you; only you can do that out of your own deep knowledge about the drivers of your business. What I have tried to do, however, is explain the methodologies we used to identify and quantify the factors driving our own business.

The latter part of the book is largely concerned with the linkages and interactions between systems and people. This is a vast subject, and again I cannot tell you how to make these connections in your specific case, but I can serve as a guide by telling you our experience. If you follow our lead here, you will put top priority on precision in defining terms and in getting people to understand the necessity for adhering rigorously to each step of the system. From reading about our experiences, you will also have learned the importance of building systems and teams of people together.

In business, as well as in private life, we are constantly sending out signals by the way we conduct ourselves. I have put considerable emphasis on this aspect of the leader's role in this book because of its importance in a service business. As I have tried to show, the wide geographic dispersal of the typical service business over many small units of people puts a high premium on personal leadership; people take their cues directly from their managers. I call attention to this because in a national service business, managers throughout the country must utilize their systems and lead their staffs; in the end, this is what makes the critical difference between success and failure. A national success is the result of many individual profit centers rolled together. For the system to work, all parts must work.

The larger story in this book—taking a losing company and turning it into a winning multinational operation—also provides some cautionary advice. An important point to bear in mind is that if you have not thoroughly learned what drives your business and developed tight systems, be careful about going abroad: Every defect in your systems will be magnified 10 times on foreign soil.

This book has not attempted to give formulas for success but rather to stimulate your thinking. I urge you to learn your business thoroughly and then apply some useful methodologies to it for greater success.

Good luck!

Index

return on investment and, 158
what the market will bear, 155–156, 159
systems-driven vs. entrepreneurial, 176
utilization, relationship with, 166
violation of, 172–173, 222
Profitability:
pricing strategies and, 156–157
revenue analysis and, 107
Promotions:
barriers to, 217–218
benefits of, 226
honeymoon period, 229–230
management success path, 229
problems with, 229–230
short-term cost, 228–229
success sequence, 231–232
two-entry program, 230–231
weaknesses and, 228
Purchasing agents, role of, 63-64

Quality, achieving, 93–94
Quality of service:
aggregation and, 105
defined, 99
disaggregation and, 105
feedback loop, 105–106
statistical approach to, 104
Quality of system, defined, 3
Quantification, importance of, 254
Questions, information-gathering and, 23, 22–23

Recession:
international expansion and, 197–197
price control and, 165–166
tradeoffs and, 92–93
Recruitment:
colleges, 232
headquarters staff, 219
market leadership, effect on, 232–233
motivated people, 232
Regional controllers, role of, 225–226
Regional maintenance manager, role of, 236
Regional managers, role of, 61, 224–225
Regional offices, functions of, 220–221
Regional sales directors, role of, 222–223
Regional vice presidents, as activists, 221–222
Return on investment (ROI):
age of fleet, 91
pricing and, 158

ROI-utilization grid, 114–115
revenue rental analysis and, 111–114
Revenue rental analysis:
components of, 111–113
computerization and, 115–116, 127
defined, 34
equipment examination and, 108
information contained in, 107–108
return on investment and, 113–114
significance of, 107, 115
time utilization, 113–114
warning signals, 112
ROI-Utilization grid, 114–115
Round-the-clock service, 3, 66

Safety:
implementation of, 69–70
performance measurement and, 133–136
Sales coordinator:
motivation, 182
role of, 179–184, 187
Seasonal business:
dealing with, 49–51, 114, 121
pricing strategies and, 157, 160
Senge, Peter M., 71, 97, 100, 106
Service dialogue, components of, 177–178
Service encounter, delivery system and, 99–100
Service productivity, 208
Service quality measurement (SQMS), 100
Shell Oil, 67–68
Slow rent report, 120–122
Small wins, importance of, 7
Source, The, 87, 184
Spain, expansion to:
accounting system, 199–200, 202
future in, 202
growth in, 199
purpose for, 198–199
recession in, 200–201
shutting down branches, 201
Standard Industrial Codes (SICs), customer base analysis and, 39, 43
Standard Statistical Measured Areas (SSMAs), location evaluation and, 31, 39, 43
Standardization, advantages of, 76
Standards:
establishment of, 56
safety and, 69

Tax Reform Act of 1986, impact of, 59–60, 165